POSTCARD HISTORY SERIES

Reedsburg

IN VINTAGE POSTCARDS

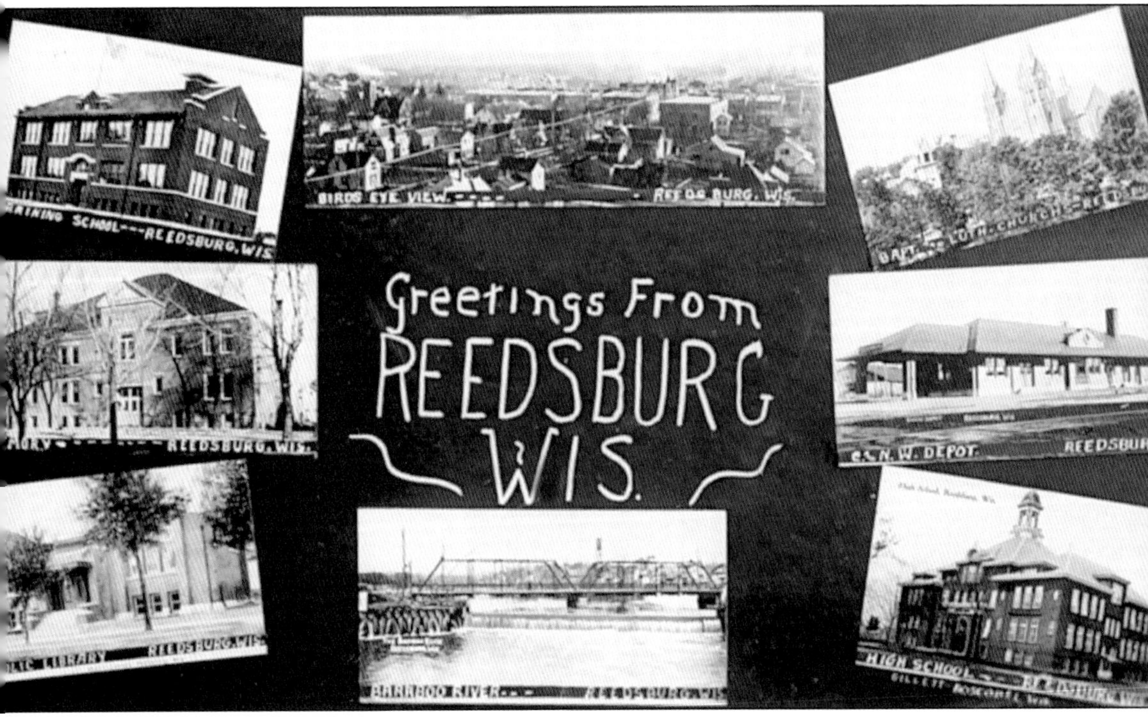
Greetings From
REEDSBURG
WIS.
BIRDS EYE VIEW
C. & N. W. DEPOT.
HIGH SCHOOL
BARABOO RIVER
REEDSBURG, WIS.

POSTCARD HISTORY SERIES

Reedsburg

IN VINTAGE POSTCARDS

Phyllis Miller

ARCADIA
PUBLISHING

ISBN 978-0-7385-3203-5

Published by Arcadia Publishing
Charleston, South Carolina

Printed in the United States of America

Library of Congress Catalog Card Number: Applied For

For all general information contact Arcadia Publishing at:
Telephone 843-853-2070
Fax 843-853-0044
E-Mail sales@arcadiapublishing.com
For customer service and orders:
Toll-Free 1-888-313-2665

Visit us on the Internet at www.arcadiapublishing.com

I would like to dedicate this book to Roger, Todd, and Marla for their understanding and patience with a Mom's hobby gone almost over the edge. I would also like to acknowledge the people before us who had the pride in their community to document the many images I have been able to acquire and enjoy.

Contents

INTRODUCTION

It's in the cards! The postcard was created in Austria in 1869. The United States passed the postal regulations allowing the card in 1872. In the early 1900s the use of postcards became prolific, as greetings were sent on postcards, and each city documented with pride the sites of their towns and villages. Messages were quickly sent to loved ones announcing news and highlighting places people had visited. The government sent a card home to announce the soldiers' arrival in Europe during the Great War. Families put photos on cards to commemorate a special occasion. Holidays were depicted on post cards. Many times people who seem to have been in a hurry promised to write a letter when they had more time. Through collections of postcards one can feel the life of a bygone era.

Reedsburg is a small town located in south central Wisconsin. The rich and rolling farmland is one of the reasons early settlers were attracted to this area. Reedsburg is only 17 miles from the beauty of the Wisconsin Dells to the northeast and 17 miles from the natural beauty of the Baraboo Bluffs and Devil's Lake. People from all over the United States travel through our town to visit attractions like the House on the Rock near Dodgeville, Frank Lloyd Wright's Taliesin at Spring Green, and the Dells of the Wisconsin River.

Products from this town are shipped to all places of the nation and worldwide. We are the home of Grede Foundries, Gerber Products, and Seats, Inc. Other small industries thrive here.

Reedsburg is full of interesting historical facts, such as when two of the "Black Sox" teammates played at our local ball field the season after they were barred from professional baseball as a result of scandals in 1919. One summer during World War II, a prisoner of war camp was located in what is now Webb Park.

There are several famous faces in Reedsburg's history, Claire Briggs, the famous cartoonist, lived here at one time. "The Old Swimmin' Hole," based on a local pond, was a recognizable feature in his cartoons. The real thing is no longer utilized, swimming pools have replaced the "hole." Agnes Moorehead had strong connections to the town, her father was a minister here and her mother lived out the remainder of her life in a little house just up the street from the post office. Agnes brought several famous friends with her when she came to visit family, on one of her trips she dedicated a new city office building.

Many firsts took place in Reedsburg as well—the first Ford dealership in the state of Wisconsin was located here, and the first sanctioned Little League was formed in the spring of 1951, with only four teams starting out.

The real heroes of Reedsburg were those very early settlers who left family, familiar things, and friends to start a new life on the "frontier." Their strengths are seen in the way the town was laid out and built up. Many of the first churches were organized soon after they arrived, and the present residents are still benefiting from their work and foresight.

From the earliest days of settlement, the settlers of this town planned for an active life. It was on the site of Reedsburg's first five shanties that the Main Street of this town now provides for a wide thoroughfare. Circumstances made Main Street what it is today. At first the business district consisted of buildings constructed of wood, because of the abundance of material nearby. However, a fire destroyed much of the town in the late 1800s, and it was decreed that all businesses be constructed of longer lasting brick.

Because of the lowland, or swamp, upon which this town was settled, it soon became apparent that the street had to be something more than dirt. Brick was used to ease the struggle of maneuvering through the business district. Cement sidewalks were installed to create easier access to the many new businesses. Years later, the people before us ,again saw the need of a better surface and blacktopping was implemented.

Main Street was the social area of the community. It was on this street that one could meet their neighbors and sell their goods. At one Market Day in 1923, several hundred people stood on Main Street to hear who would be the proud owner of a new Ford to be raffled off.

Main Street was also the site of a visit from a little-known senator from Massachusetts by the name of John Kennedy. In town to campaign for the presidency of the United States, he and his entourage held a rally on the east end of the business district at the Badger Theatre. In a newspaper article, his brother, Robert, received a larger spot on the front page as he spoke to the Kiwanis Club about the abuses of Hoffa in the office of labor.

Parades were a big part of an earlier era. Crowds gathered to send off and welcome back soldiers of the different conflicts which our local men fought in. In the 1960s, the men of the national guard were sent to Fort Lewis, Washington, because of turmoil in Berlin. Reedsburg played host to photographers of Life Magazine as they came to town to record the events, trials, and tribulations from a small community's sacrifice to keep a nation safe. For a few years Reedsburg played host to the Miss Wisconsin Pageant, which also included a parade. The event eventually outgrew our small community.

Merchants and general stores were the most visible businesses on the street, but a closer look revealed signs above the stores, marking the locations of the professionals. Many doctors, dentists, and lawyers had their locations above these stores. Also above the stores were halls such as the Opera House, Germania Hall, and Brooks' Hall, which were used for large meetings and entertainment events.

On Main Street you could find jewelers, boot and shoe makers, cigar makers, tailors, milliners, and barber shops alongside the drug stores, restaurants, saloons, butchers, and movie theatres. The Main Street of yesterday resembles the malls of today in as such so many diverse needs could be found in a very close area. Everything from soup, to the grocer, to nuts, or the hardware store, could be found on this two block section of downtown. While shoppers spent their day in town, the horse and buggies were cared for in livery stables and feed barns located within easy reach of the Main Street stores.

One

Just For Fun Greetings

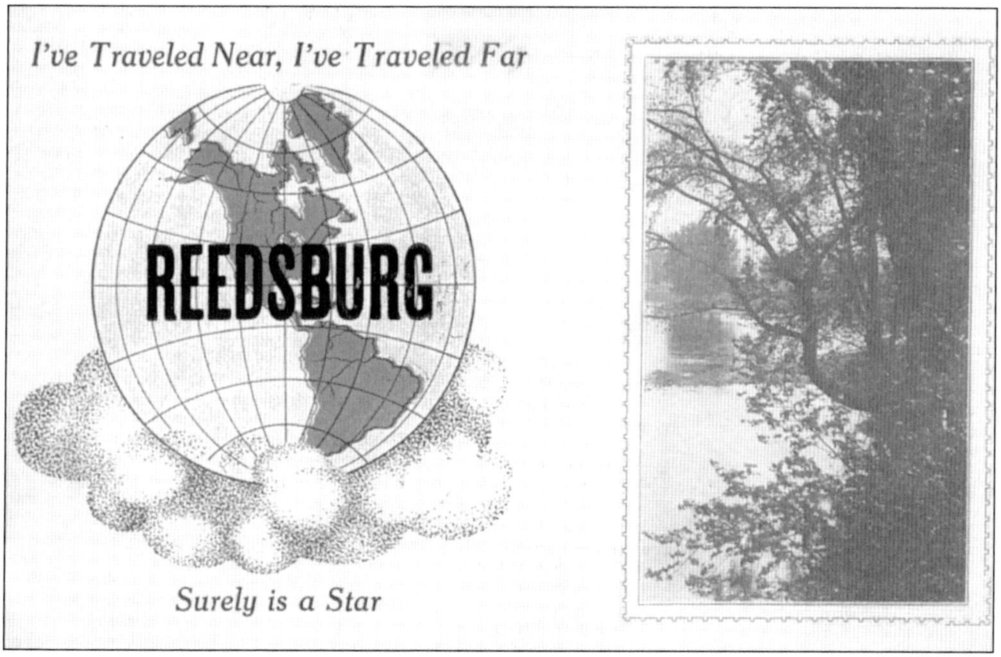

The following cards need no additional comment, they speak for themselves. They also define the humor of earlier days in a small Midwest town. It appears the senders of these cards wanted to remember the good days they had with family and friends.

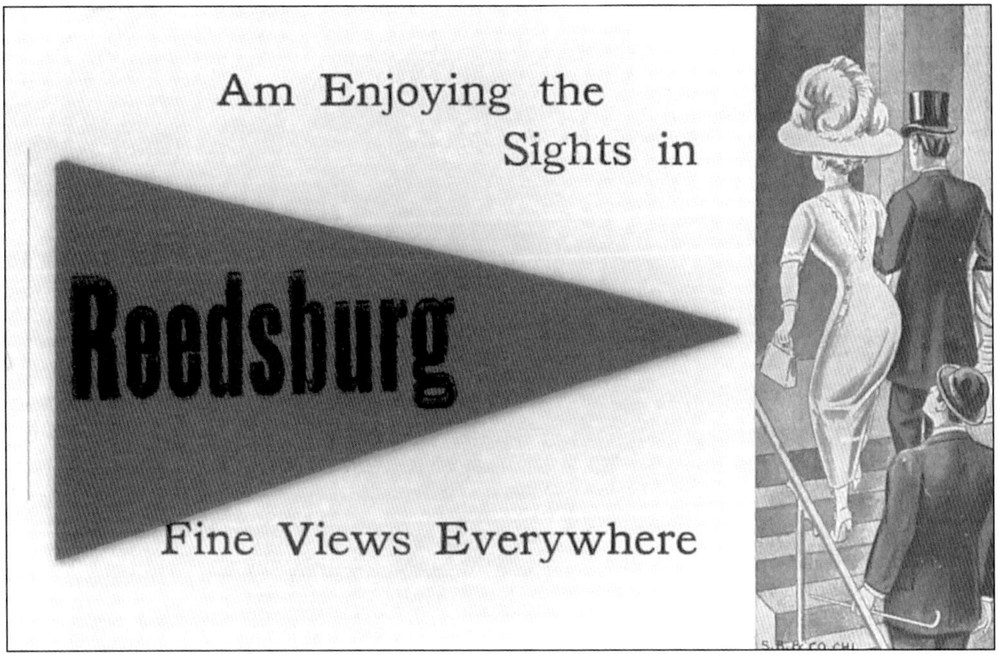
Am Enjoying the
Sights in
Reedsburg
Fine Views Everywhere
S.B.R.CO.CHI.

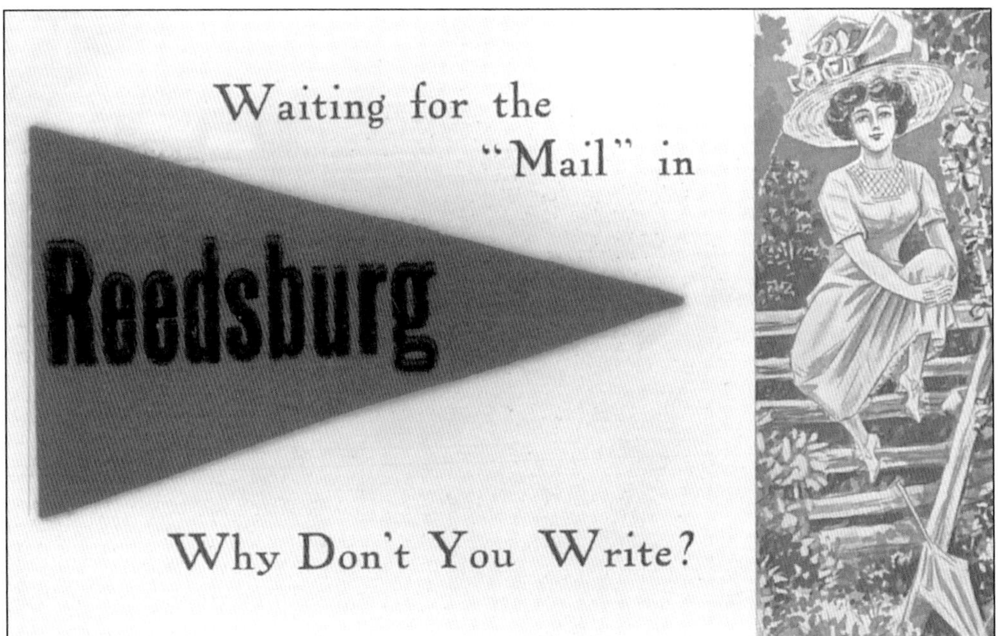
Waiting for the
"Mail" in
Reedsburg
Why Don't You Write?

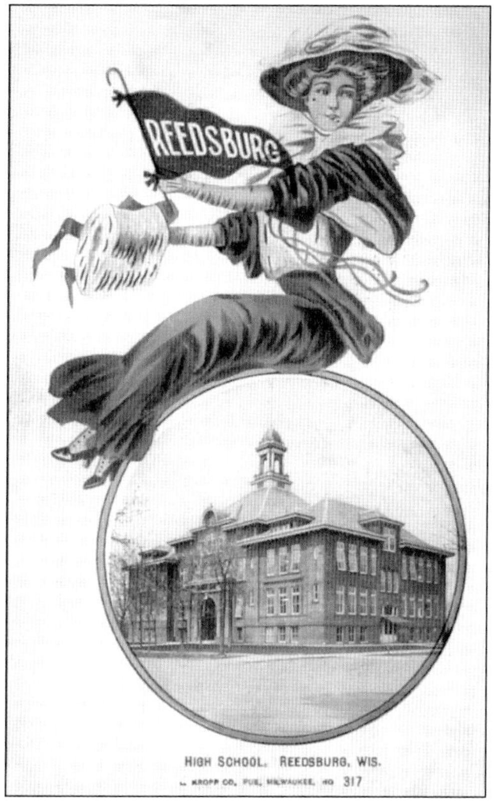
REEDSBURG
HIGH SCHOOL. REEDSBURG, WIS.
317

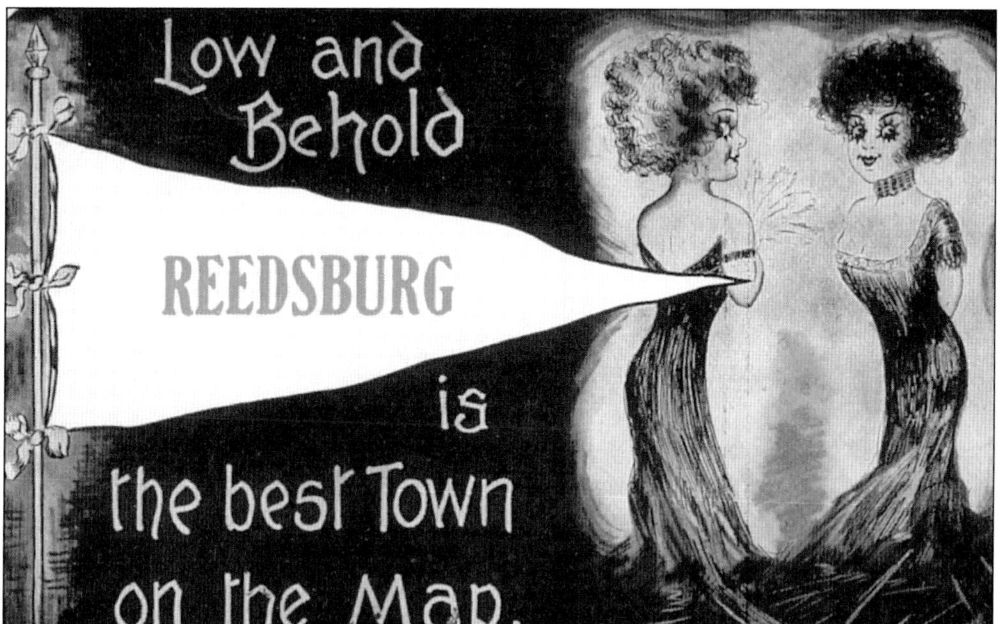
Low and Behold
REEDSBURG
is
the best Town on the Map.

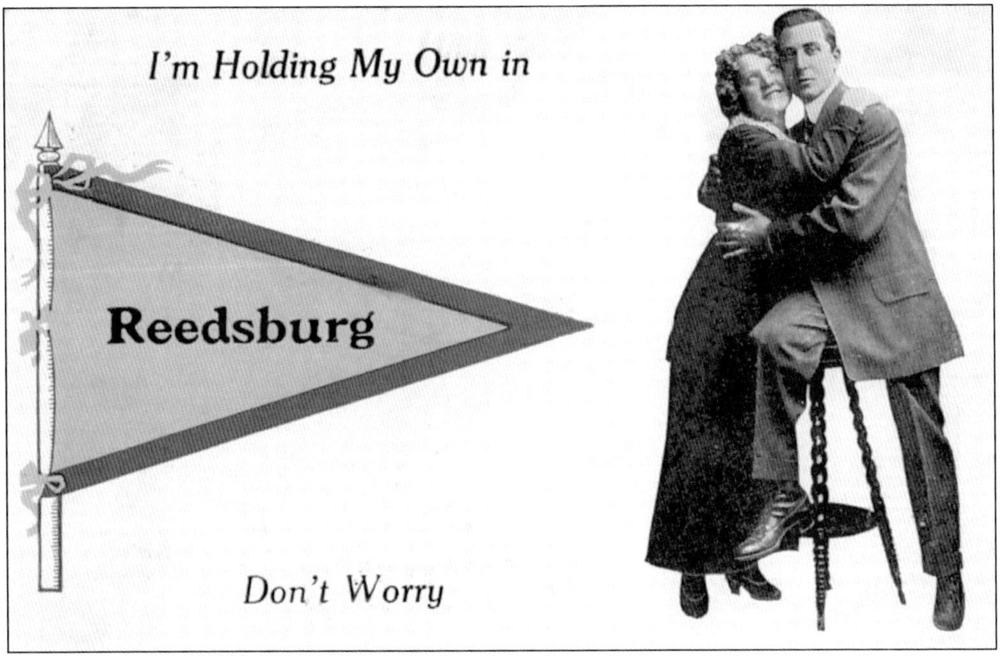
I'm Holding My Own in
Reedsburg
Don't Worry

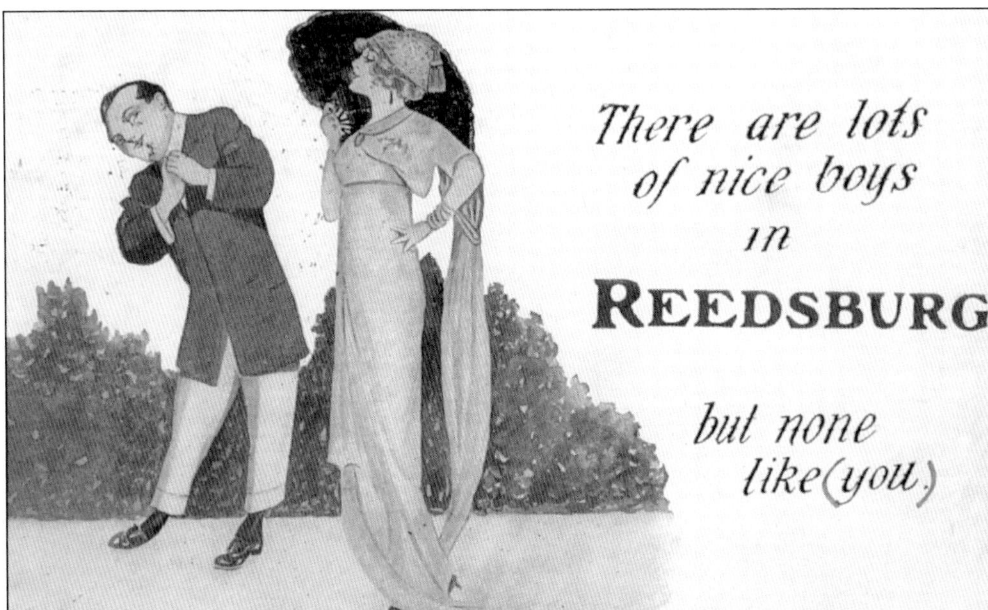
There are lots
of nice boys
in
REEDSBURG
but none
like (you)

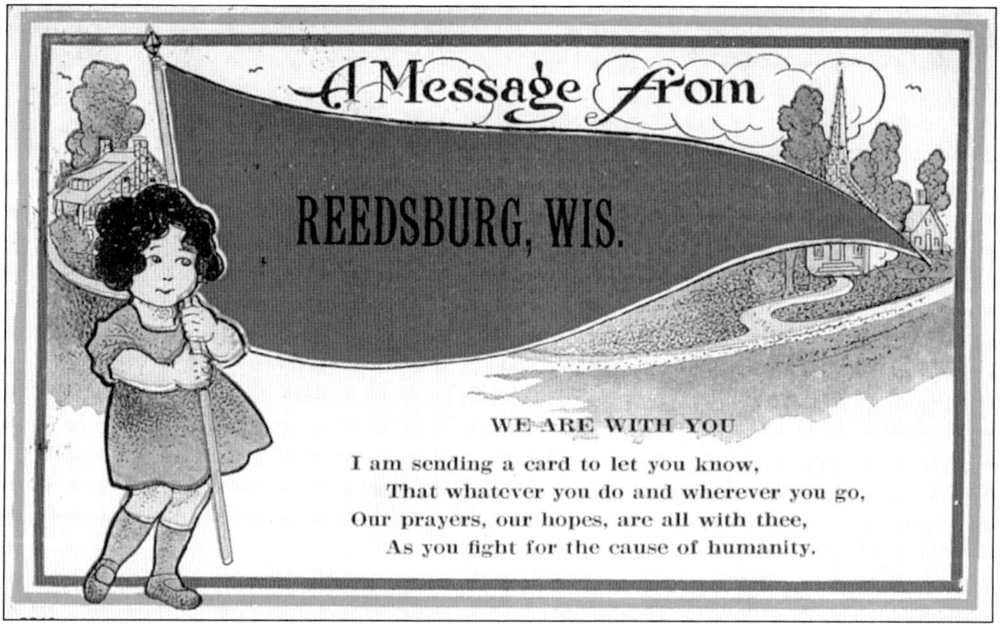
A Message from
REEDSBURG, WIS.
WE ARE WITH YOU
I am sending a card to let you know,
That whatever you do and wherever you go,
Our prayers, our hopes, are all with thee,
As you fight for the cause of humanity.

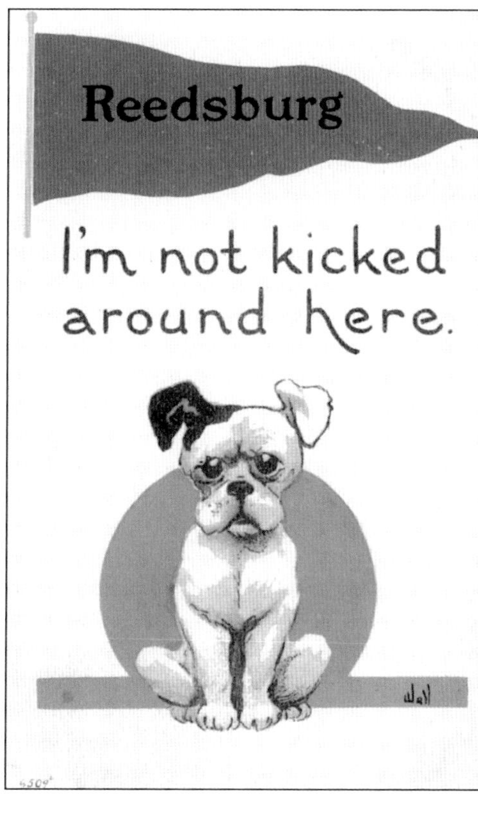
Reedsburg
I'm not kicked
around here.

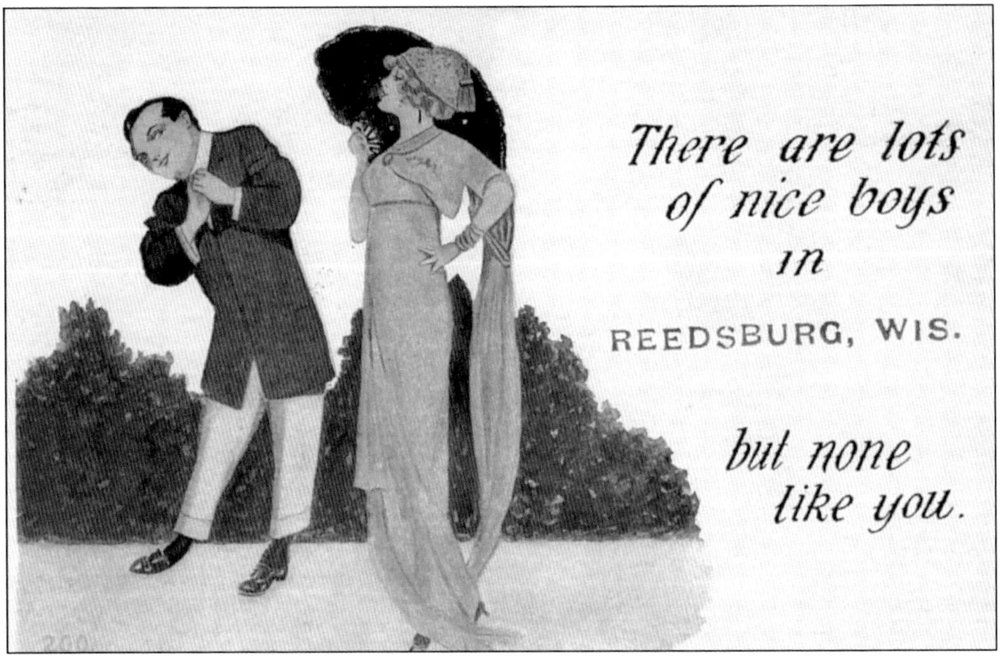
There are lots
of nice boys
in
REEDSBURG, WIS.
but none
like you.

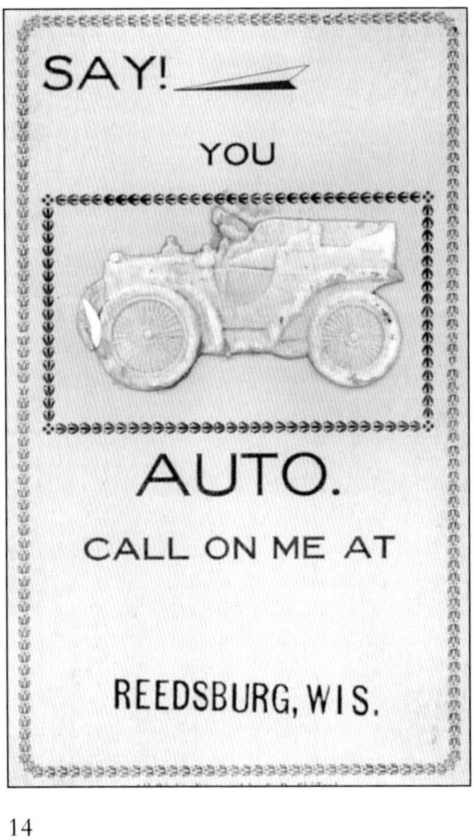
SAY!
YOU
AUTO.
CALL ON ME AT
REEDSBURG, WIS.

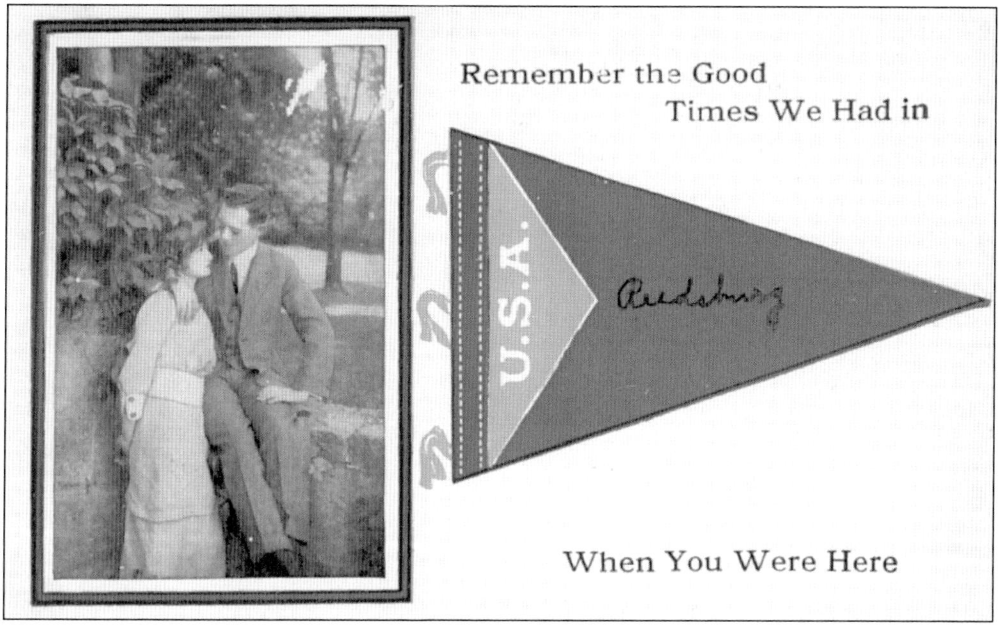
Remember the Good
Times We Had in
U.S.A.
Reedsburg
When You Were Here

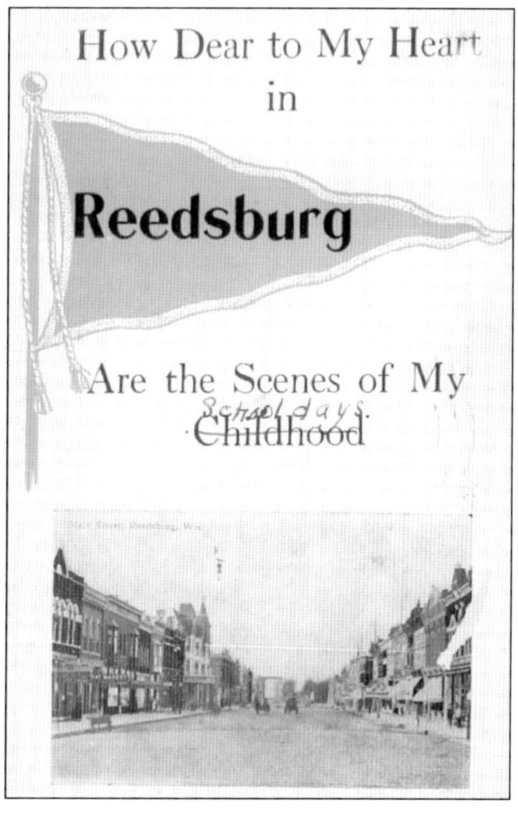
How Dear to My Heart
in
Reedsburg
Are the Scenes of My
School days.
Childhood

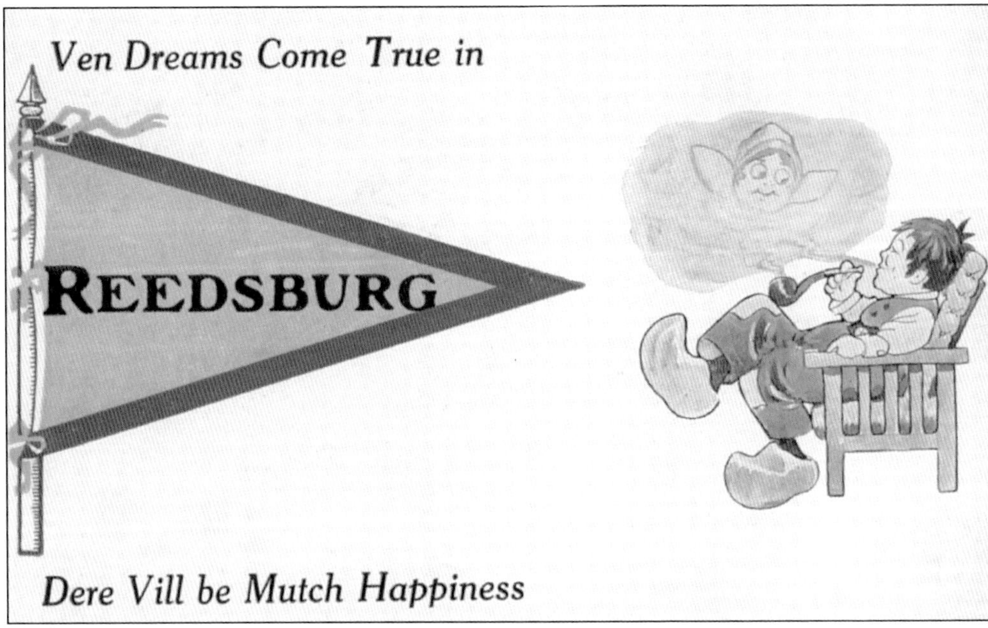
Ven Dreams Come True in
REEDSBURG
Dere Vill be Mutch Happiness

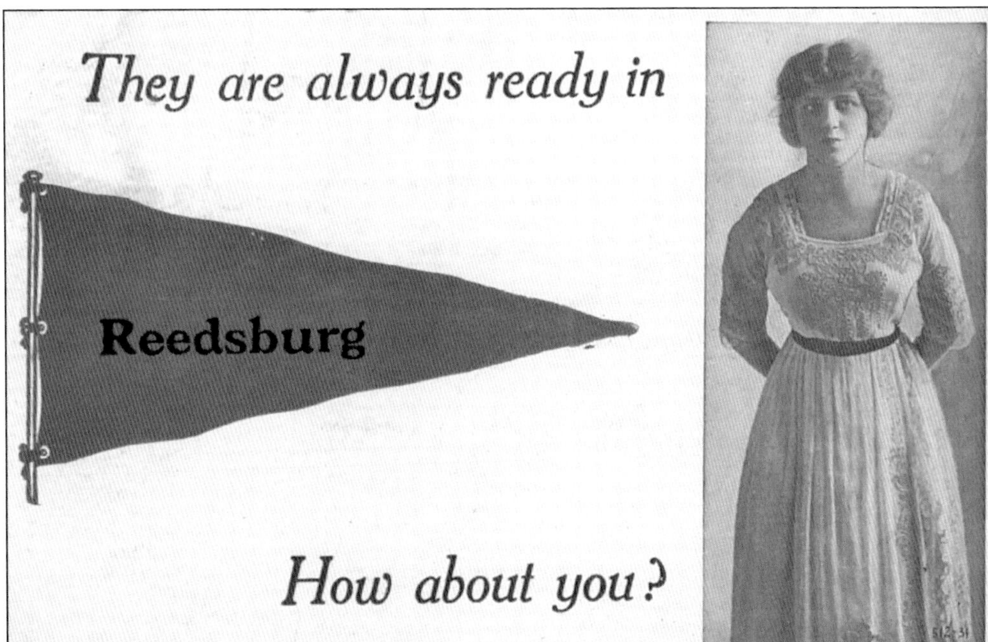
They are always ready in
Reedsburg
How about you?

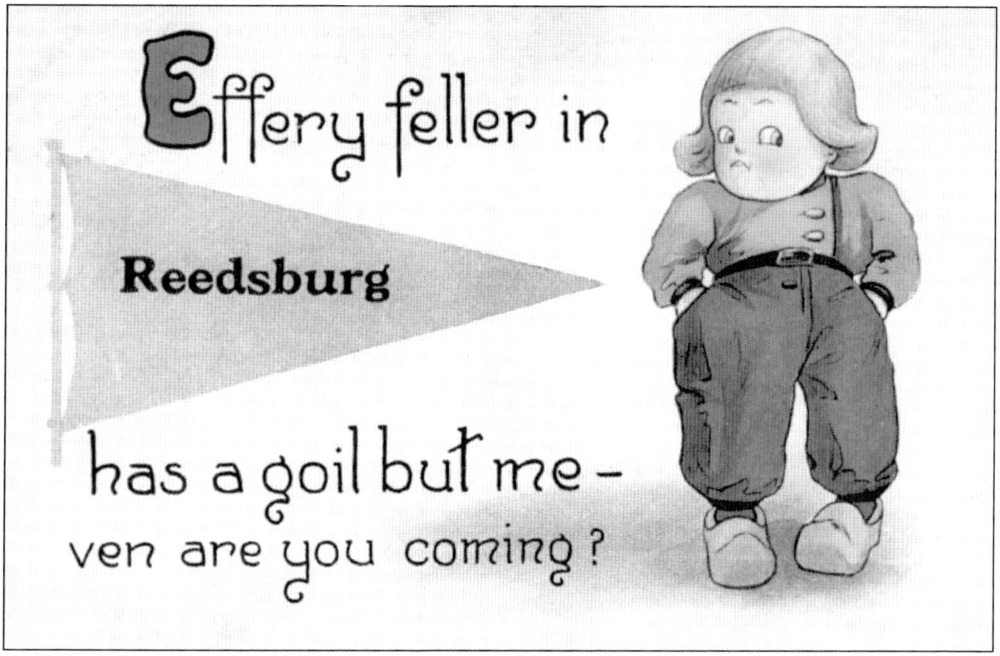
Effery feller in
Reedsburg
has a goil but me -
ven are you coming?

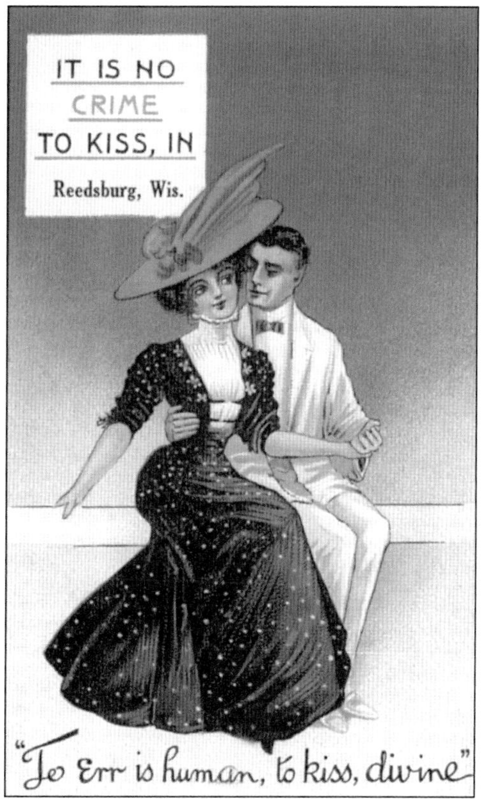
IT IS NO
CRIME
TO KISS, IN
Reedsburg, Wis.
"To Err is human, to kiss, divine"

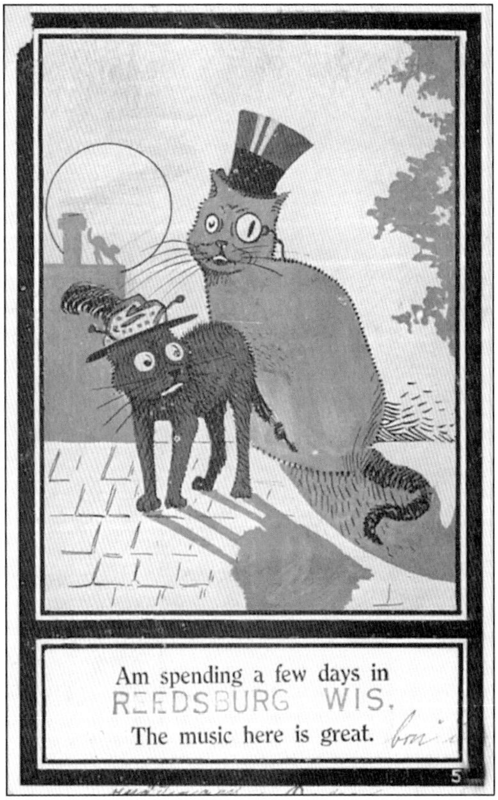
Am spending a few days in
REEDSBURG WIS.
The music here is great.

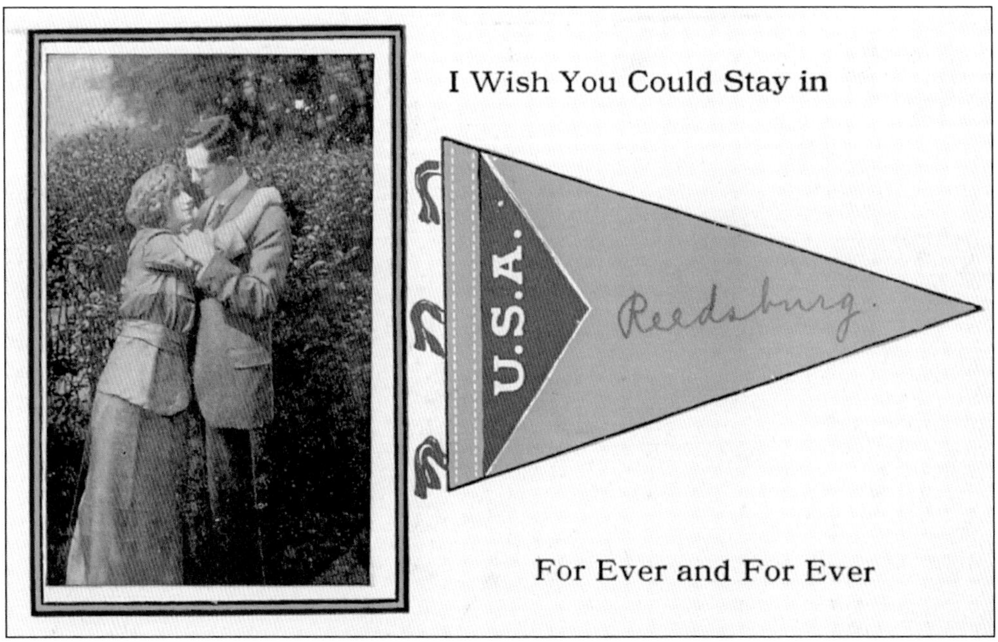
I Wish You Could Stay in
U.S.A.
Reedsburg.
For Ever and For Ever

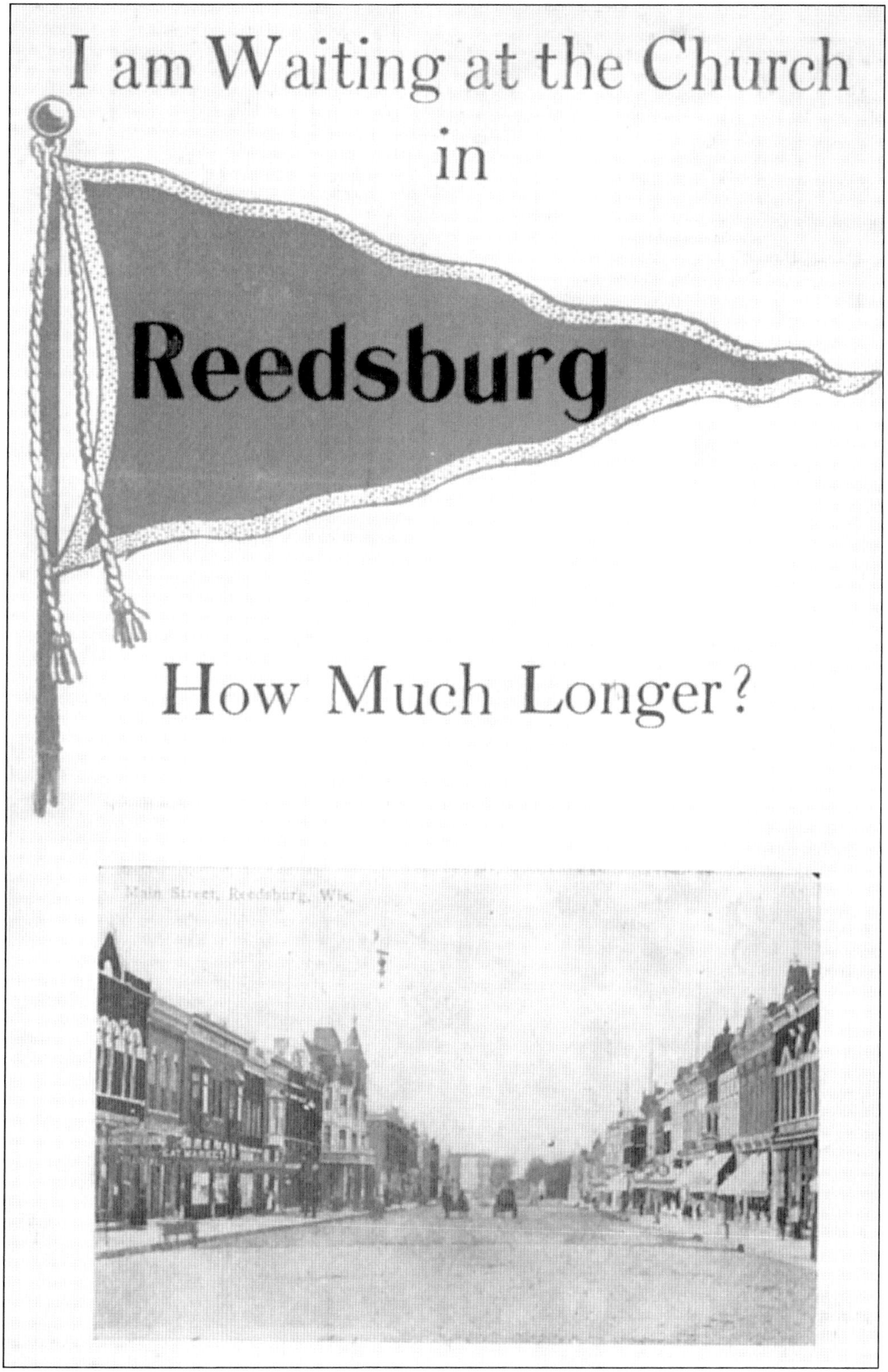
I am Waiting at the Church
in
Reedsburg
How Much Longer?
Main Street, Reedsburg, Wis.

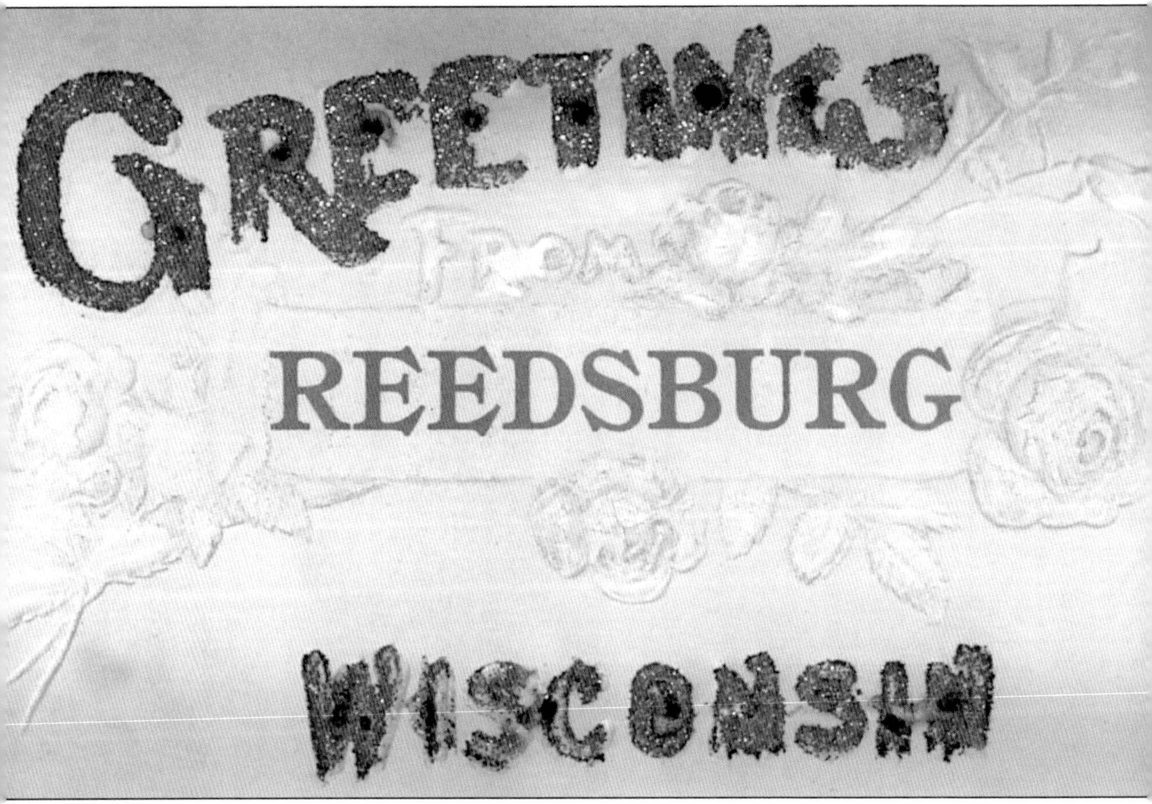
GREETINGS
FROM
REEDSBURG
WISCONSIN

Two

The Parks of Reedsburg

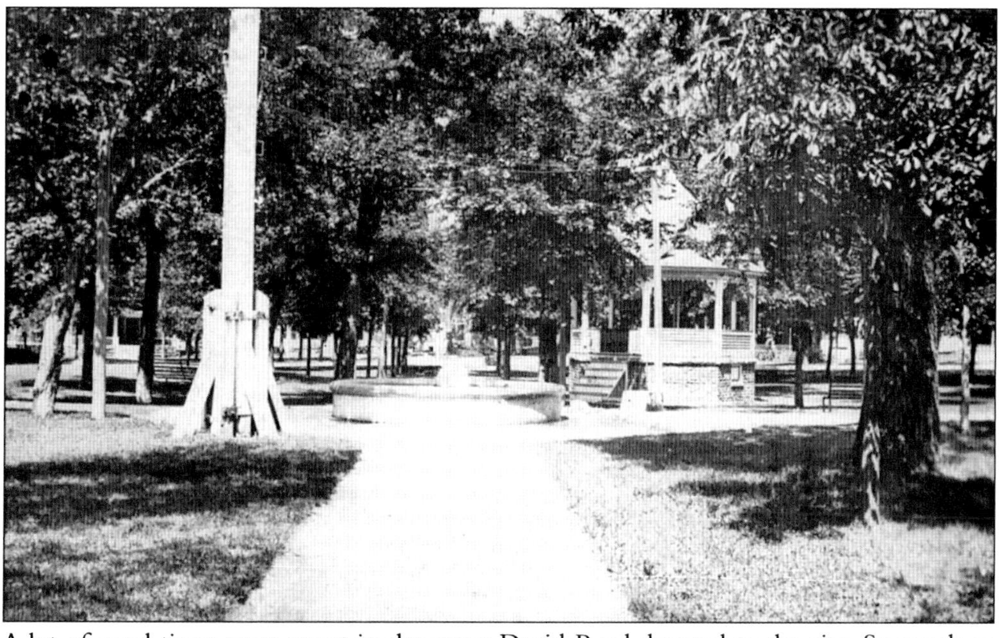

A lot of good times were spent in the space David Reed donated to the city. So much so that at one time there was a plea in the local paper to either repair or repaint the worn fence which once enclosed this area.

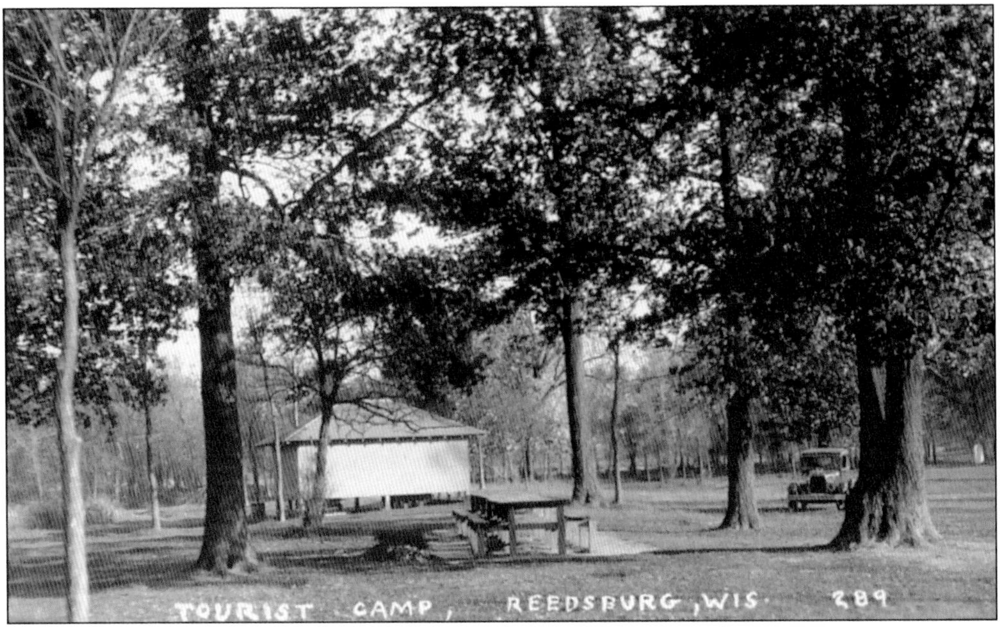

Before the days of motels, a city would provide travelers a place to encamp for the night. This park in Reedsburg was located at a flowing well and on the banks of the Baraboo River at the end of South Pine Street. The area was donated to the city by the members of the Reedsburg Land and Improvement Company in 1911. There was a shelter with picnic tables, and you could fish in the river or the pond created by the flowing well. This camp became known as South Park.

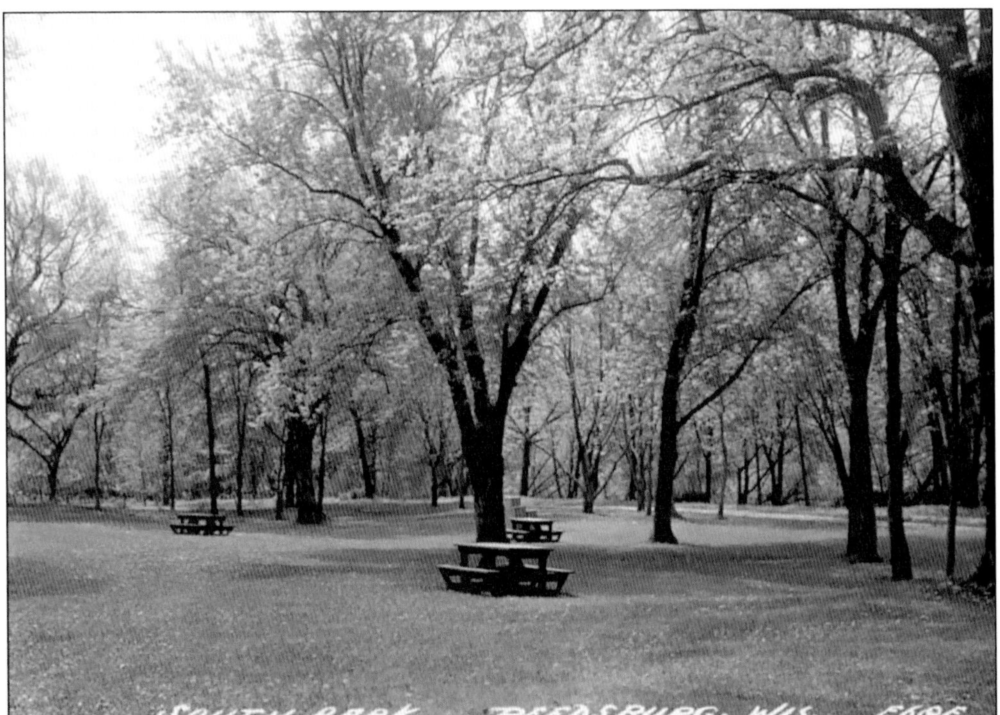

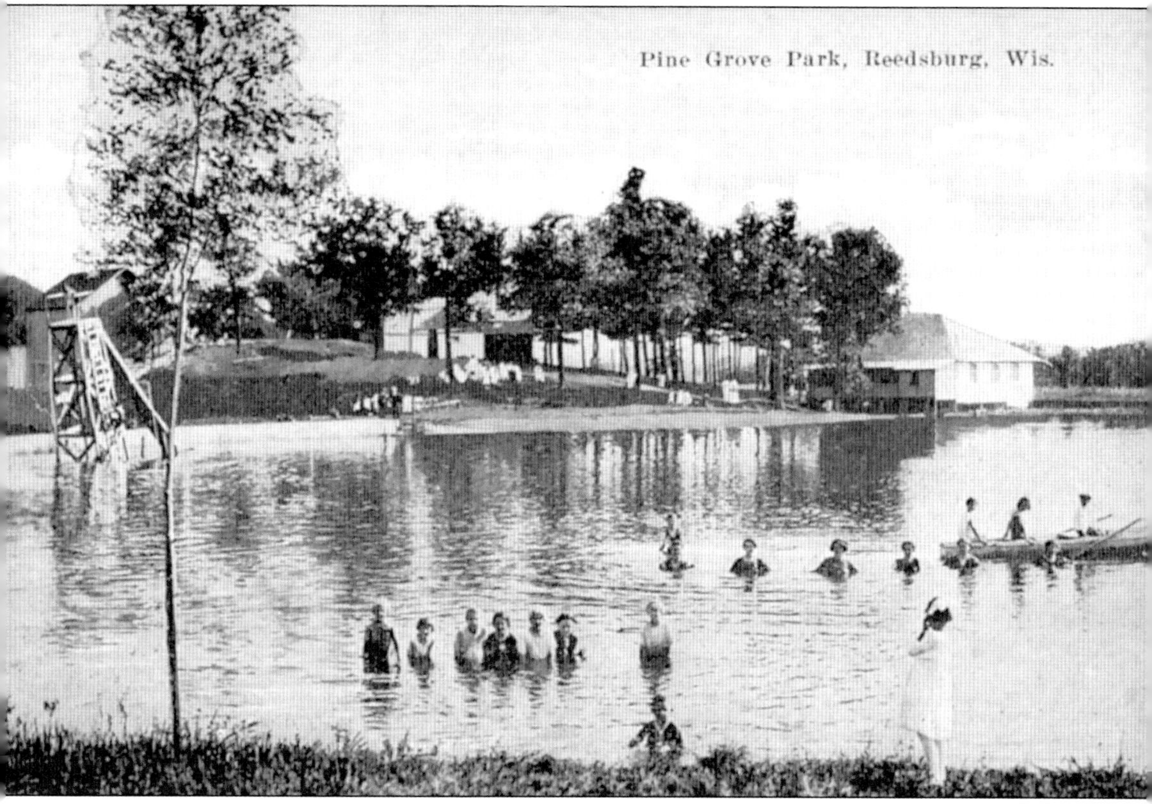

This park was located about a mile from Reedsburg. Mrs. A.F. Taylor started this resort area in the early 1900s. Everyone looked forward to the opening of this resort each year. Besides swimming in the lake, there was also a dance pavilion.

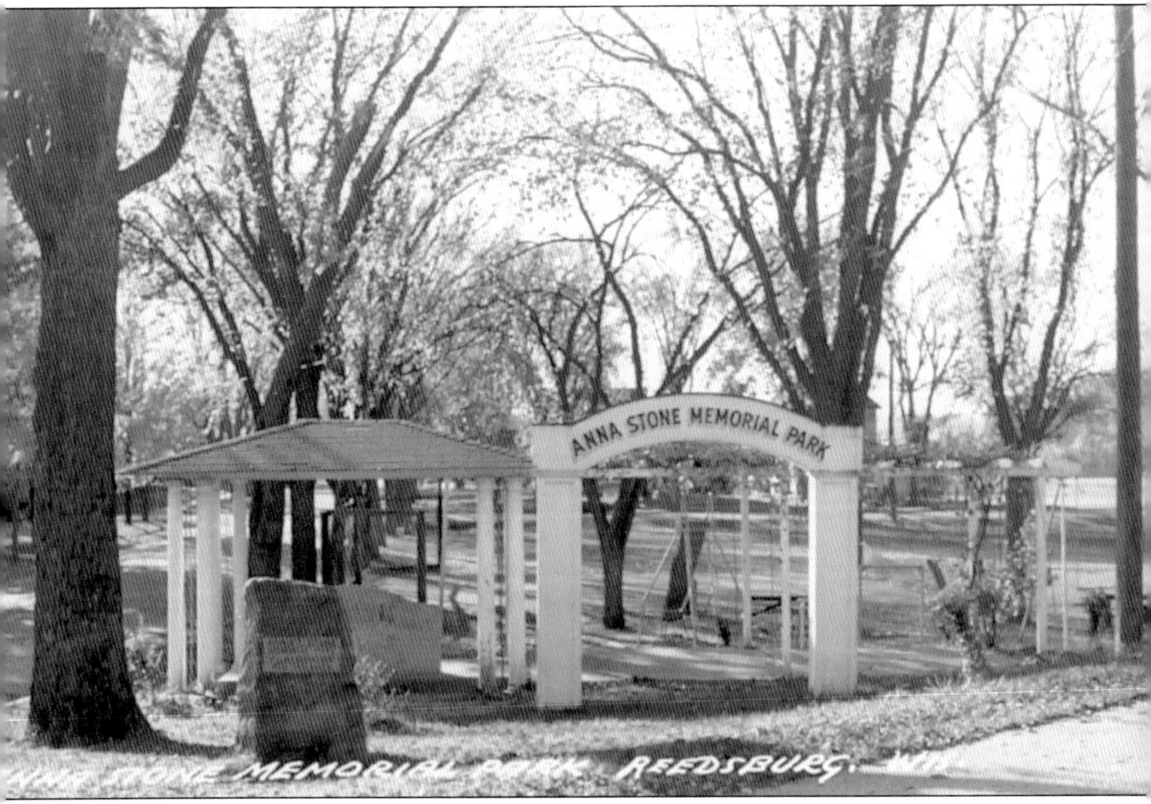

James A. Stone, a prominent attorney, donated a triangular parcel of land to the city in 1917. It was a memorial to his daughter, Anna, who died at a young age in 1913, and was buried in the Greenwood Cemetery. The land was used as a neighborhood park and playground. Many ballgames were played in this park, and during one winter the city flooded the area for a skating rink.

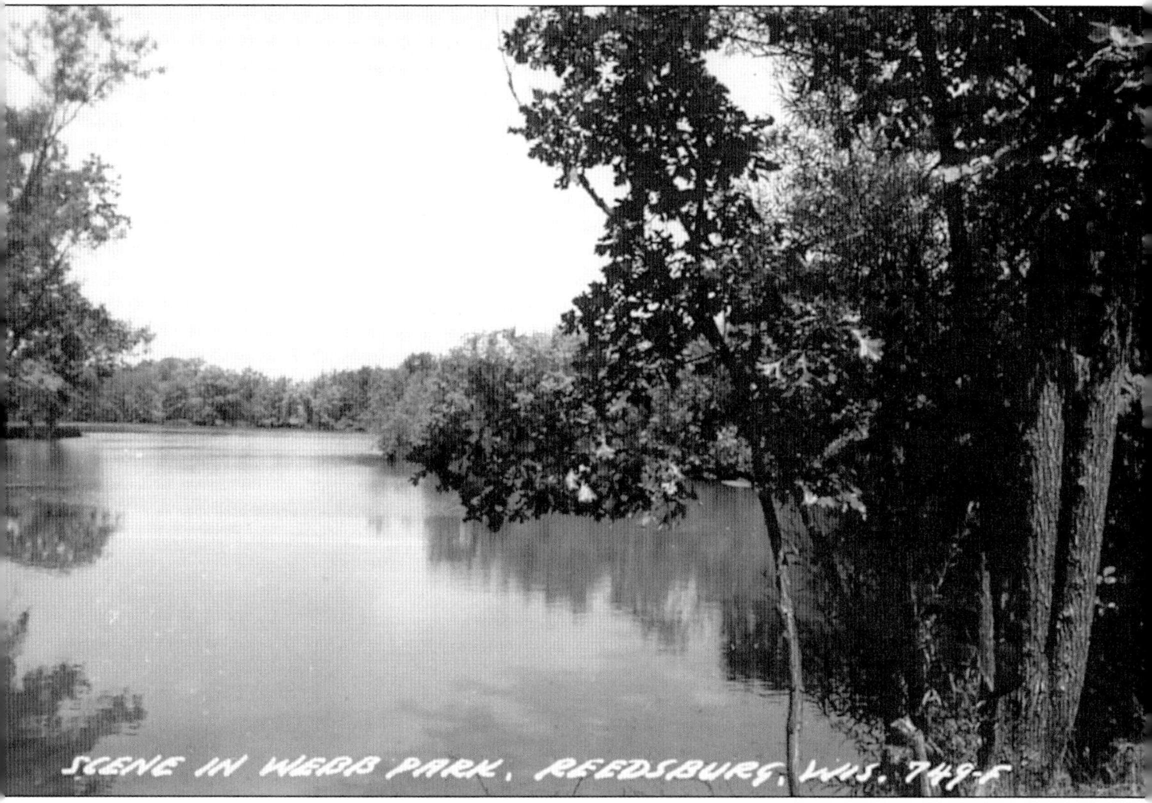

Herbert Webb left monies to the city of Reedsburg to be used for public purposes. At the earliest days of settlement, this area was a swamp land. During World War II, near or on this site, a prisoner of war camp was built. The prisoners were fenced in at night and only during the day were they released to work at the canning company or on nearby farms. More recently, the area has been improved and is now the site of Webb Park, with the largest picnic area, a swimming pool, tennis courts, playgrounds, and hiking trails.

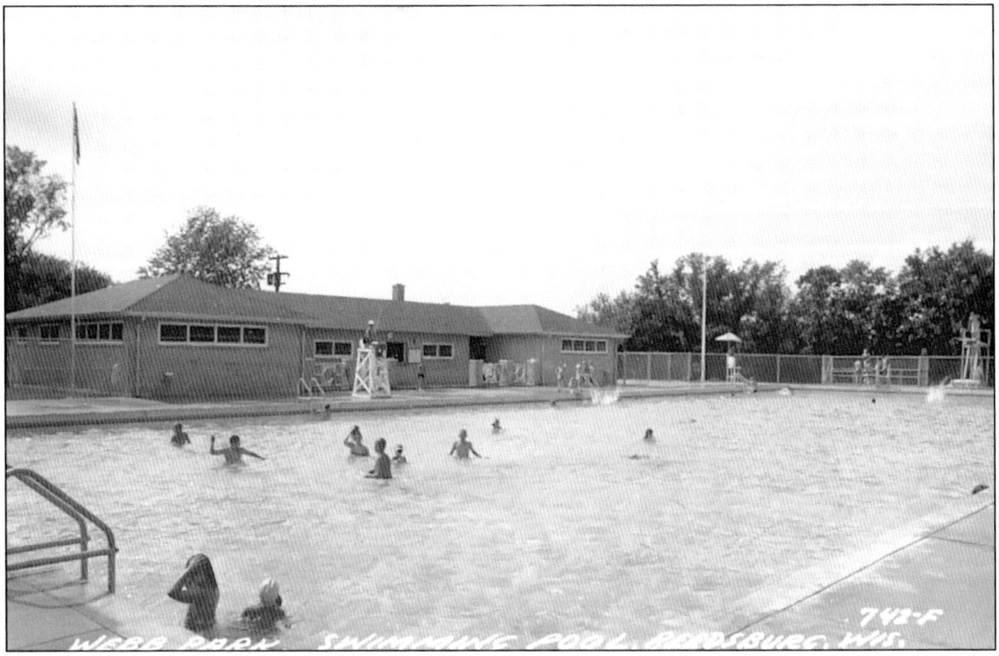

The squeals of delight ring through the rest of Webb Park as children cool off on a summer day and take their lessons to become the next generation of Life Guards.

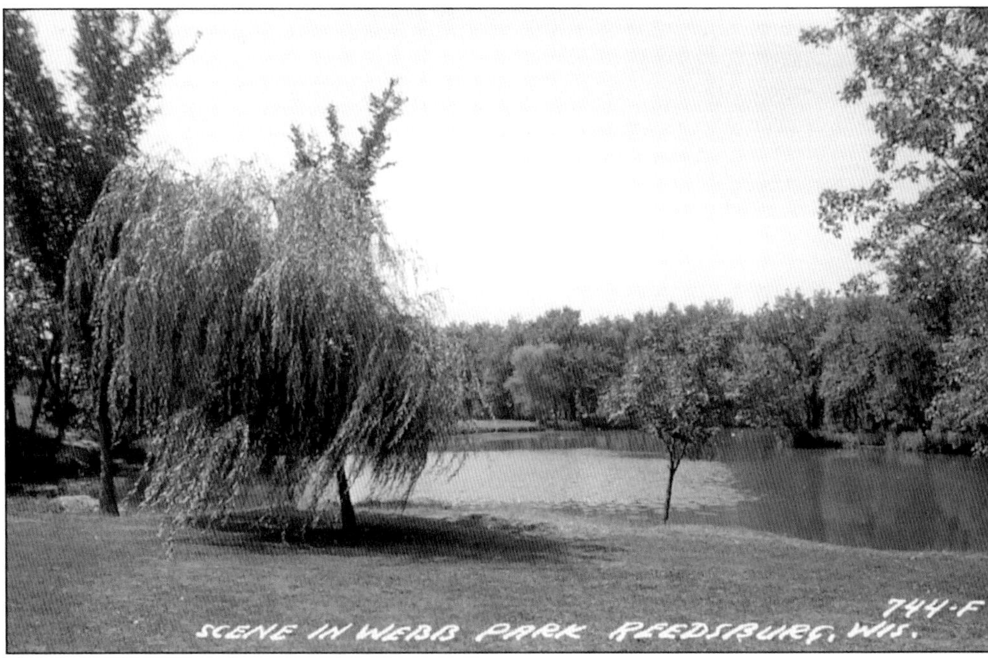

A lazy afternoon can be enjoyed by the river in Webb Park as it winds its way through Reedsburg to join the Wisconsin River, ending its journey in the Gulf of Mexico as the Mississippi River.

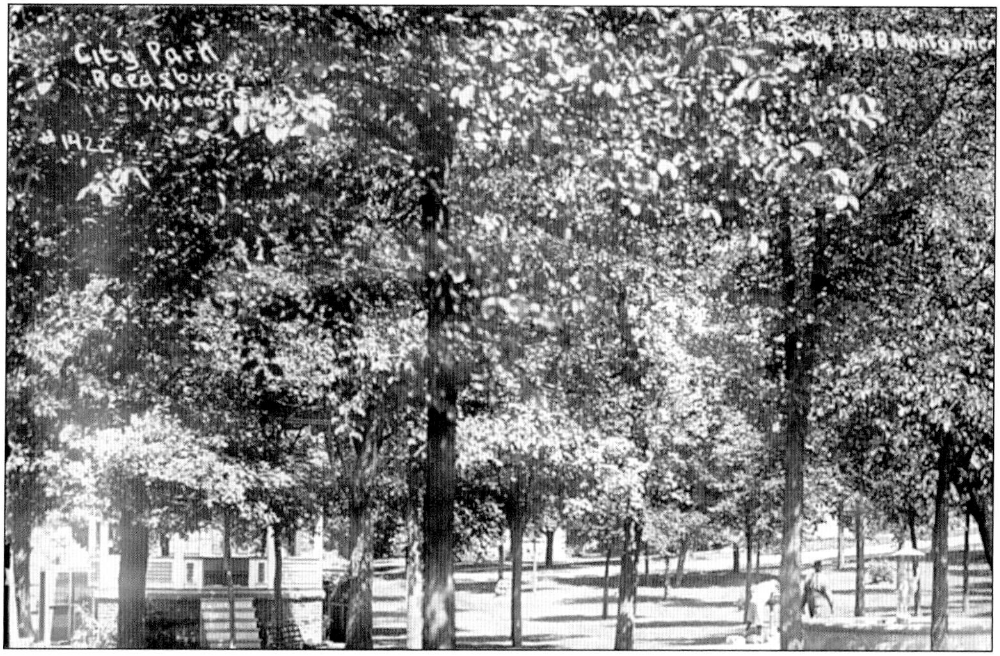

David Reed, the founder of Reedsburg, donated a complete square near the business district on Market Street, now Park Street, to be used as a village square. The park had shade trees, a drinking fountain, and a cement fish pond. A bandstand was erected *c*. 1910. The area was used for concerts, community picnics, and public meetings. Through a works project in the 1930s, the city replaced the wood and brick bandstand with a stone band shell. The stone was quarried just north of town.

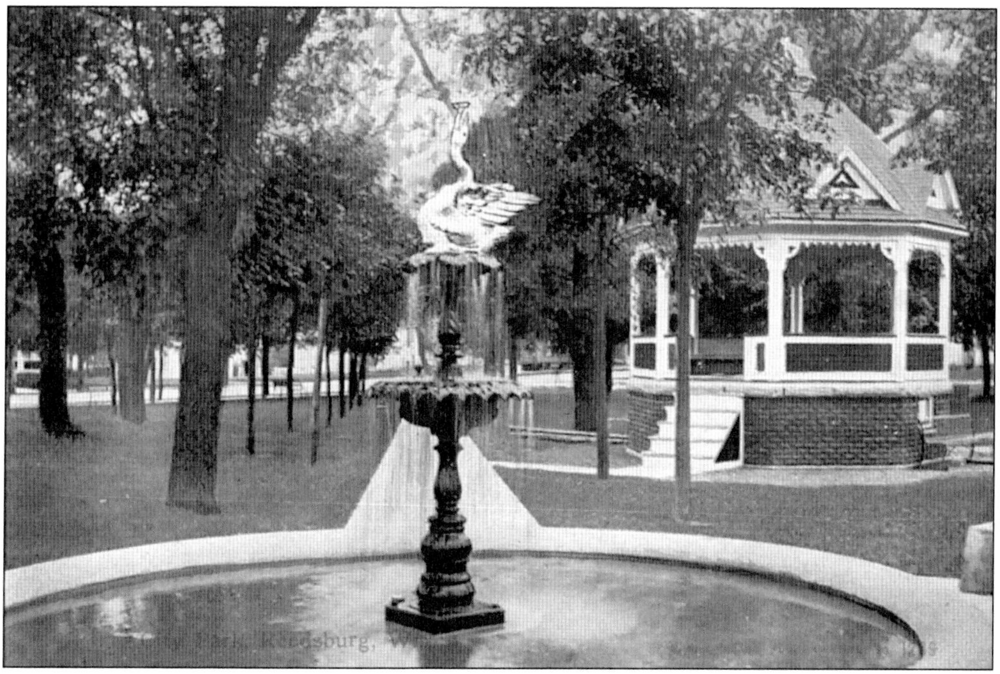

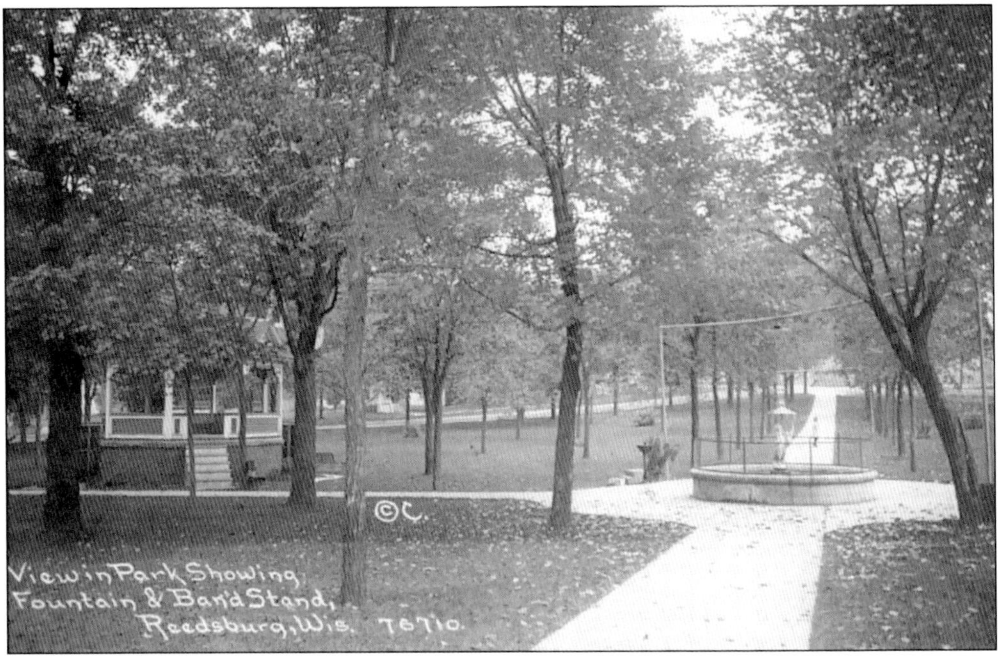

The park was a playground for children as well as a lovely place for public functions. This was the starting point for many Memorial Day parades to the Greenwood Cemetery in which children carried flags and flowers to be placed on the graves of the veterans that rest in peace at this burying ground. One of the graves visited was that of the little drummer boy, who at the age of 12 went to fight in the Civil War and returned to live his life out here in Reedsburg.

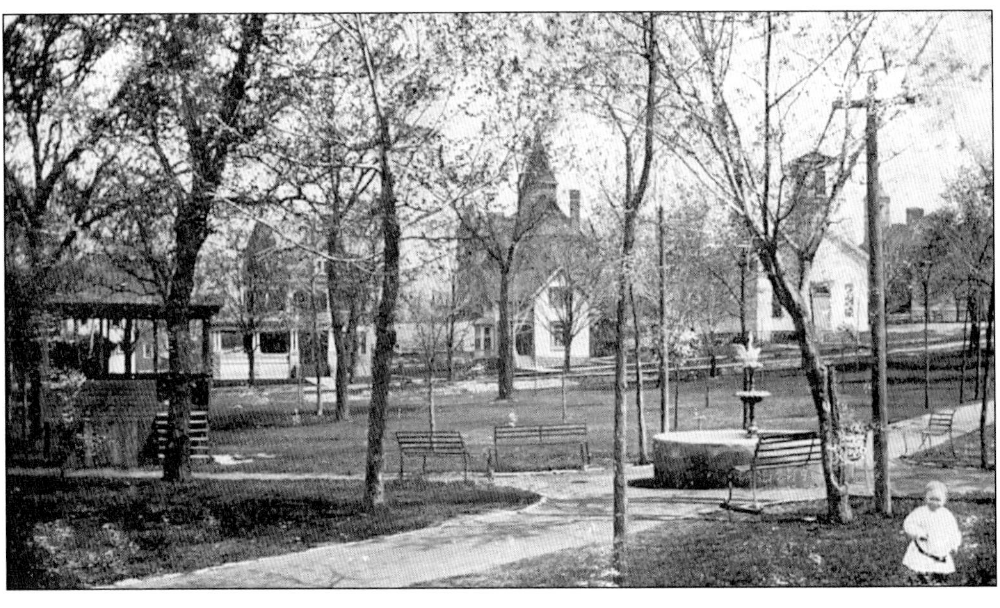

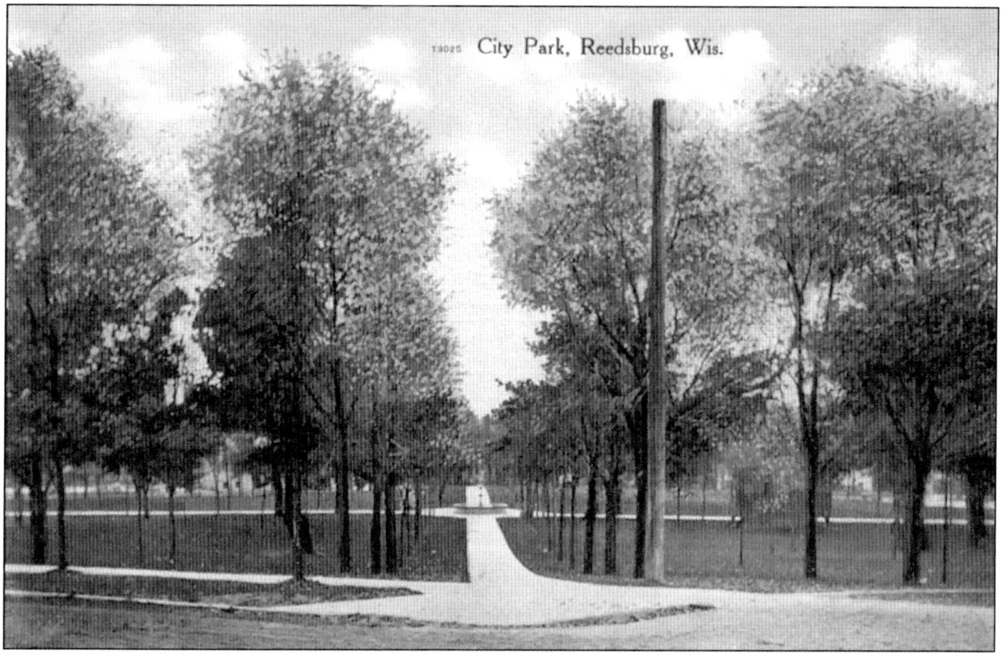

This park has walkways around the circumference, as well as cement sidewalks (previously dirt paths) cutting diagonally through the grounds. A fountain was erected in the middle of the city square. There is no remnant of the old fence which once enclosed the park. Loving care and the watchful eye of early residents have kept this park in pristine condition.

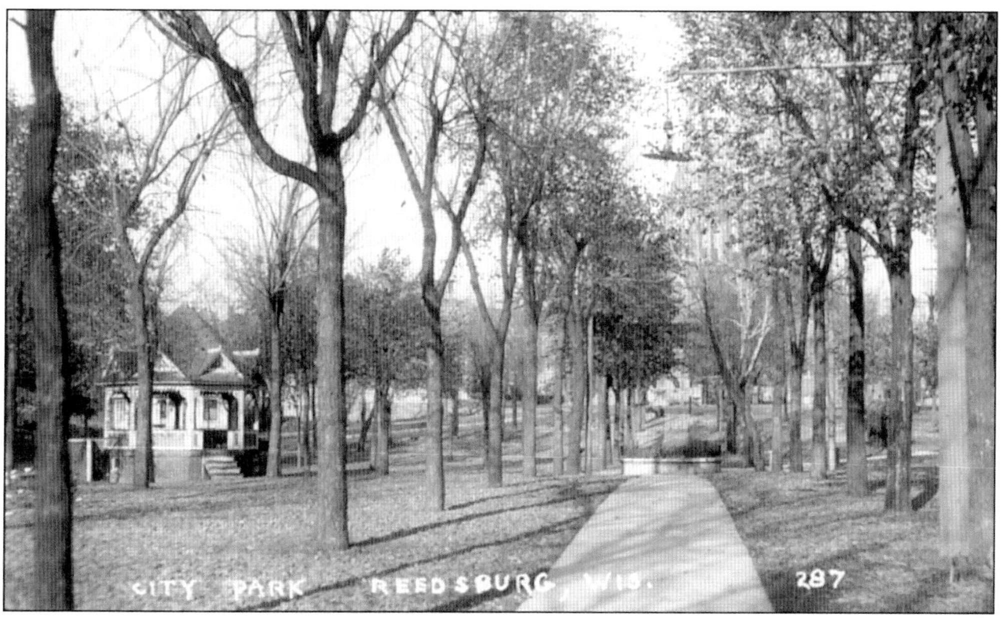

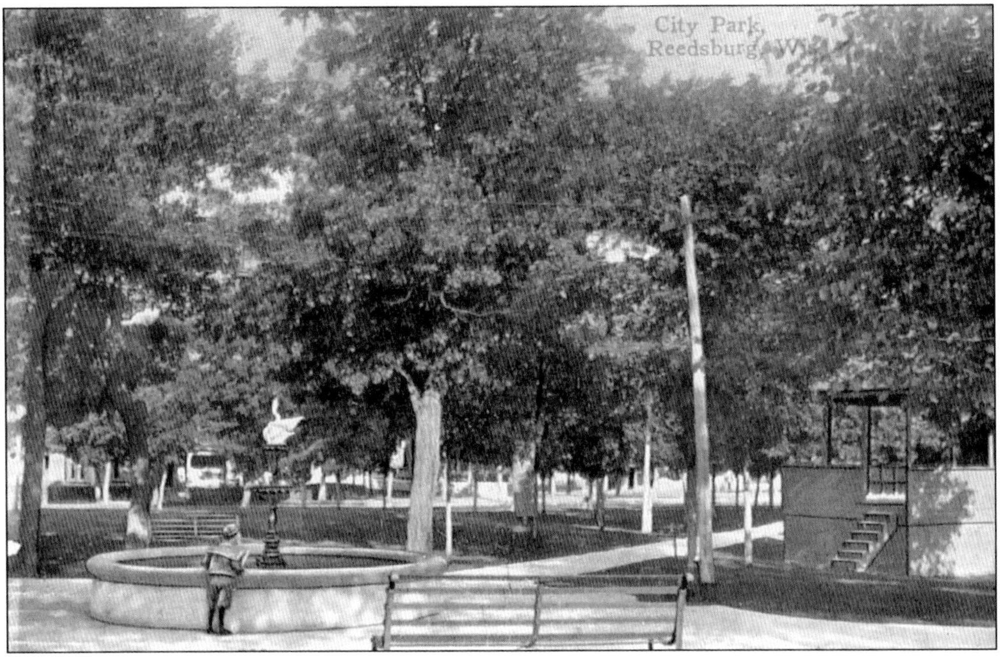

The shade of the elms around the goldfish pond can be seen in this photo of the park. What a wonderful way to spend a hot summer afternoon. Many of the features of the park have changed because of the passage of time, but the little boy on this card, daydreaming of things to come, could be from any time.

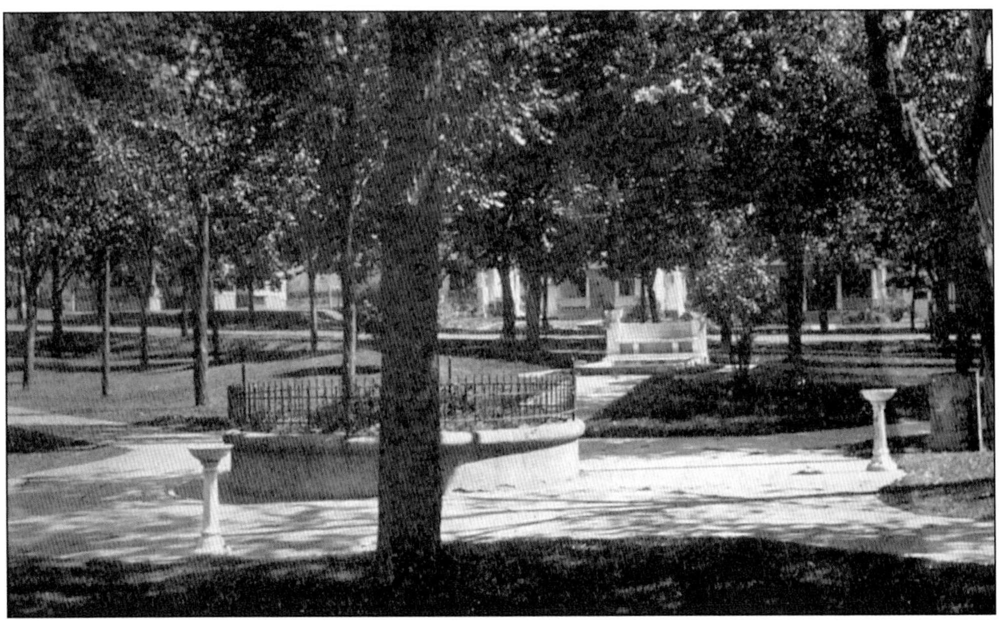

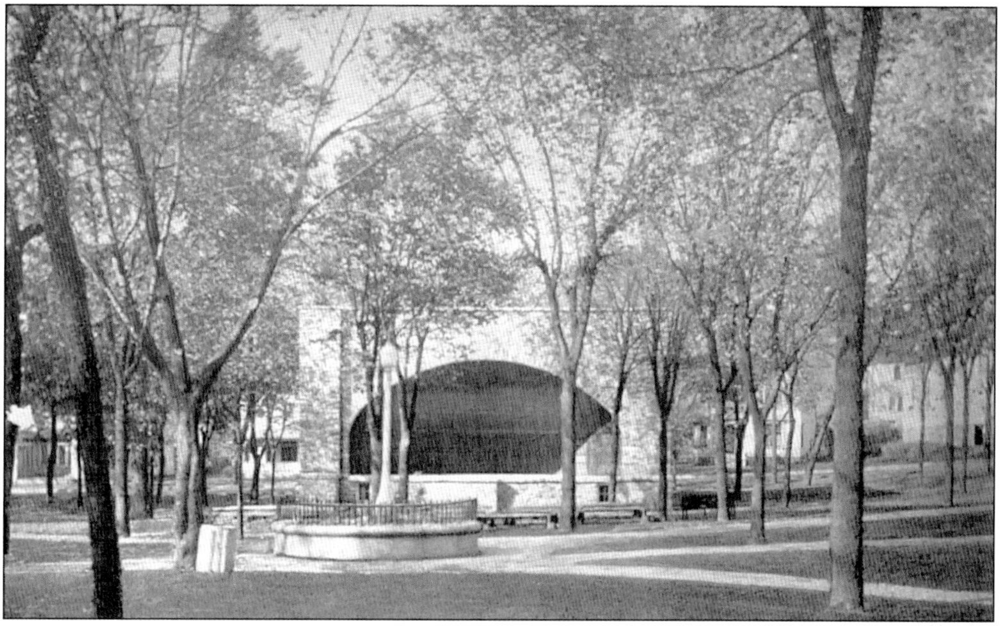

The stone band shell was the site of many concerts throughout the years, some from the local high school band. Many an evening was spent enjoying the music and cool of the evening. When electricity came to Reedsburg, the walkways and benches had marvelous lighting for an evening stroll through the park.

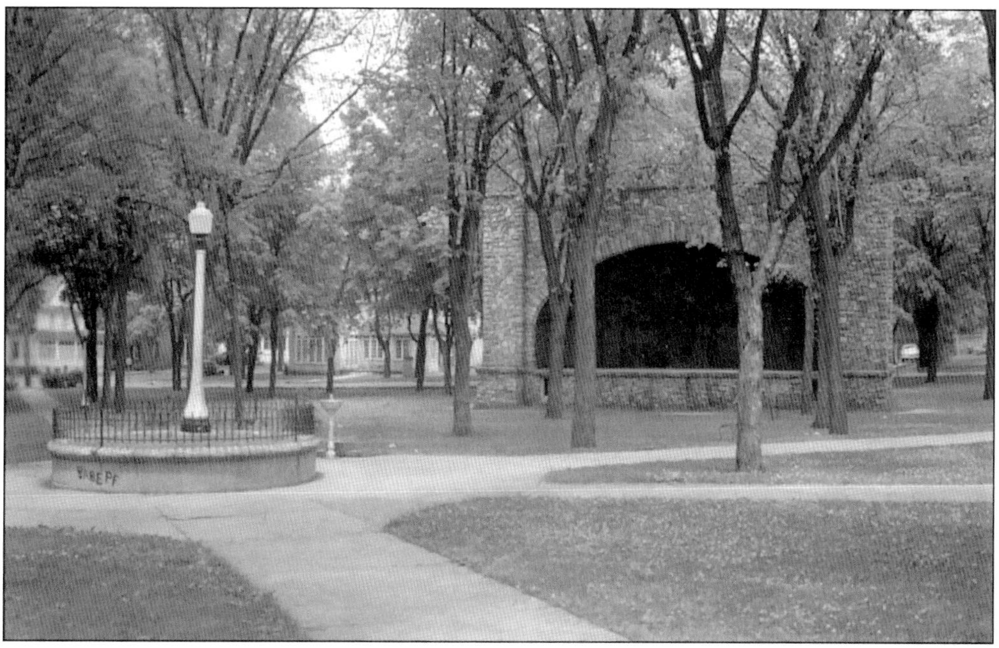

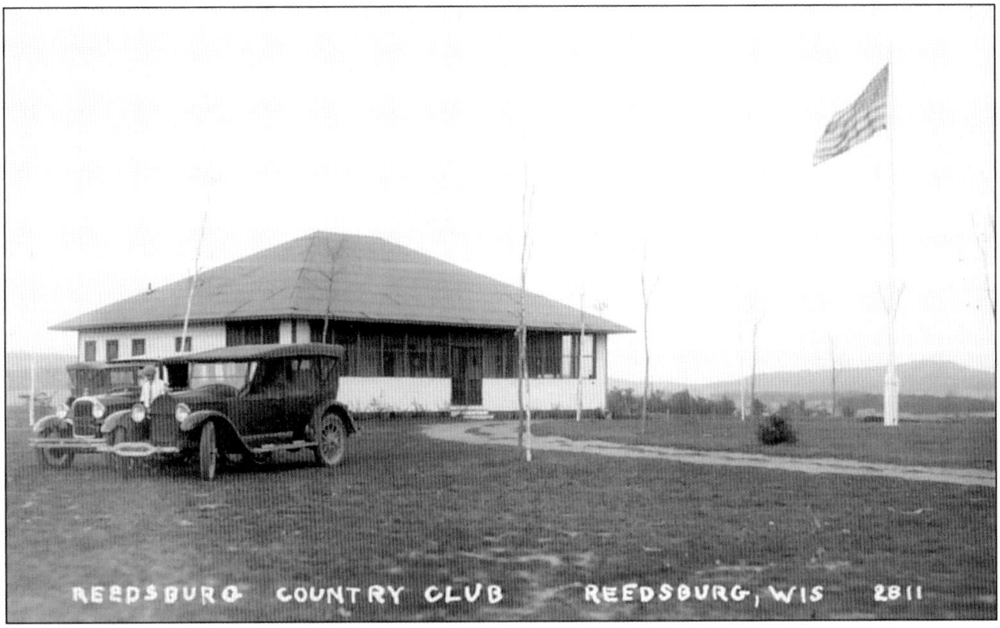

The country club was started in 1924, when a group of men built a nine-hole golf course on about 60 acres of land just east of Reedsburg on Highway 33. The first clubhouse was a meager wooden building on a knoll overlooking the course. As time passed, the clubhouse was improved with additions, and today overlooks a full 18 holes of golf, in place of the original 9.

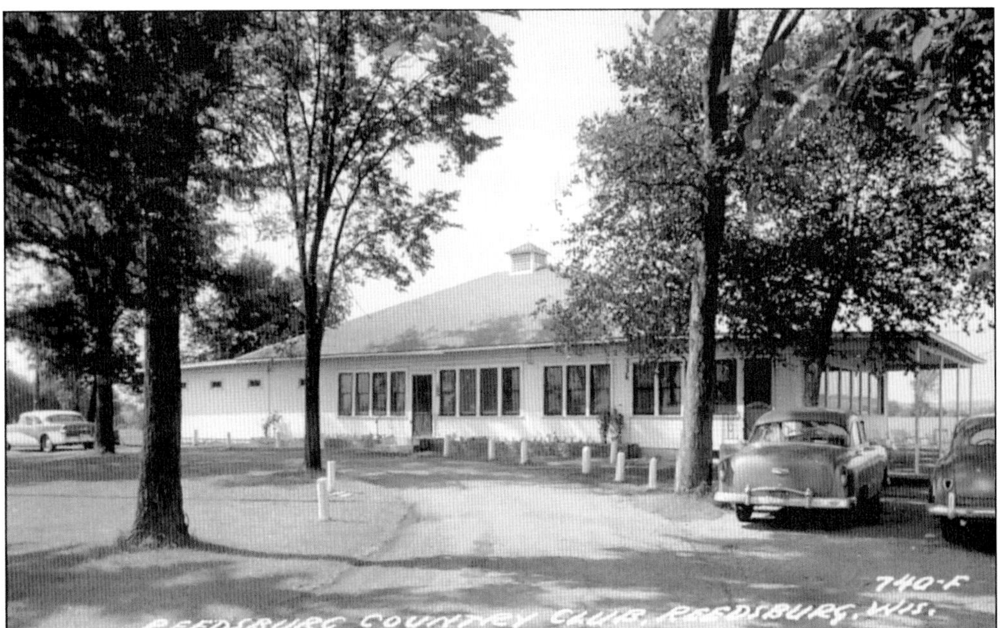

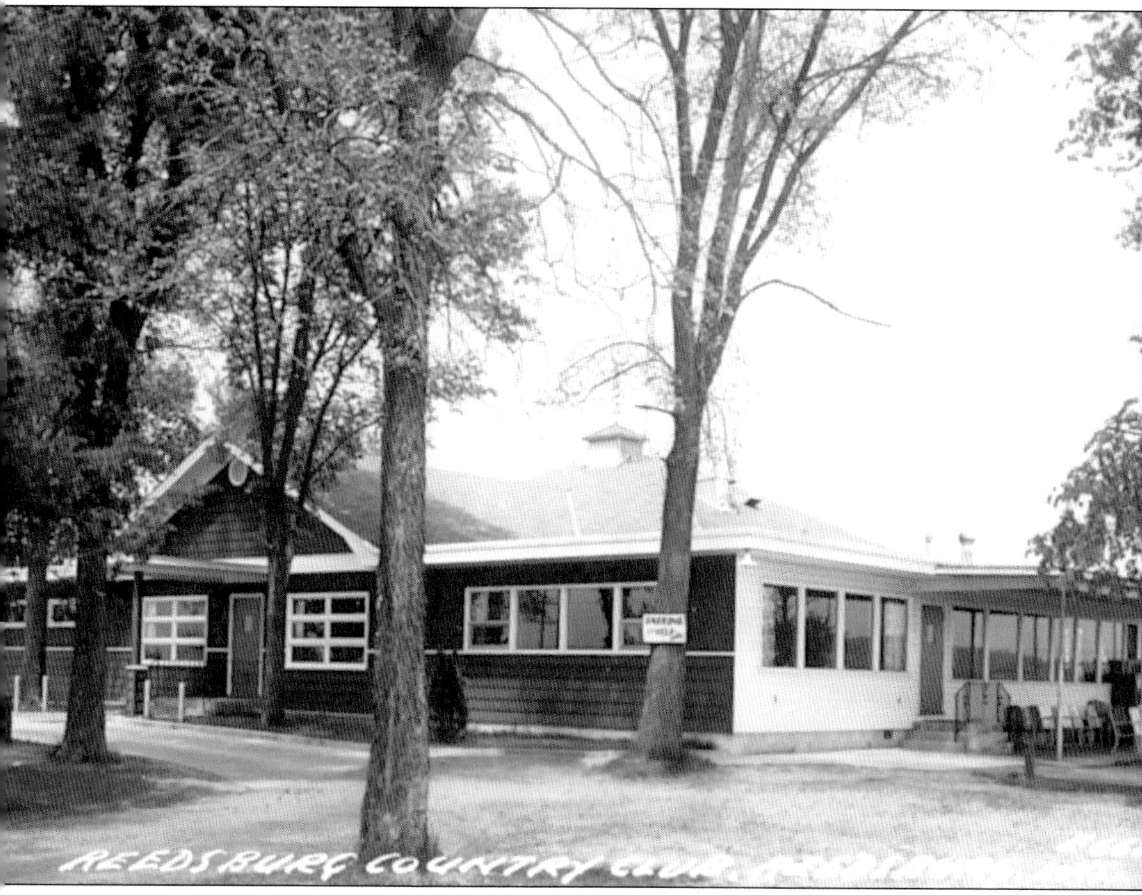

Another innovation in the remodeling of the clubhouse.

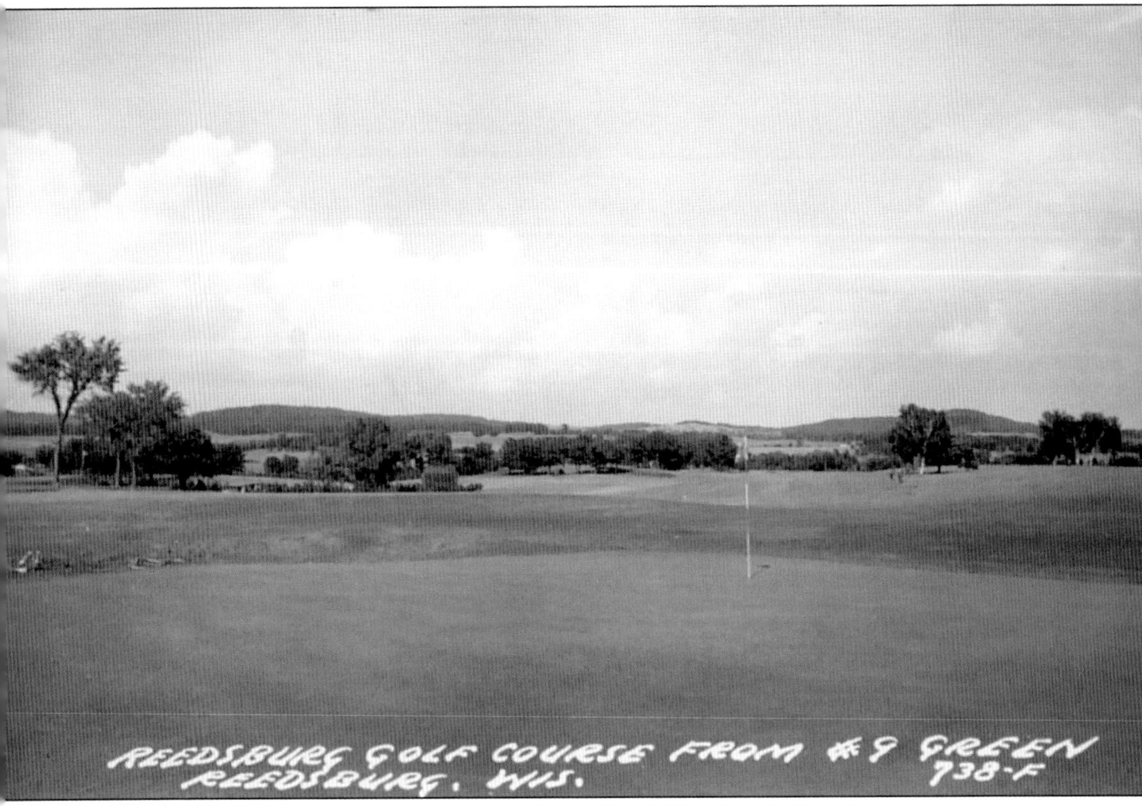

The "birdies" and the "eagles" live on in the rolling hills of rural Reedsburg.

Three

Public Buildings

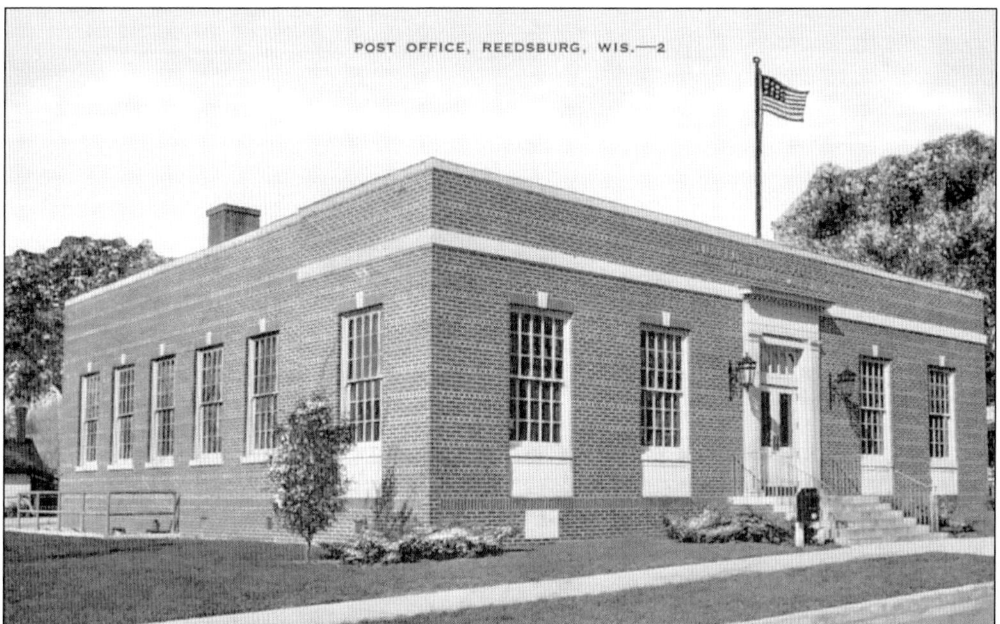

Postal deliveries to Reedsburg have come in many forms. Early on, mail was brought on foot from Baraboo. Eventually the mail came by stage and finally by train. Other changes have taken affect, such as the spelling of the town, from Reedsburgh to Reedsburg, and the discontinuation of twice daily delivery. The Reedsburg post office had many locations before this building was constructed on North Walnut Street in 1938. A beautiful mural painted in the lobby can still be viewed today.

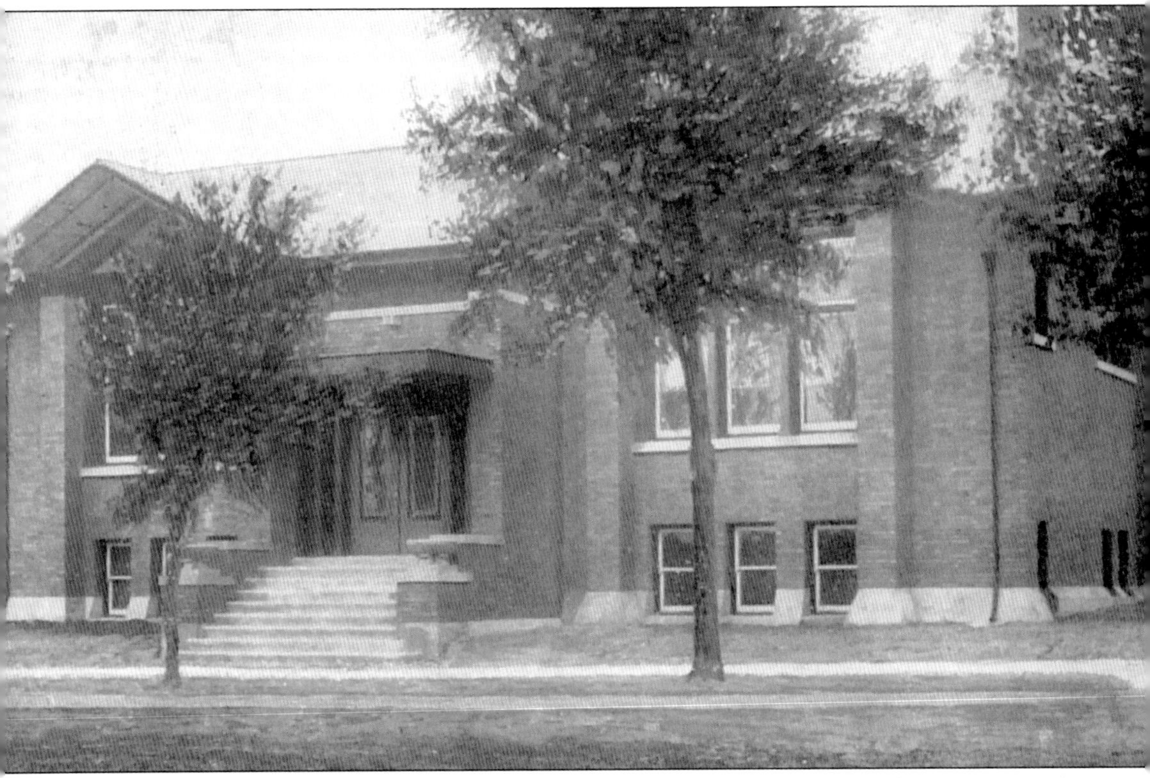

In 1898, the Woman's Club of Reedsburg invited a woman of the State Library Commission to come to town and speak about the importance of a free library in the community. The meeting was held at Brooks' Hall and was well attended. It took a year to secure funds and arouse interest, with the first space donated by Mr. and Mrs. Stine in a building that still stands on Main Street today. As the library grew, it found a new home in the upper level of the fire department building. Mrs. George Morse donated a lot near the downtown business area in order for the library to construct a building of their own. Application was made to the Andrew Carnegie Library Fund for help with the project. Ground was broken in 1911 and on January 1, 1912, an open-house warming was well attended. By 1998, circumstances required a newer and larger facility, but the Carnegie still stands, throwing its shadow toward the new Reedsburg Library. There are plans to refurbish the building and continue its use as a library of sorts.

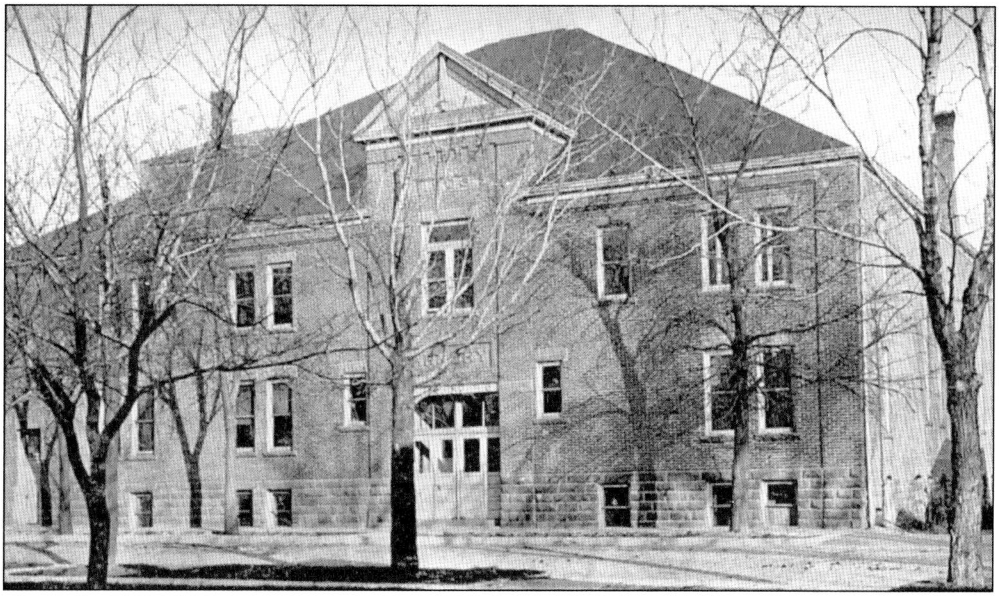

The armory was built in 1903 at a location on South Park Street. Besides being the home of the National Guard, it was also used for social events connected with the Reedsburg Military, like the balls held to give our boys a good send-off for the World Wars. The guards have served the state from 1899 until the present time. At one time there was roller skating for the young people of the area at least once weekly. The building housed the National Guard, which has served the state for over 100 years, until 1965 when a new building and the site of the armory was replaced with a commercial building.

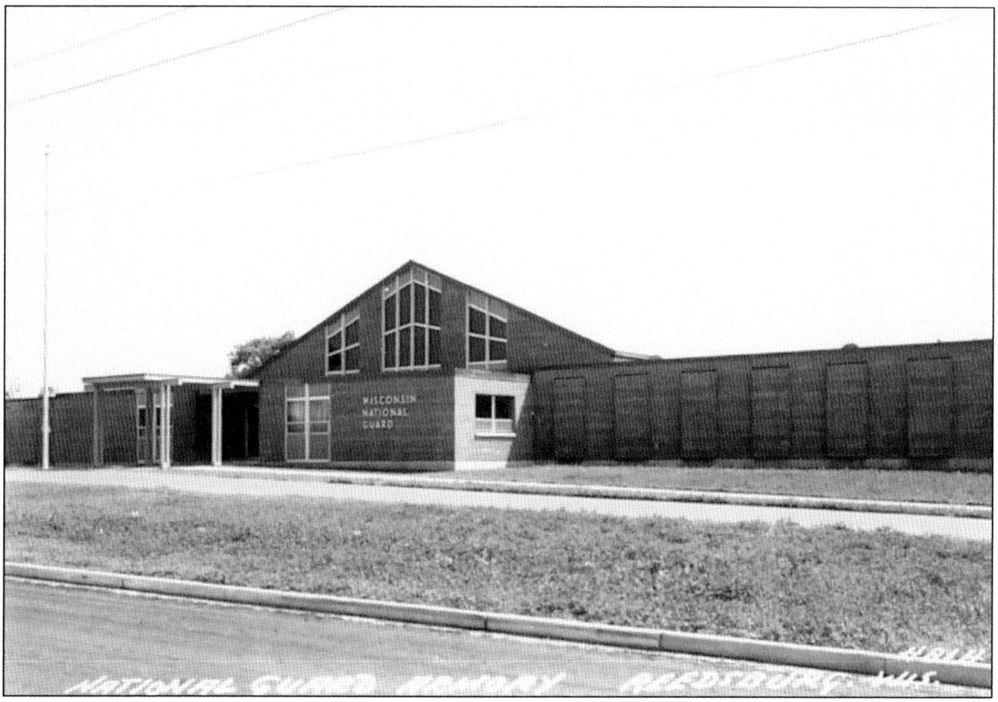

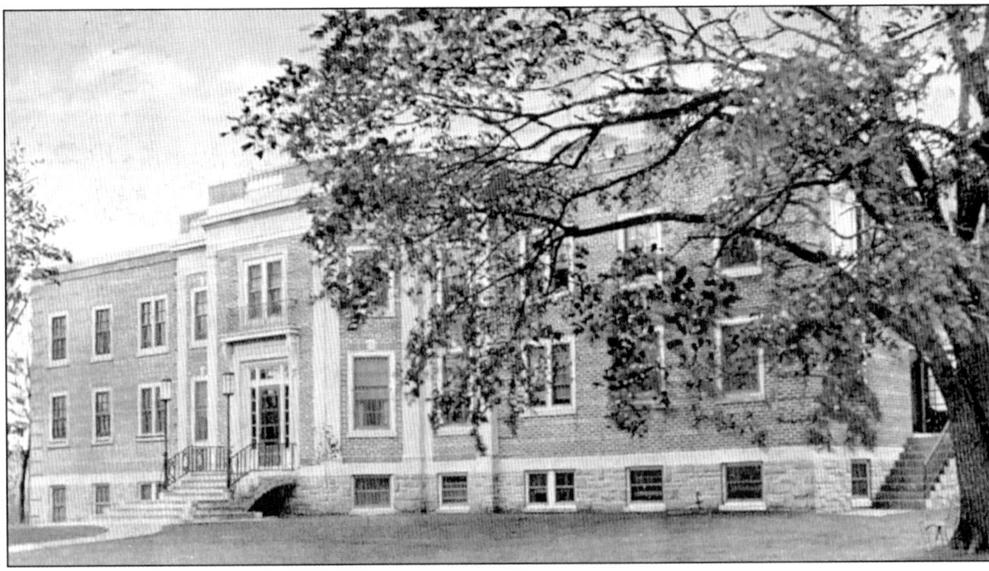

At a meeting of the Kiwanis Club in 1930, a group of men banded together to explore the idea of building a municipal hospital. In 1932, a public meeting was held at the old armory, with a great crowd responding. A referendum to build a hospital was held, and after a vote of 1,053 to 203, the construction of a building proceeded. Mrs. Freda Nishan donated a parcel of land on North Park Street large enough to build a good-sized building set back from the street. That year at the Old Settlers' Association meeting it was decided that the group would donate a room to be known as the Old Settlers' Room. Nine other people followed their lead. Construction began with the bulk of the labor hired locally. The hospital opened on January 27, 1933, with Miss Ida Larson as the first superintendent. This building served the community until 1976, and is still standing today, remodeled as an apartment building.

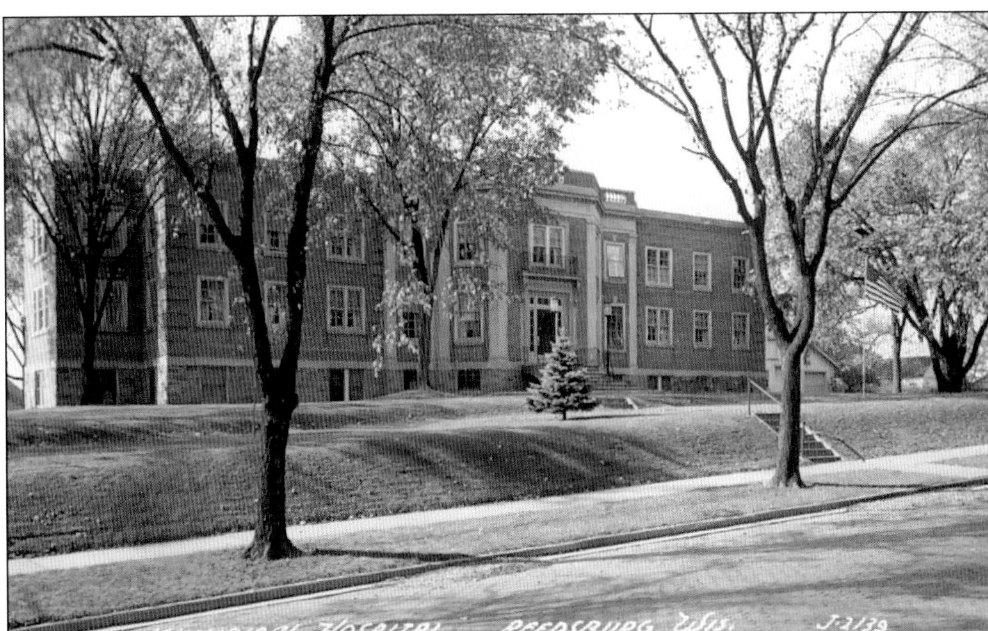

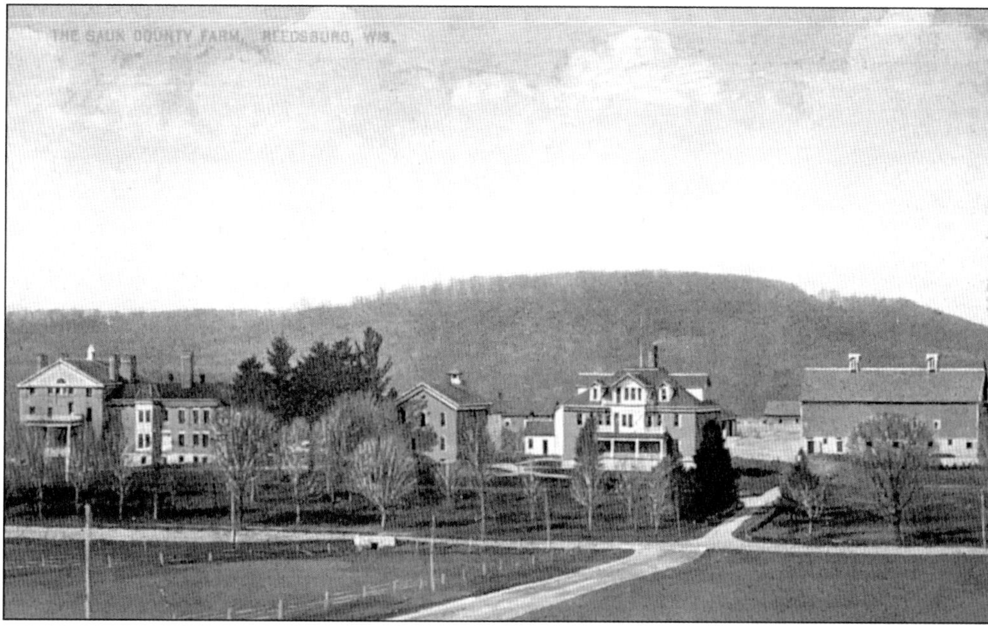

About 4 1/2 miles south of Reedsburg off of Highway 23 is the Sauk County Health Care Center, once known as the Sauk County Farm and the County Poor Farm and Insane Asylum. The land for the original building was first purchased in 1871. The first admissions to the hospital were recorded in 1887, with a total of five residents. Depending upon capability, the residents performed many of the chores on the farm. Cattle were kept in the barns, gardens were grown, and goods were preserved and baked. The farm had its own fire department and there was an industrial building on the premises in which inmates could weave on a loom. The patients were taught upholstery work and furniture repair, as well as basket weaving and brass pounding. By 1918, about 75 percent of the patients were from Sauk County. Those outside the county were accepted, but had to pay more for their care. Though many changes have been made, the quiet rural setting, with abundant shade trees, stayed the same.

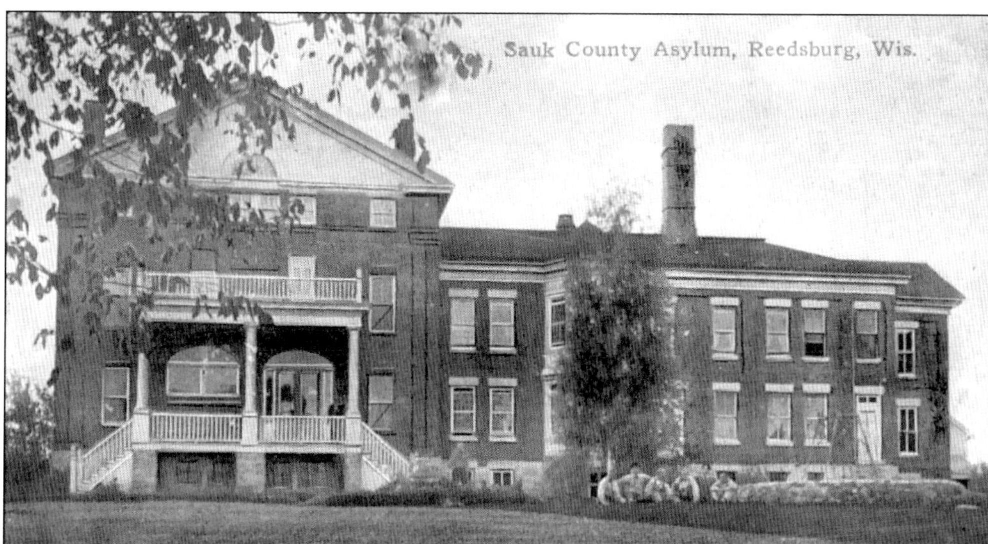

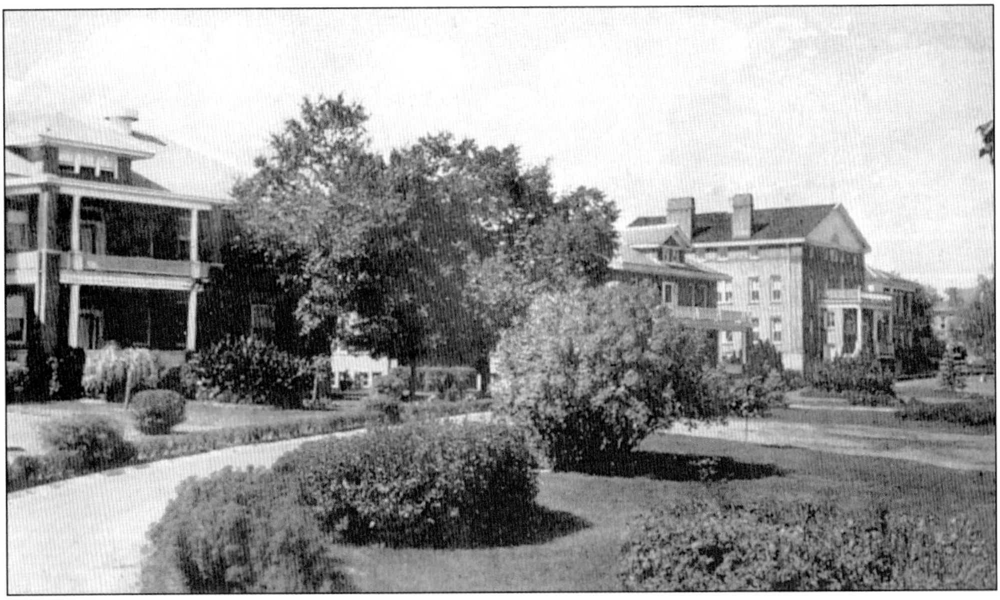

This is an image of the Sauk County Hospital and Home.

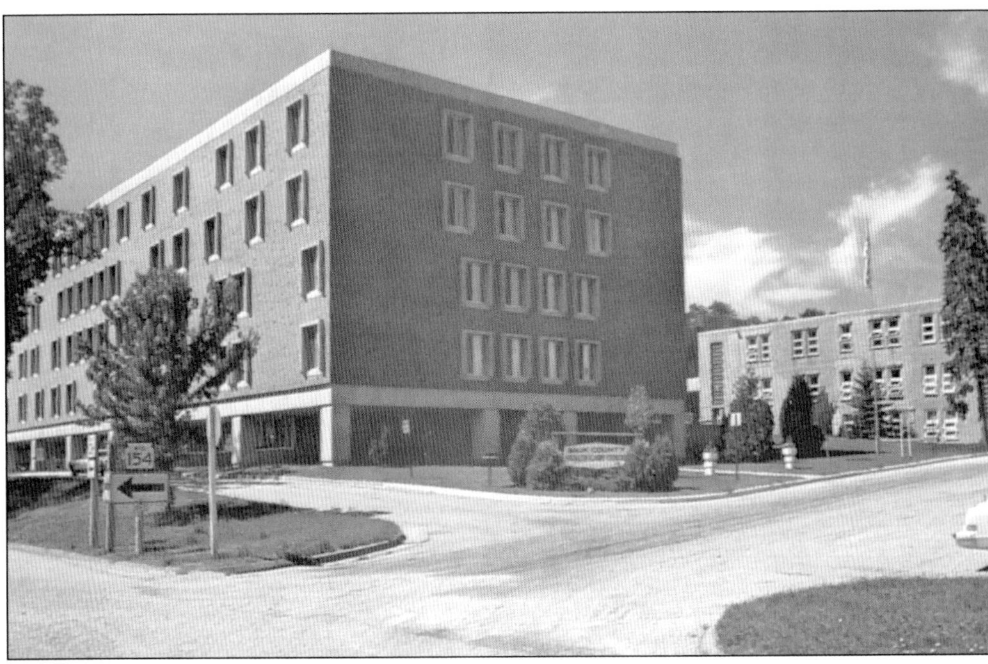

The Sauk County Health Care Center as it looked in later years after construction of new buildings.

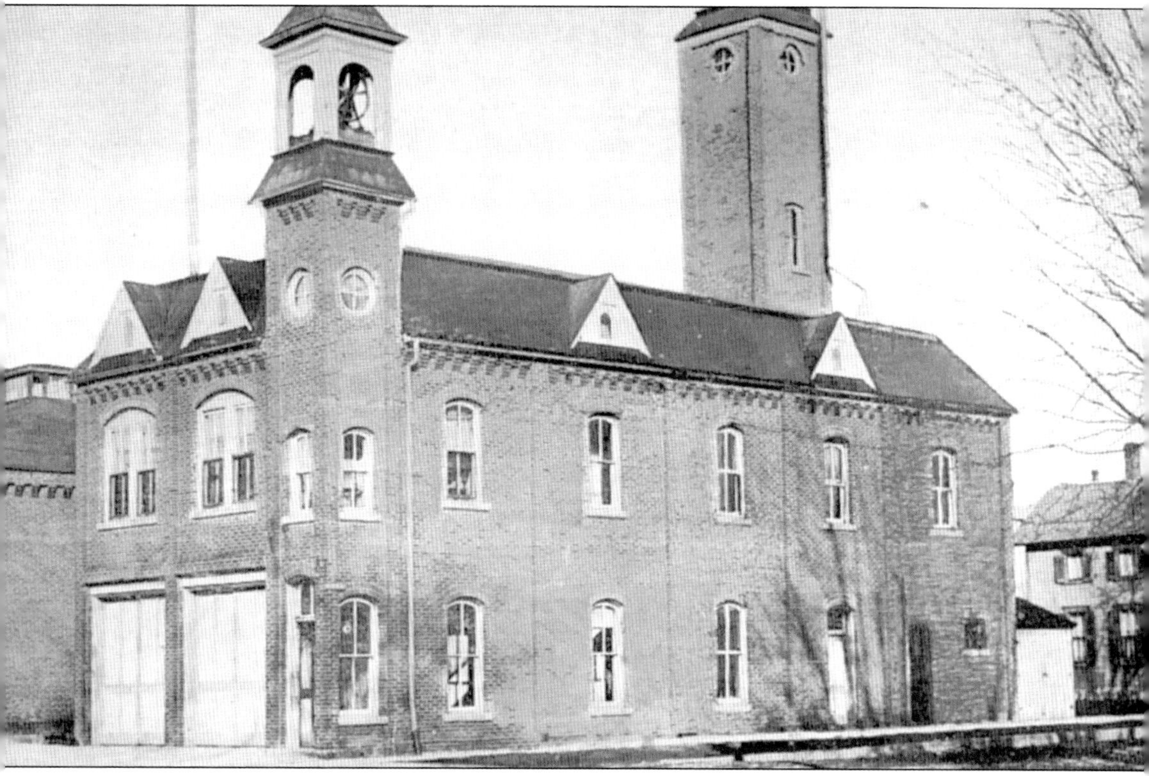

In 1888, the lower level of the City Hall was constructed to house the fire department and jail. By 1900 a second story was added, along with the tower on the east side of the building for drying the hoses. Council rooms and a public library were on the new second story. The library was used until a new building was completed at the corner of South Locust and Vine Street. Until much later in the 20th century, the top floor was used as a recreation center for the youth of the area, and was known as "The Hive." By the 1970s an entirely new municipal building was erected at the eastern portion of the block and this building was razed to build a new fire station and police department. In the days before trucks were used to fight fires there was a barn behind the fire department that housed the horses used in pulling the pumps, hoses, ladders, and tools that were needed to fight the blaze.

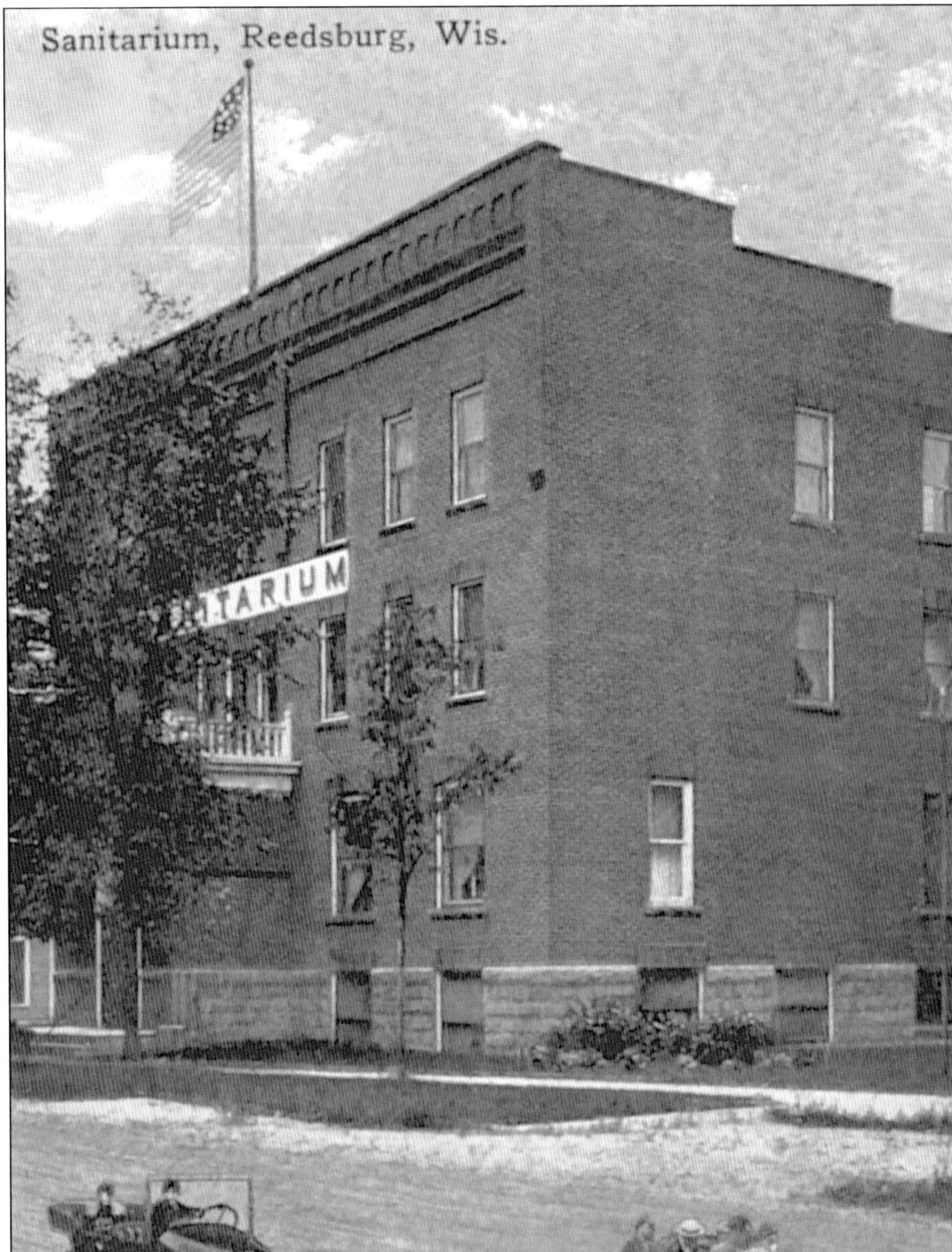

The Bates Hotel was built *c.*1900 on Vine Street near South Walnut. In 1902 the hotel had 40 rooms, parlors, sample rooms, steam heat, electricity, and baths. Laborers, retirees, businessmen, and others listed the hotel as their residence in a 1902 directory. Dr. T.R. Hastings, formerly of Lime Ridge, purchased the Bates Hotel and opened the Sanitarium in 1912. He saw a need for in-house care and a nursing staff to care for patients on a round the clock watch. The Sanitarium provided Turkish baths, hot air baths, massages, etc. Being built of brick it was less prone to fire, and Dr. Hastings installed a new ventilating system, one of the grand features of the new business.

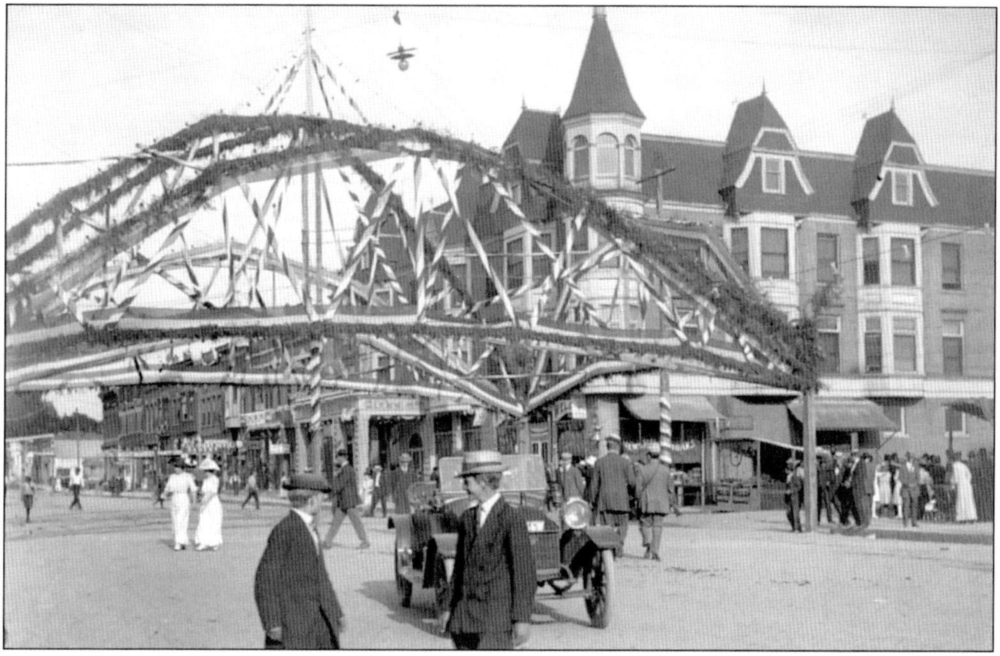

In 1912, a department went all out to insure the success and enjoyment the Wisconsin State Fireman's Tournament. About $2,500 was raised by local, state, and association funds to be used in the celebration, some as prize money. Local papers boasted of the city's ability to host such a celebration on its paved streets, and advertisements were used to find rooms for rent in order to accommodate the thousands of visitors. The fire department dressed in their protective rubber suits for the state competition. A team of horses present answered to the names of Pete and Charlie, and were a very important part of the fire department. On a previous response to a fire during a storm, a team of horses met their death when accidentally electrocuted by a voltage wire.

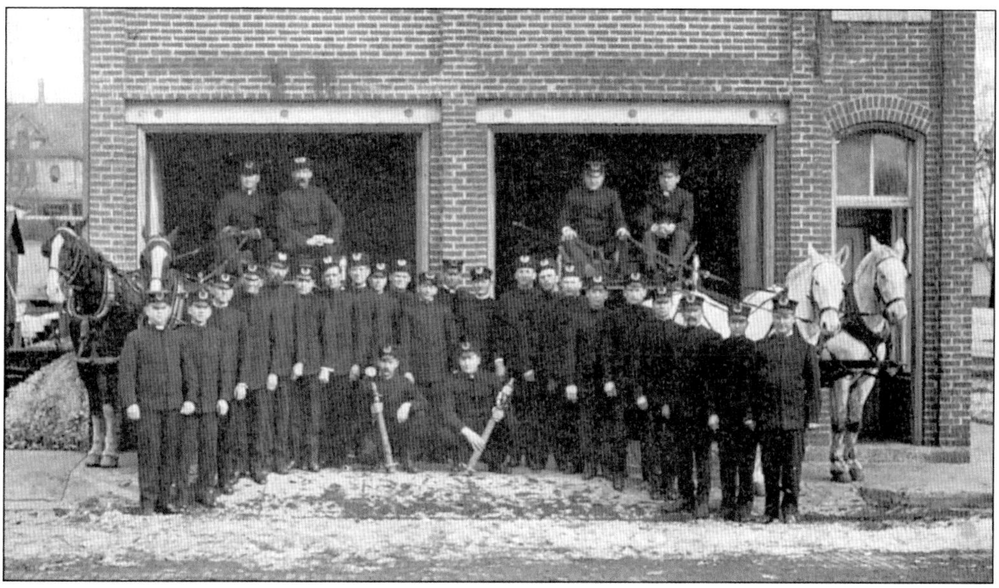

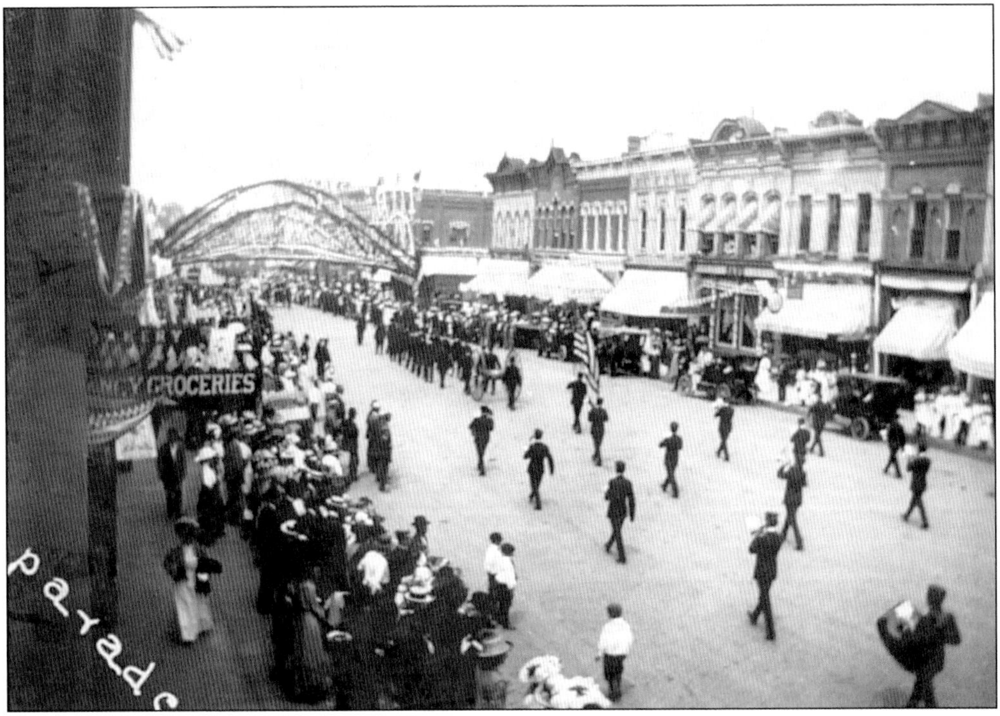

A large attendance was at the parade for the Firemen Tournament as it headed from east to west on Main Street.

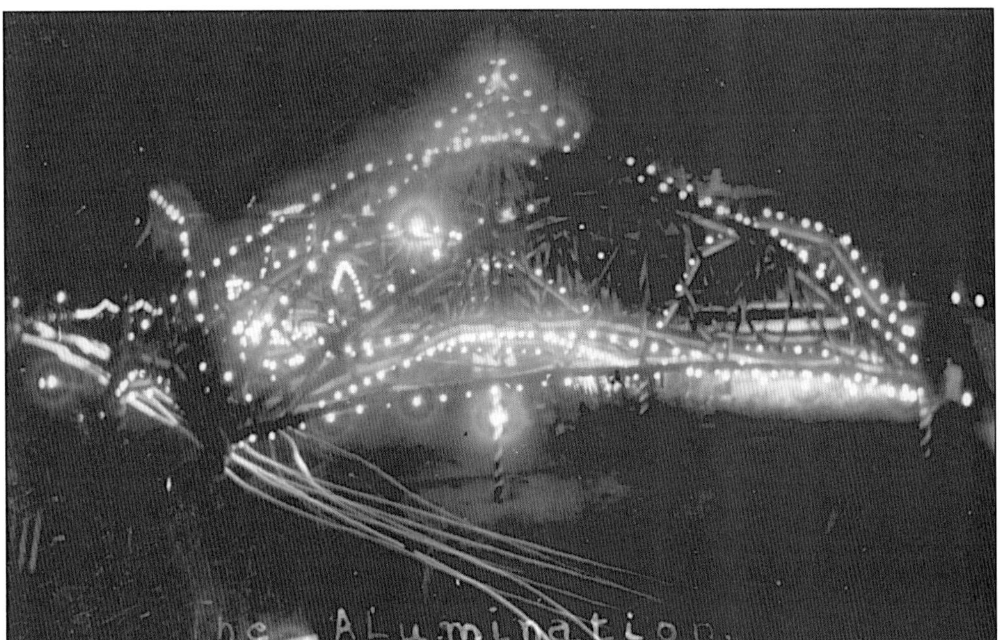

At the intersection of Main Street and Walnut Street a canopy was constructed for the Tournament. The glow of the lighted canopy was an attraction at the evening festivities.

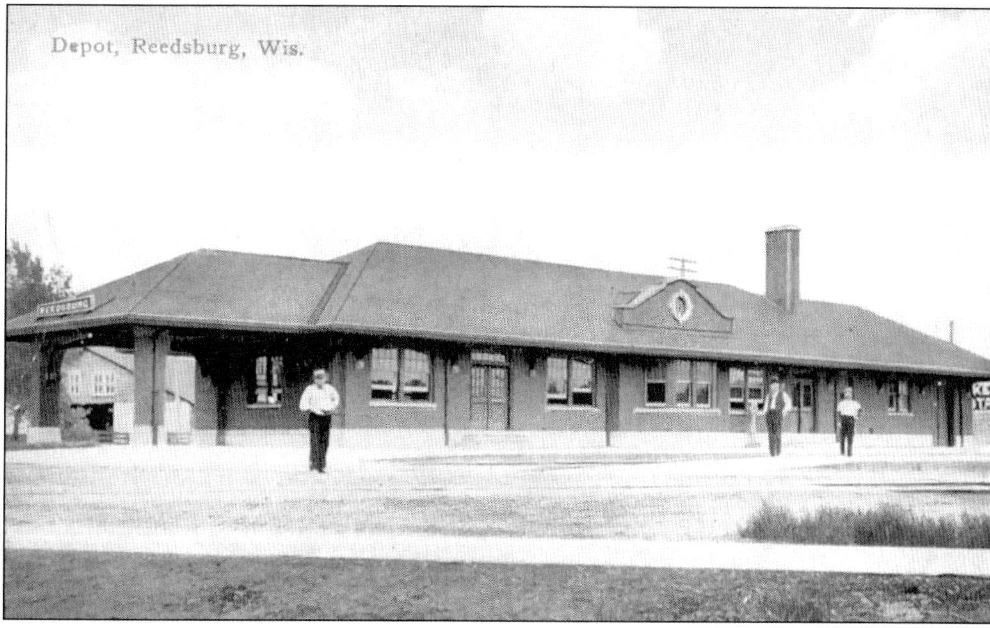

Thanks to the efforts of Colonel Abelman, the railroad reached Reedsburg in 1872. The growth of the city very much depended on the location of the railroad. In a 1924 newspaper schedule there were five westbound trains and five eastbound trains. The depot was an area of much activity and the trains served many purposes. Hops was shipped from Reedsburg in the 1860s. Lore has it there is at least one house in the city that was shipped by train; an order delivered from an early Sears catalog. The town's military men left for the Mexican War, and both World Wars via the depot. Even as late as the Berlin Call-up in 1961, the National Guard left this city by train.

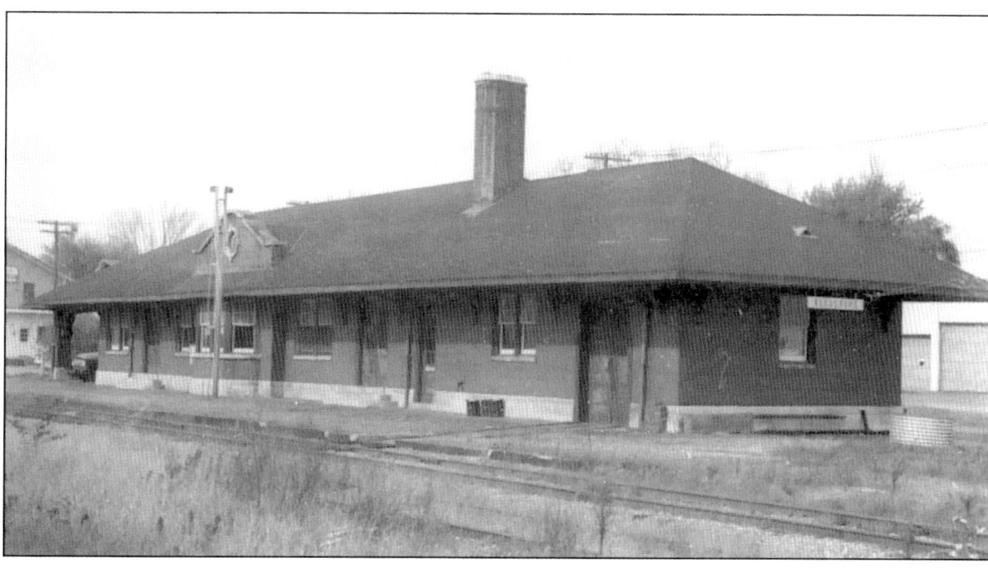

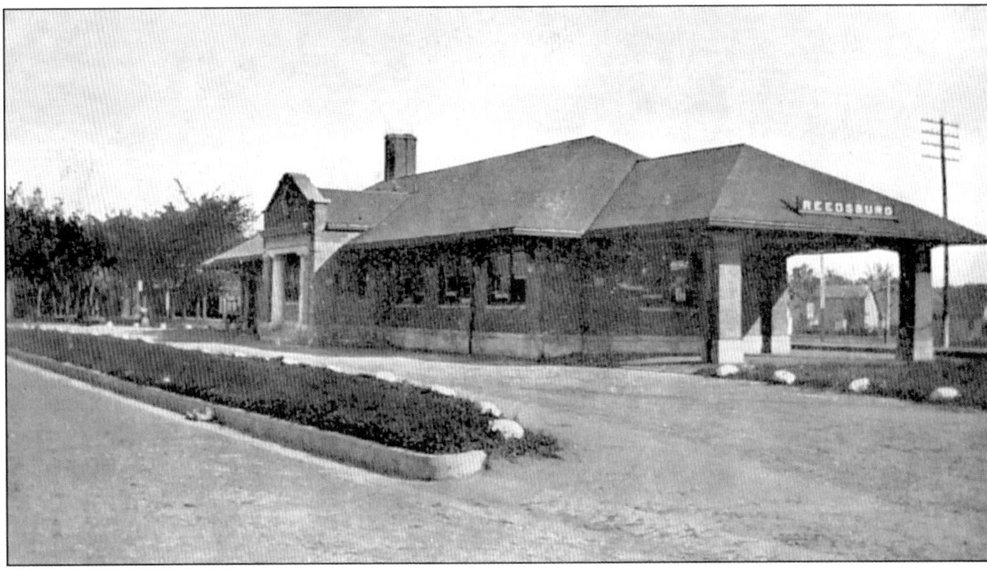

The Chicago & Northwestern Depot (CNW) awaits the arrival of passengers at its front door.

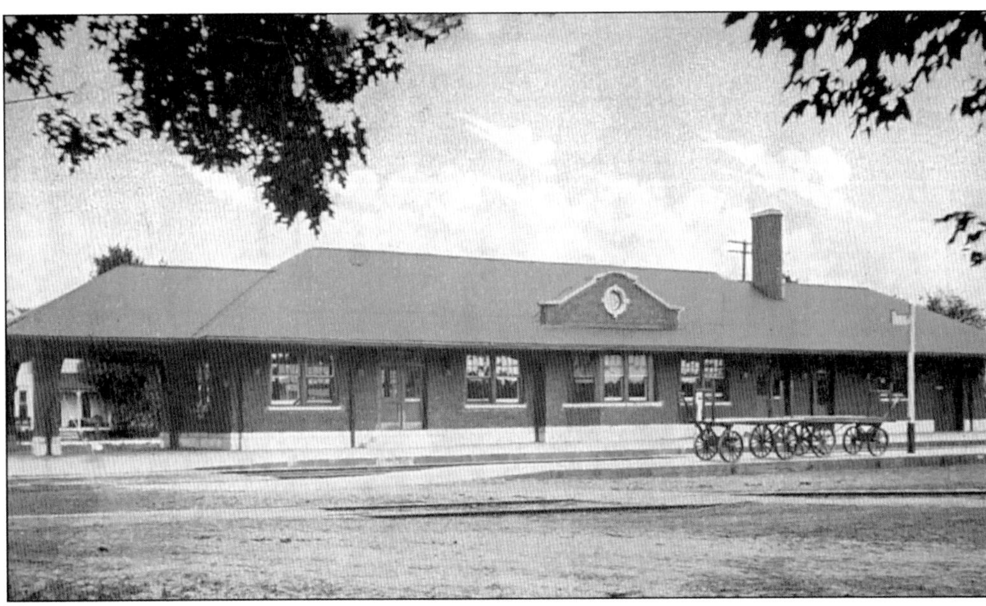

A freight cart sits awaiting its next shipment. Note the pole that received the mailbags as the train passed by.

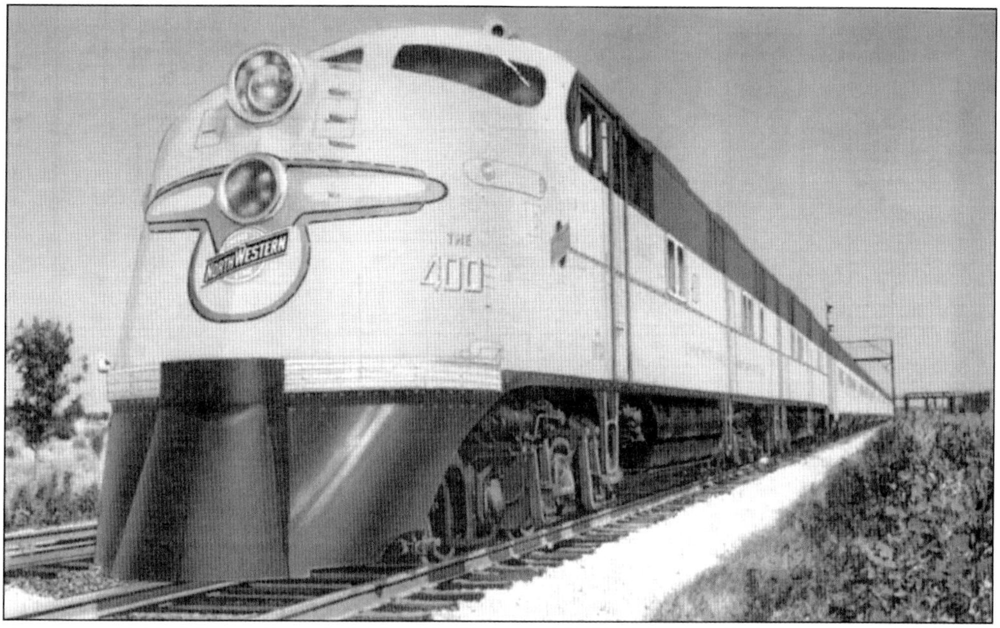

The *400* was a CNW streamliner. The train ran through town on a regular schedule. Many people would board the train in the morning, go to Madison to shop, and return in the evening. You could afford both the time and money instead of traveling by car, which was difficult in the days when the train ran. Today the train has long retired and the tracks have been removed, but in its place there is a lovely bicycle trail—known as the 400 Trail.

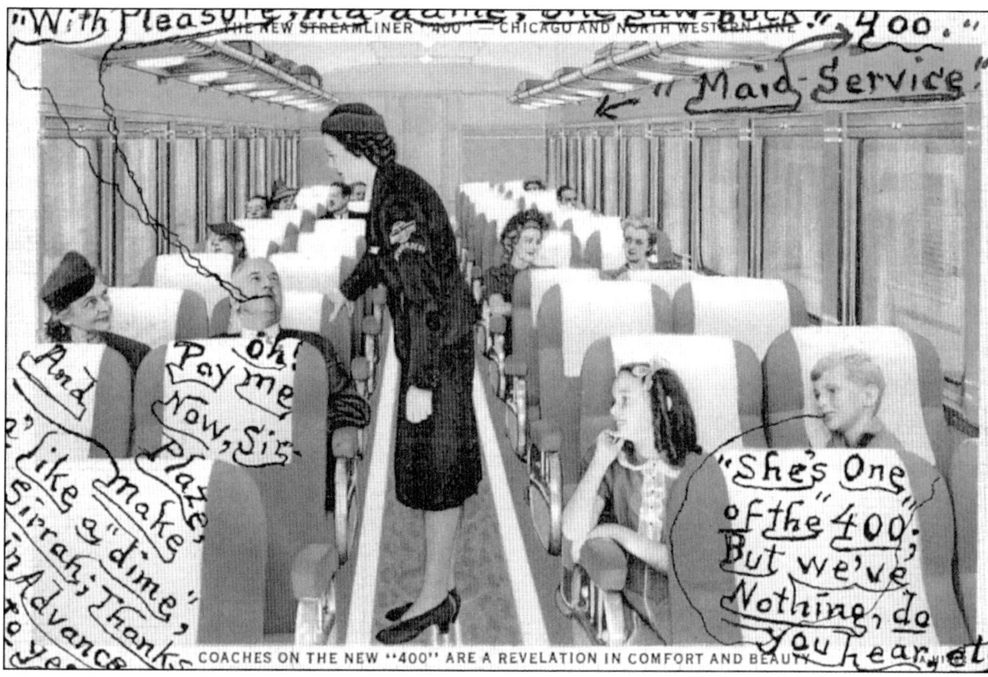

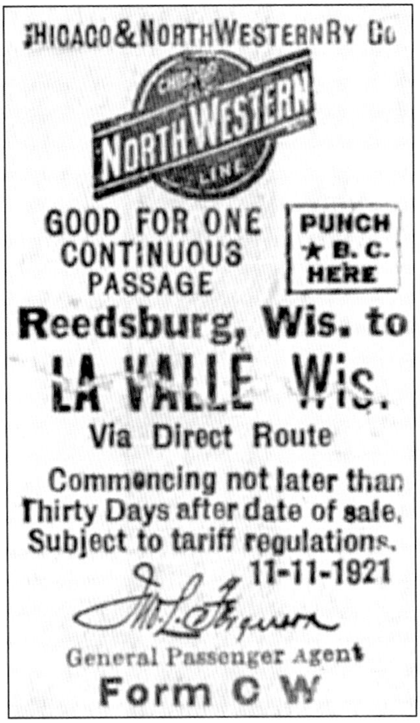

This ticket is dated January 1922, the passenger traveled by train to LaValle, Wisconsin, which was a distance of only seven miles by road. Today that same trek can be made on a bicycle trail constructed on the former bed of the old railroad. Gordon Station once stood in this area of the track, built by CNW as a service spot for their trains.

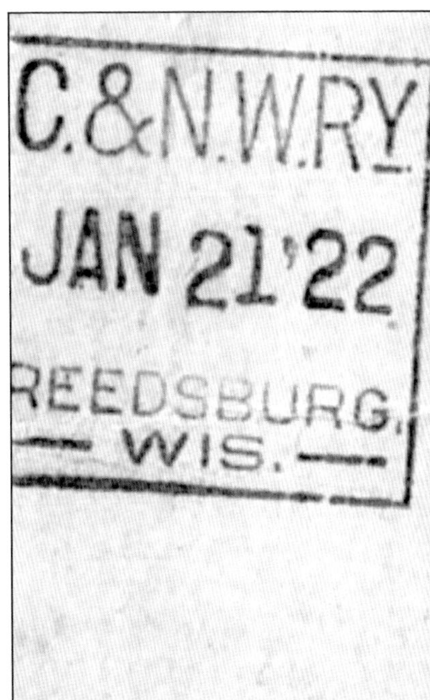

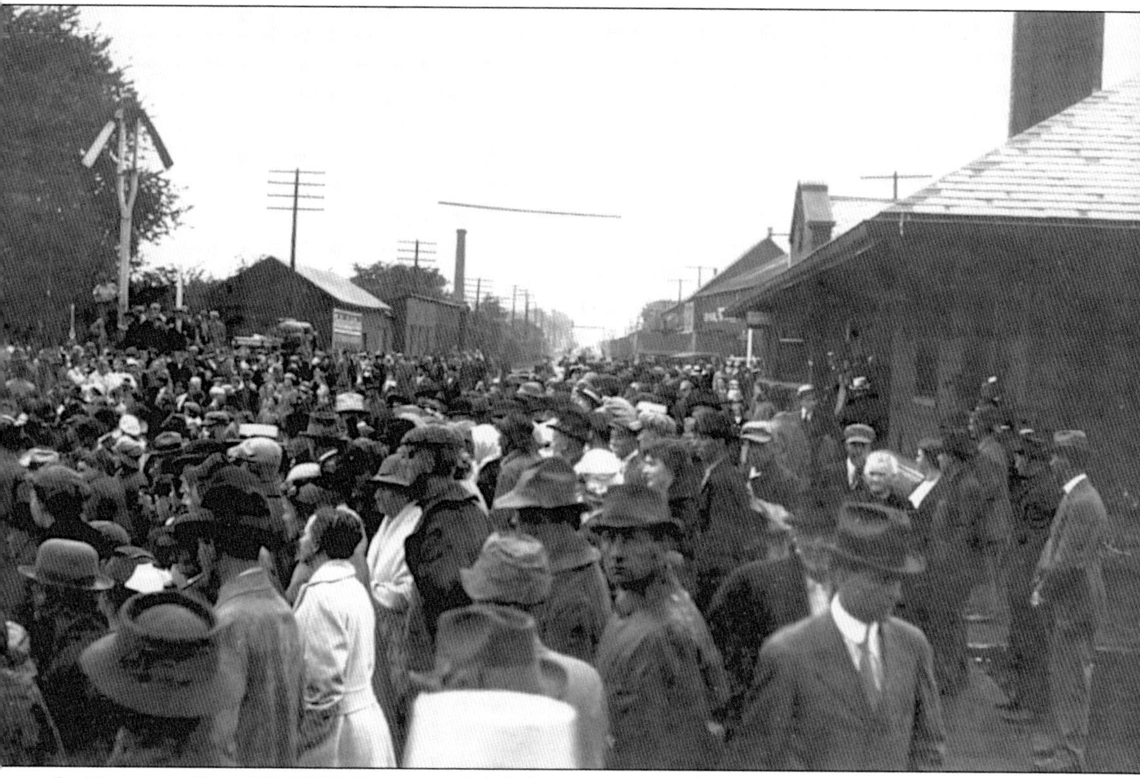

At 10 a.m. on June 22, 1916, Company A left for Camp Douglas to report for World War I. The crowd clearly shows the support that these men met from their family and friends.

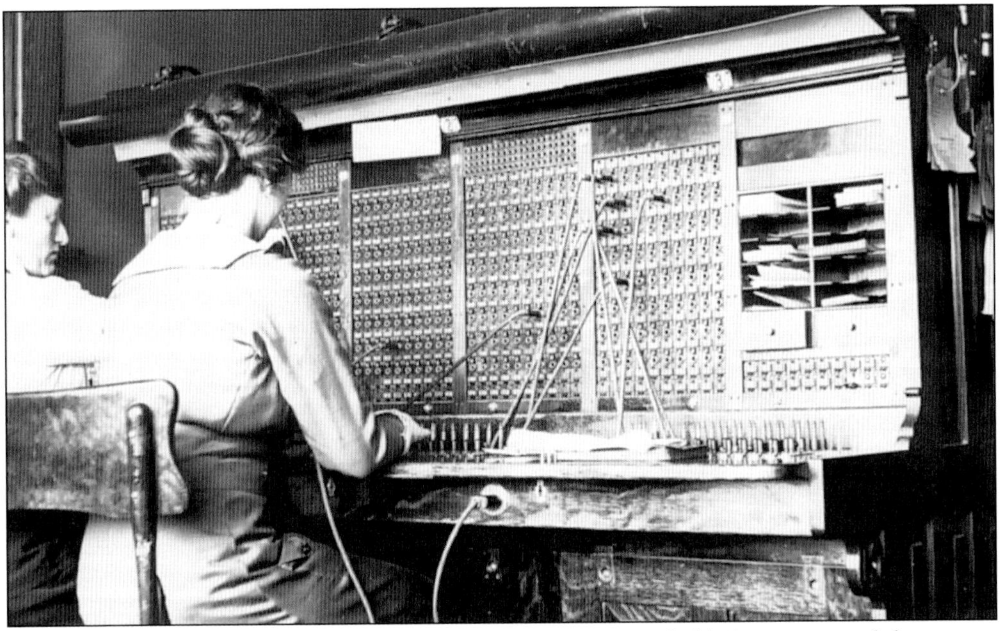

This photo postcard dates back to a time when the operator probably knew you and the person you were calling. This was long before the time of "menus" and long recorded messages. In a small town a child could tell the operator that they wanted to talk to their mom or dad, and would soon actually talk to them! She may ask about you and your family's health as she was connecting the long cords to complete the call. In times of emergencies the switchboard operator was the person who could promptly come to your assistance.

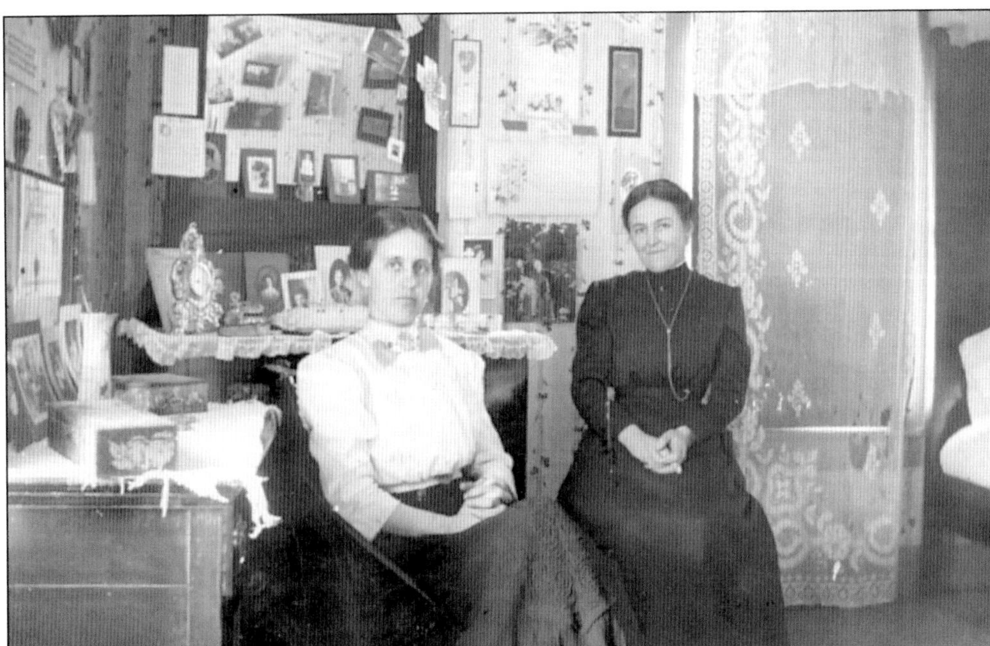

On a card dated March 1912, women sit in a typical living room of that time period. Photographs such as these immortalized families and were proudly displayed.

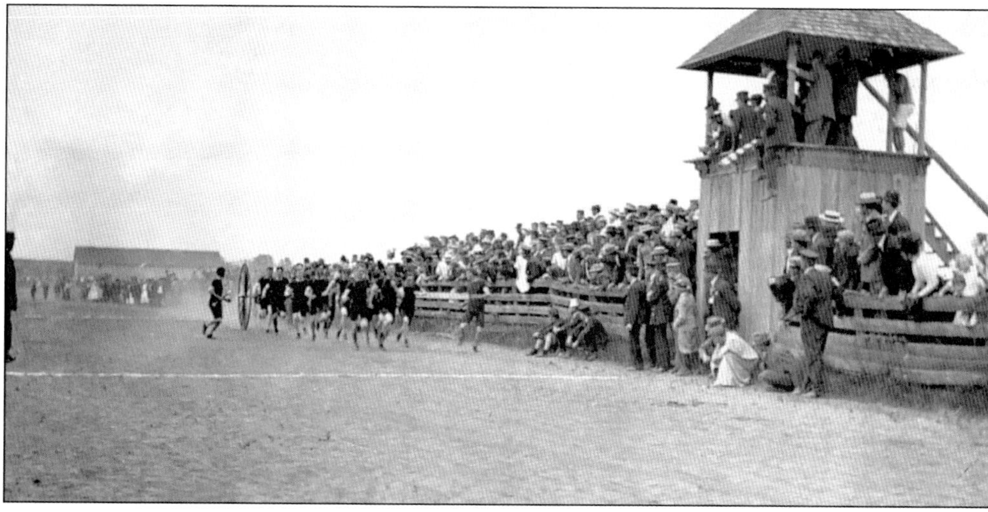

A.P. Ellinwood came to the area as a teacher. He fought in the Civil War, served on the county board, and as a state assemblyman. On a plot located south of LaValle Street and west of Preston Avenue Ellinwood he built a fairground. This was only a small portion of the 200 acres he owned. In 1874 he held his first fair, complete with an exhibits hall and race track. His wife was very involved with the fairs and was also an admirer of the local wild flowers, thus the exhibit hall came to be known as Floral Hall. In an early fair book Ellinwood advertised the admission as 25¢ for adults, 15¢ for children under 12, and 10¢ for a single horse or double team. The fair was open to residents of Sauk, Juneau, and Richland counties. In 1908, a tornado touched down at the fairgrounds and leveled all of the buildings. A column in the local paper stated that there was not enough timber left from the buildings large enough to construct a chicken coop. Ellinwood died in 1901, but with the satisfaction that he had turned "Ellinwood's Frog Pond" into a thriving enterprise. The fair continued to be held until 1919 under the management of several different local businessmen.

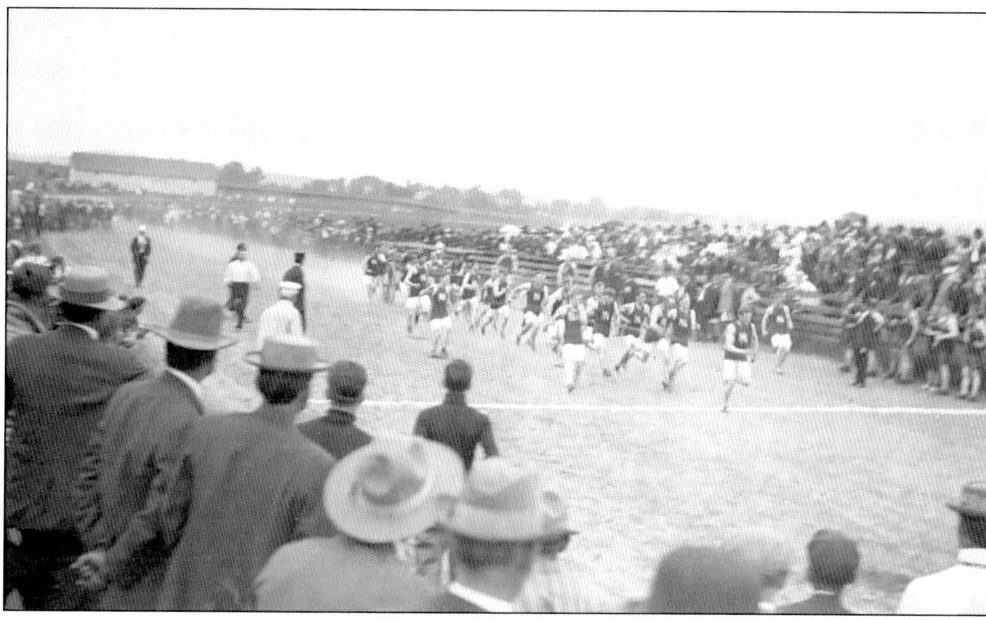

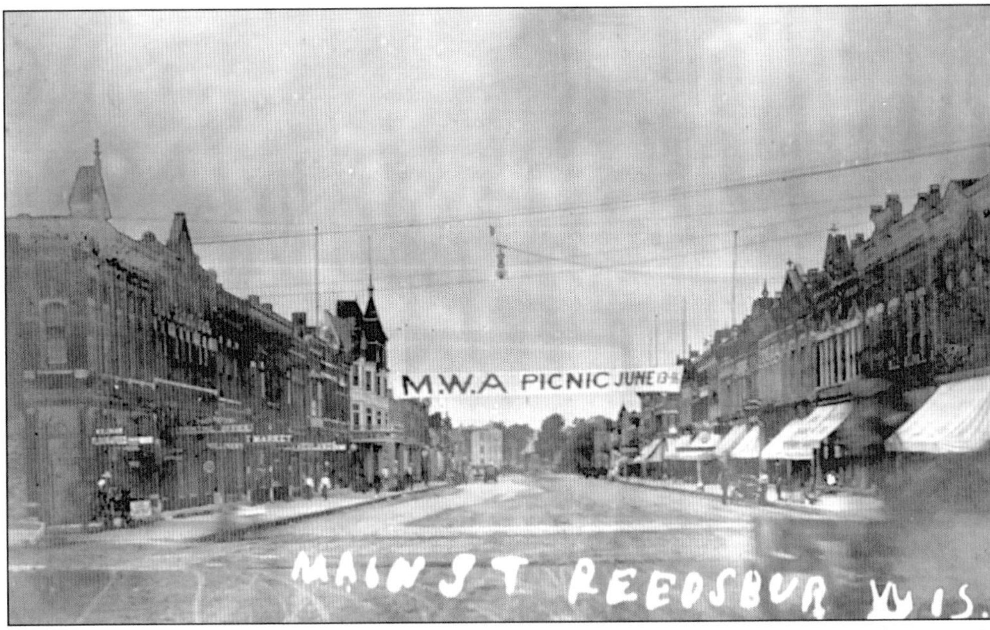

On July 13, 1906, the Modern Woodmen of America had a large meeting and picnic in Reedsburg, as can be seen by the large banner that spanned Main Street. This fraternal life insurance company was founded in Iowa in 1883, and exists today to fill the needs of thousands of people.

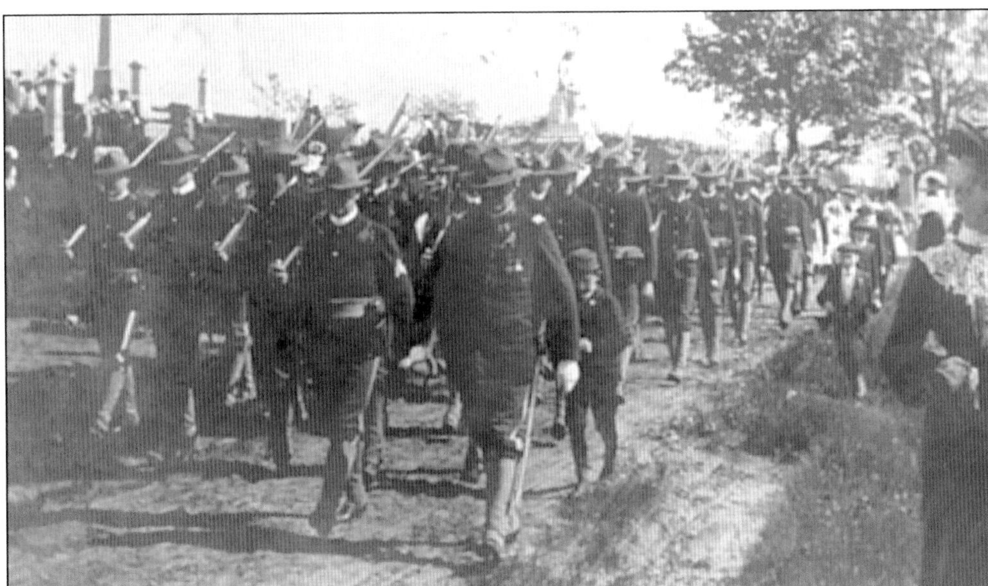

There was a strong feeling among the residents of this city to hold a service on Decoration Day (Memorial Day) each year. After the building of the Civil War monument at Greenwood Cemetery, the service was moved from the City Park to the cemetery. Visible is the monument behind the veterans as they marched to the service. A large, tiered amphitheater is located in the cemetery and to the north of this road where people of the community come each year to remember our fallen servicemen.

Four

Main Street

From the early days of settlement, Reedsburg has tried to have an aggressive attitude toward establishing businesses and drawing the local residents to do business in their home town. The people who designed the business district also designed a wide Main Street that allowed for traffic to flow smoothly and provided ample parking. In a 1912 brochure, the promoters were proud to announce the "entire business district is made up of solid brick buildings which does not contain a single stingy feature." Each building was noted to have good display windows so the visitors could view the wide variety of goods available for purchase. Streets were paved with bricks and sidewalks were made of cement. The clerks were well practiced when it came to courtesy to their customers. Main Street, just east of the river, was once just five small shanties. These "houses" stood where the wider main street is now located. Pioneers were constantly moving and by 1900 the population of Reedsburg was 2,225. That population has more than doubled, with the present population of Reedsburg at almost 8,000 and growing.

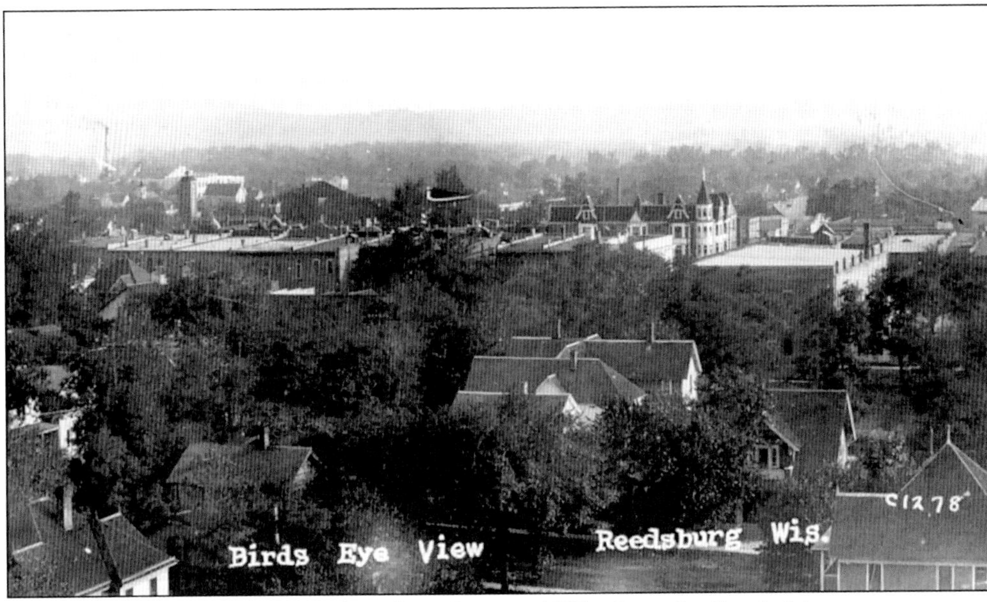

This scene of Reedsburg was taken from Brewery Hill where the first brick water tower was erected. We can see the large number of trees in the residential area. The buildings of downtown are visible with the Hotel Stolte predominant in the downtown area. The far background displays the beautiful bluffs that surround the town. The Baraboo River meanders just in front of the bluffs.

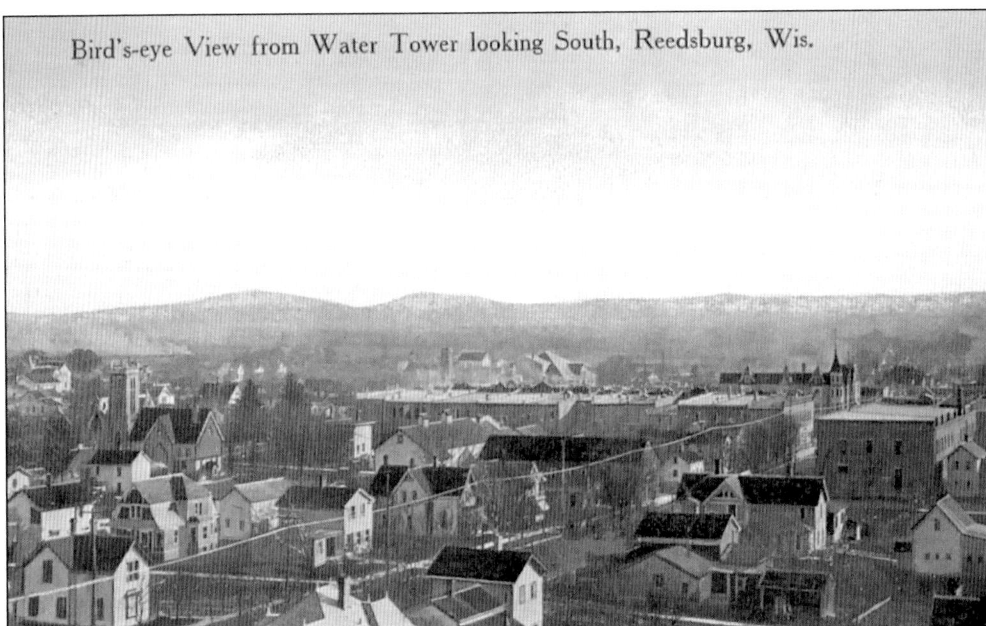

Another view of a residential area as it edged up against the downtown business area. In 1912 it was noted in a local publication that the building of homes was exceptionally hectic. Also notice that there were a few carriage barns still around at the time of this postcard. A large icehouse was still standing at the corner of Second and North Walnut Streets.

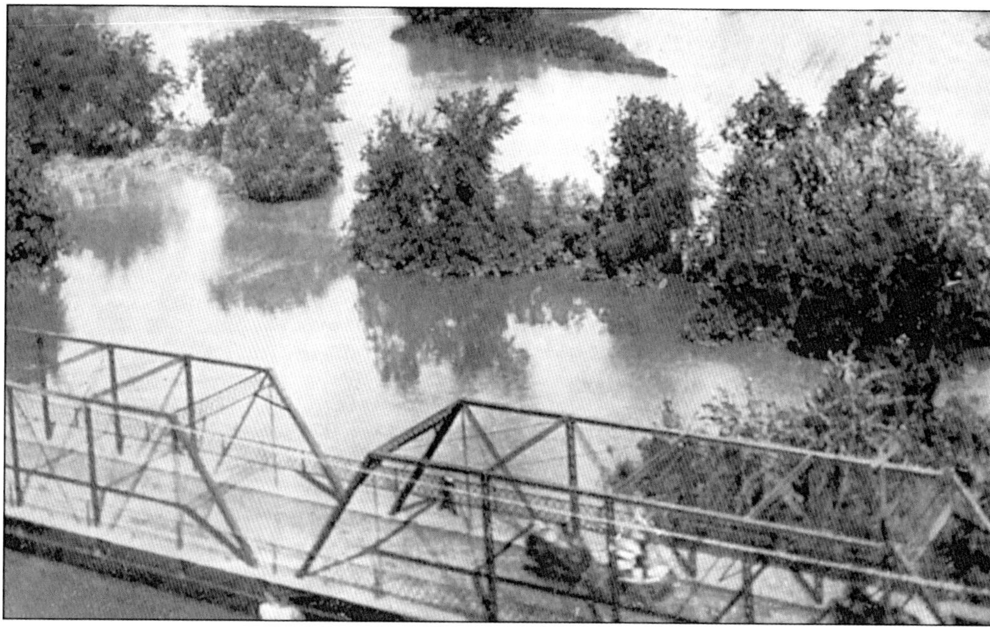

In May of 1845, James W. Babb arrived from Ohio and became the first white settler to make a permanent home at what later became Reedsburg, Wisconsin. He crossed to the west side of Baraboo River at approximately this site and claimed 1,500 acres of land. The Native Americans used this site in their hunting excursions many times. At the age of 67, Mr. Babb started a new life for himself at Reedsburg and generations of his family followed. The potential of the river soon became the allure of other settlers, with Mr. Reed and Mr. Powell harnessing the power in the summer of 1847. They built a mill and settlers started to arrive. By the time Mr. Babb died in 1875, a bridge had been constructed to join the east to the west. The early bridge had a sign posted on it stating that a $5 fine would be incurred by anyone riding or driving faster than a walk. It was reported that across this bridge on a Sunday morning in 1872, several Prairie Schooners were seen passing through town.

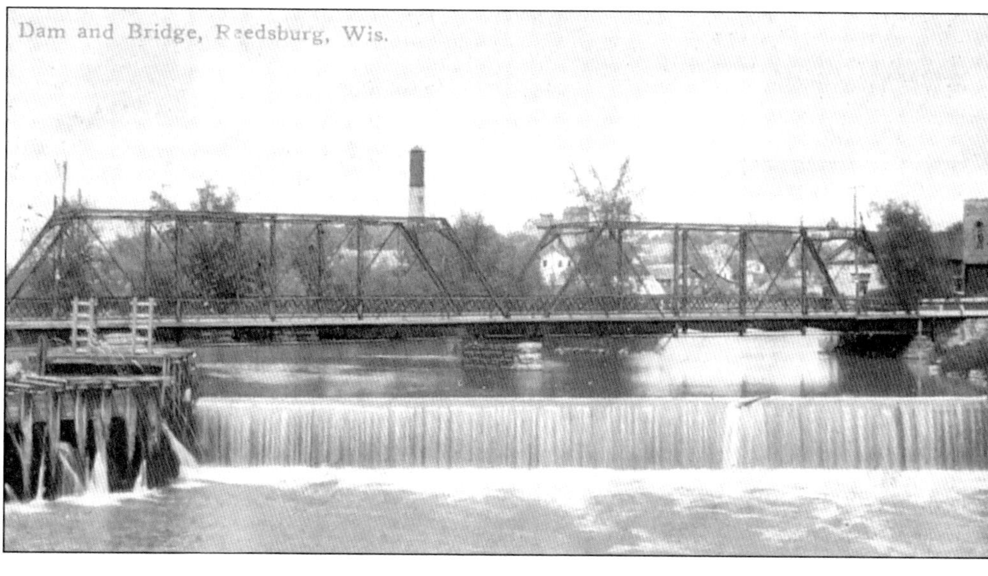

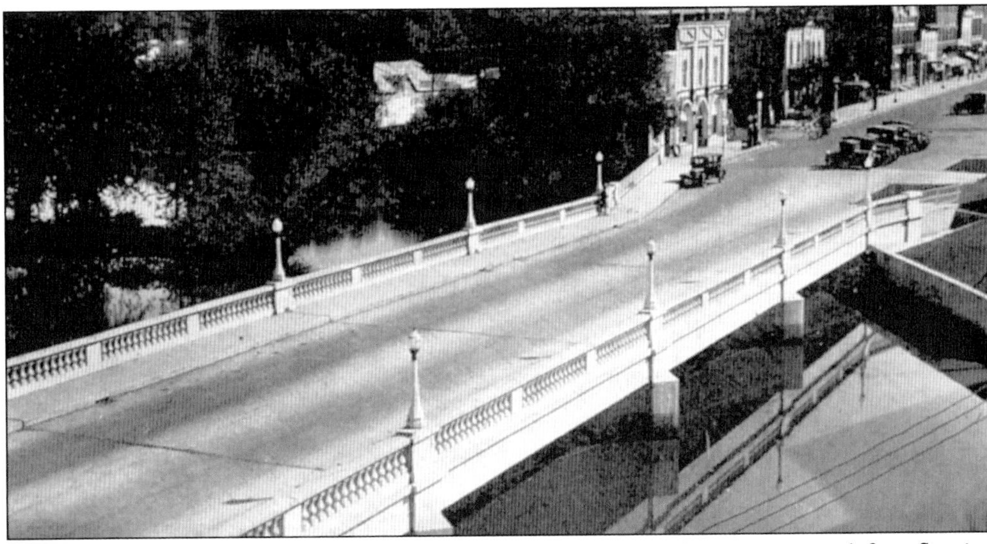

In October of 2001, the Baraboo River became the nation's longest restored free-flowing river. Through the years, dams had been built on the river to encourage industry. Those were removed from the Baraboo River, making the river flow from its headwater north of Elroy to where it meets the Wisconsin River in Portage. It flows 115 miles unobstructed. At one time there were 100 structures on the river. The river gave power to many mills along its banks, which are no longer needed. At the time of settlement in the area, the river was a source of power, necessary to build many of the towns along its banks. Today we may wonder what would have happened to our town had we not been able to harness the river.

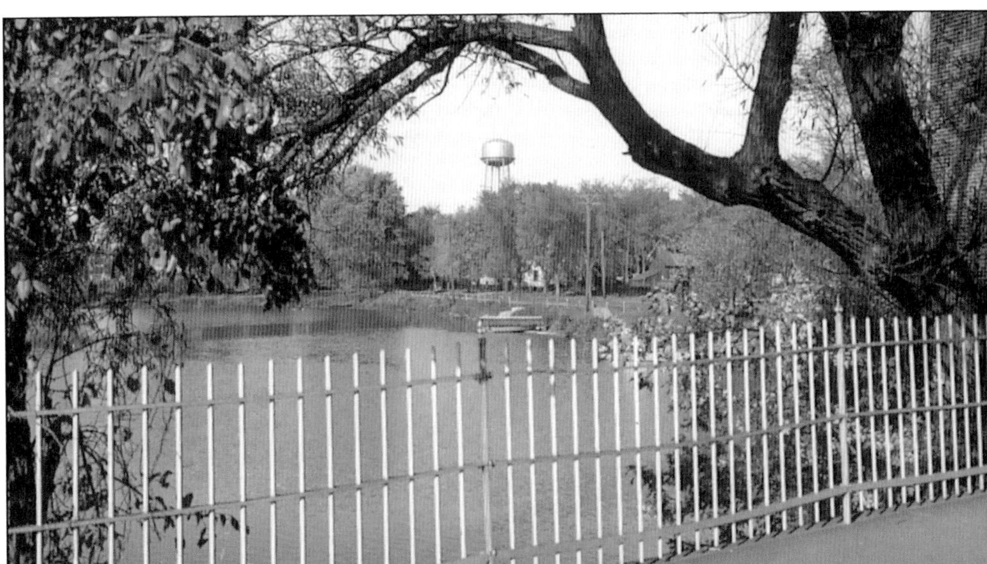

The river provided food and recreation for the settlers of Reedsburg. Not only power for the mills came from the Baraboo River, but ice was harvested in the winter and stored in several ice houses in the city before the days of electric refrigerators.

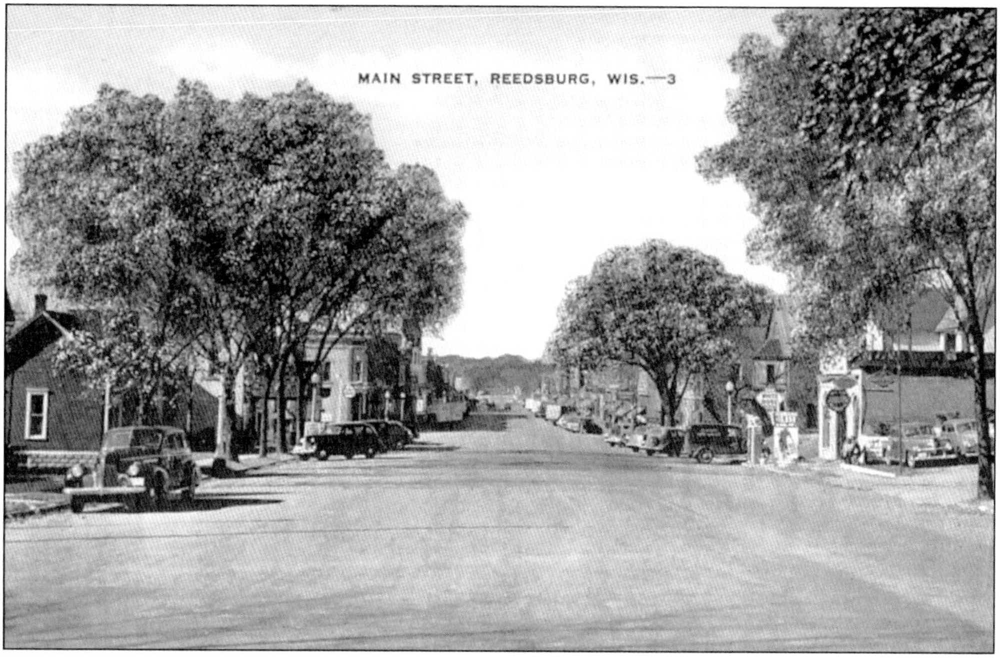

Looking west from Main Street toward the business district.

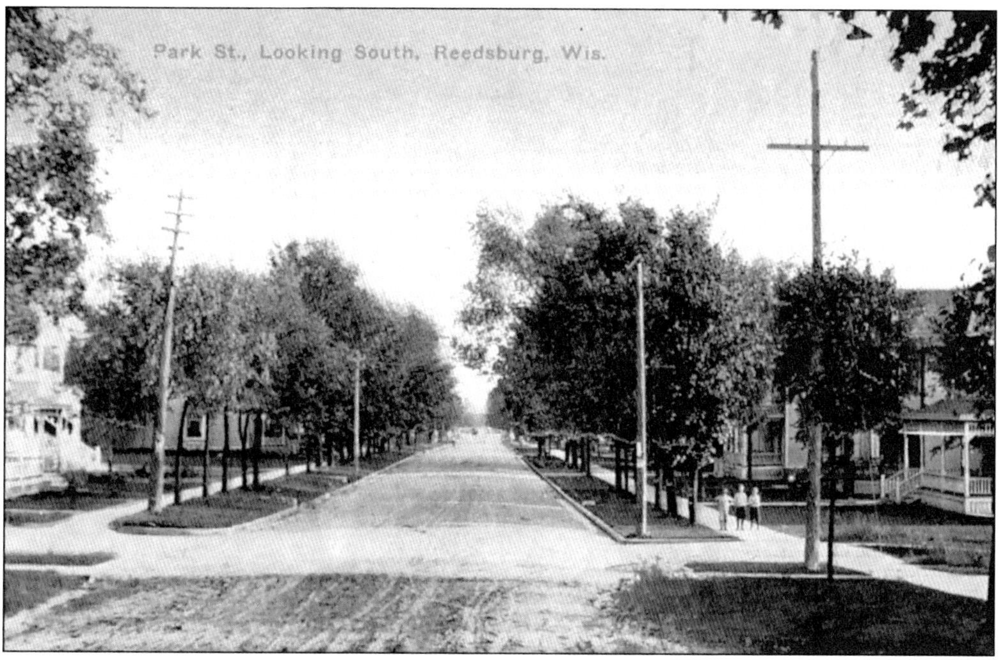

Looking south on North Park Street.

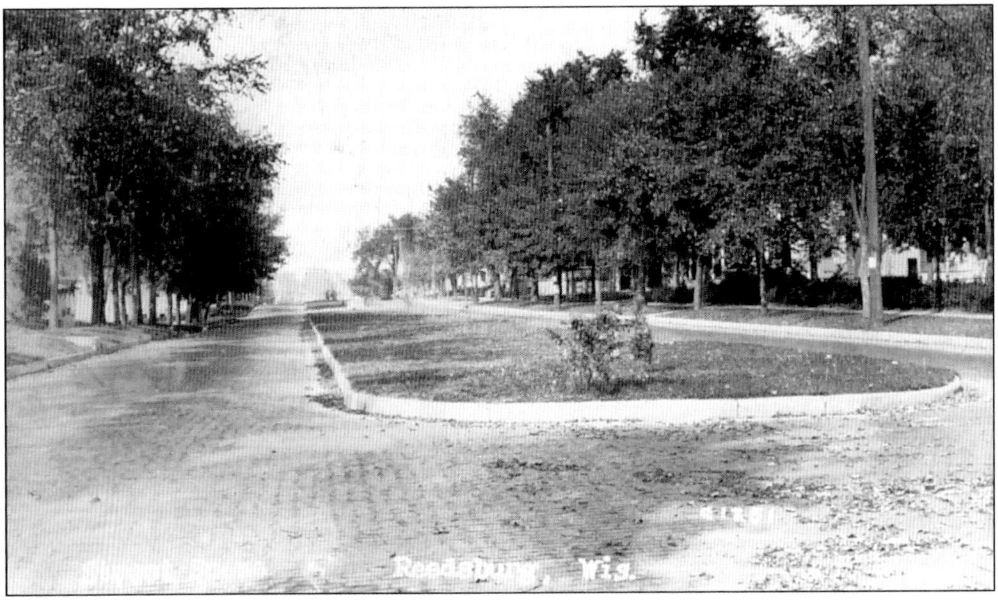

On the east end of the downtown business, our city forefathers planned a boulevard that runs for two blocks. On the west end of the boulevard stands a flagpole, where at one time a cannon was placed in remembrance of our soldiers who fought in the Great War. During World War II this cannon was donated for its metal. Notice the brick streets in the postcard. The residential area had lovely shade trees on both the north and south sides of the street.

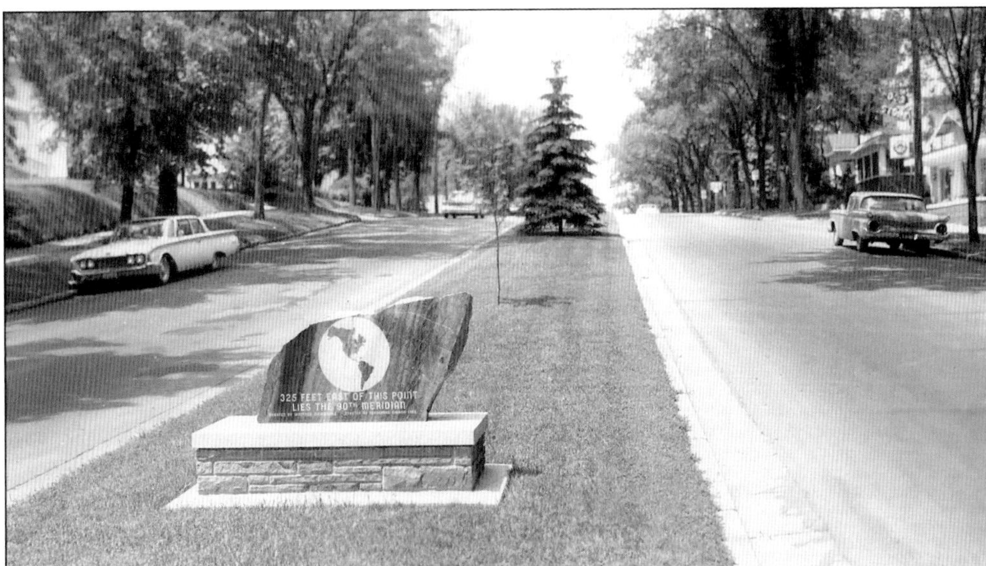

The city of Reedsburg is located on the 90th meridian. Hilbert Kleeber, mayor in 1959, marked the exact location of the 90th meridian with the help of Roger Friede and Conrad Steinweg. In 1963, the Reedsburg Kiwanis club funded the marker on the east end of the boulevard on Main Street. The marker is located 325 feet west of the exact location of the meridian. Today as you drive on East Main you not only see the monument, but you can see the wide stripe painted on the highway as you drive directly over the meridian.

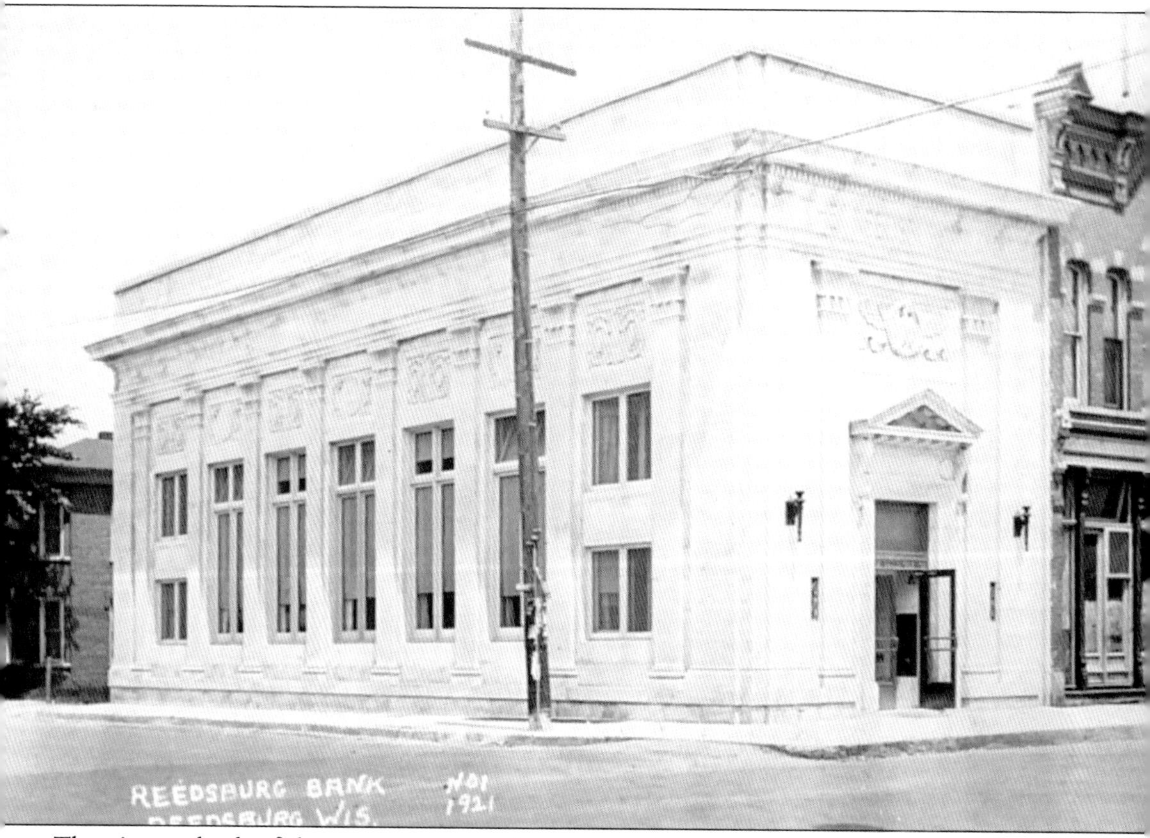

The pioneer bank of the community stood sentry on the corner of Main Street and North Walnut Street. In 1867 the Reedsburg Bank was established as a private bank founded by J. Mackey, E.O. Rudd, and J.W. Lusk. With the consolidation of the State Bank of Reedsburg and The Citizens Bank they operated under the name of The Reedsburg Bank. The site of the bank had moved from time to time until reaching its final location at this site. Throughout the years the bank has expanded the building to the east, but it stands in the same spot today.

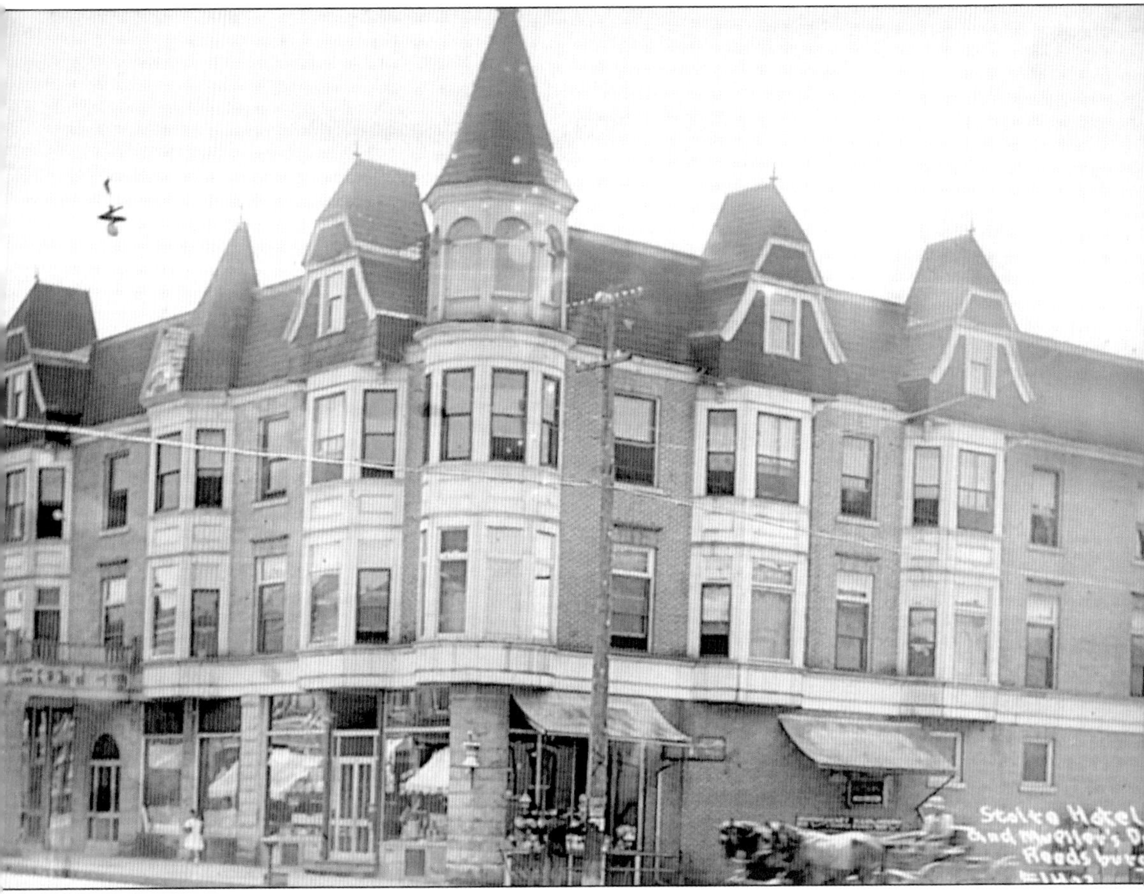

The Central House was a large wooden structure that stood on this site previous to the building of the Stolte Hotel in 1896. The Central House, or Alba House, was destroyed by fire. In this postcard you will notice the activity of the town. There is a woman in a buggy, being pulled to her destination. On the corner a gentleman reads a poster, posted on the utility pole, about a fair. A sign for the sample room in the building's basement is on the side of the building. On the side corner is the emblem of the pharmacy, located in the hotel overlooking Main Street and South Market, or Walnut Street.

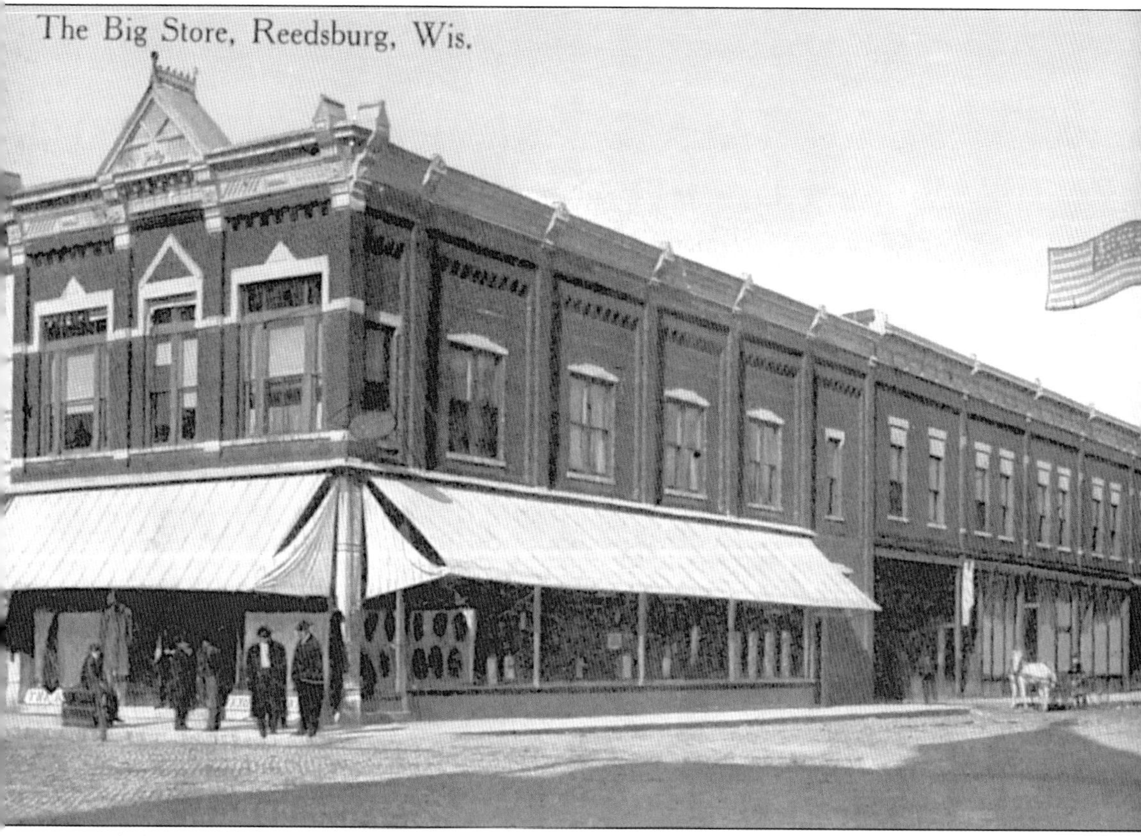

Founded in 1883, The Big Store was the biggest store in Sauk County. The store extended from Main Street for an entire block to Second Street. You could buy groceries, clothing, gifts, jewelry, home repairs, and even buggies at this location. Spaces for professionals were on the second floor from Main Street to the alley. A tunnel under the alley connected the entire business. In its early days, customers could sell eggs in exchange for needed supplies. This store was one of the first in Reedsburg to candle eggs. Mr. Schweke, the founder of The Big Store, was stricken with an illness and died while on a trip to New York to sell hops that were grown in this area. During the night hours in August 1957, a fire started in the building. The fire department did their best, with the help if neighboring fire departments, but could not save the structure. Several businesses found new places to relocate to, but the memories of The Big Store live on in the minds of those growing up in this area.

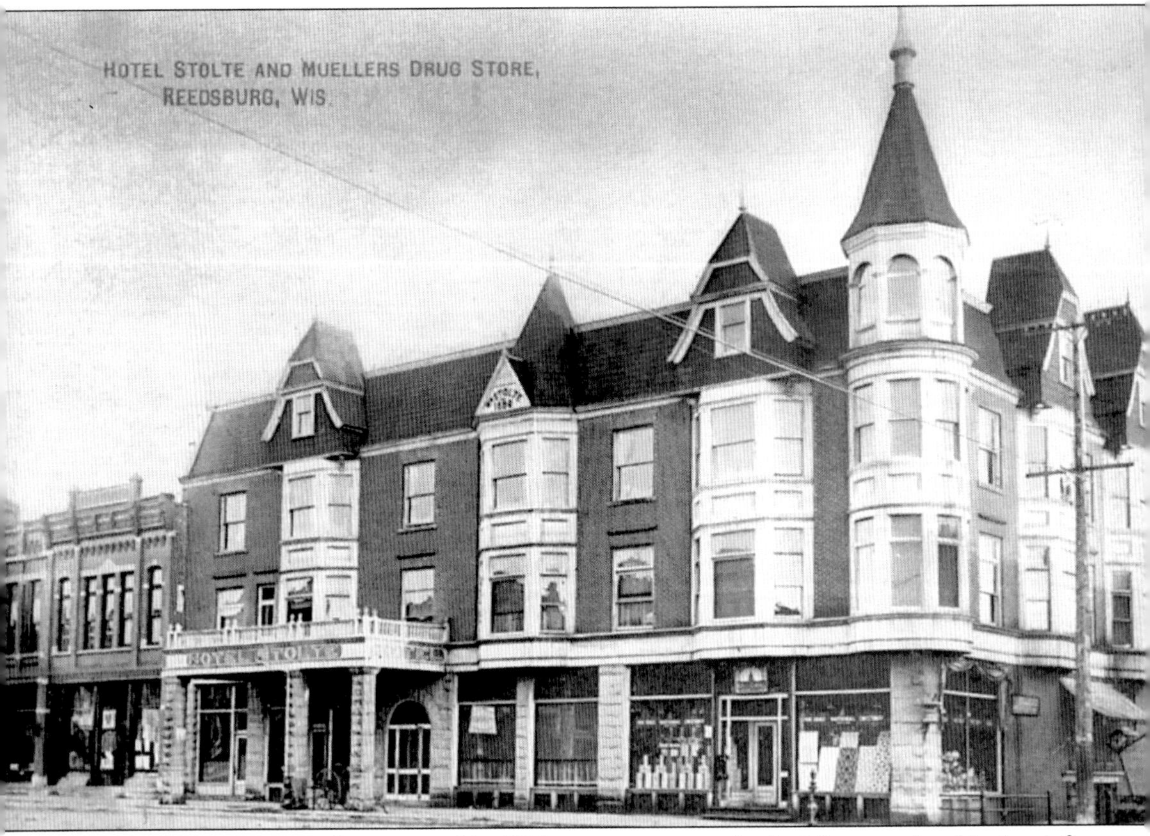

Before the Stolte Hotel was erected in 1896, a two-story wooden building stood at this site. A fire destroyed the Central Hotel in the spring of 1896 and the new hotel was constructed the same year. In 1915 Scott Huntley bought the hotel and constructed additions, making a courtyard on the second floor of the building. This exists still today. Sidney Ashworth bought the building and operated it until sometime in the 1970s, when it was sold to a Mr. Helms. Today the structure has been excessively remodeled, and houses a restaurant, dress shop, beauty salon, and offices in the basement and first floor. The top two floors are apartments. According to the back of this card, found in the lobby of the hotel, room 47 rented for $19 per week.

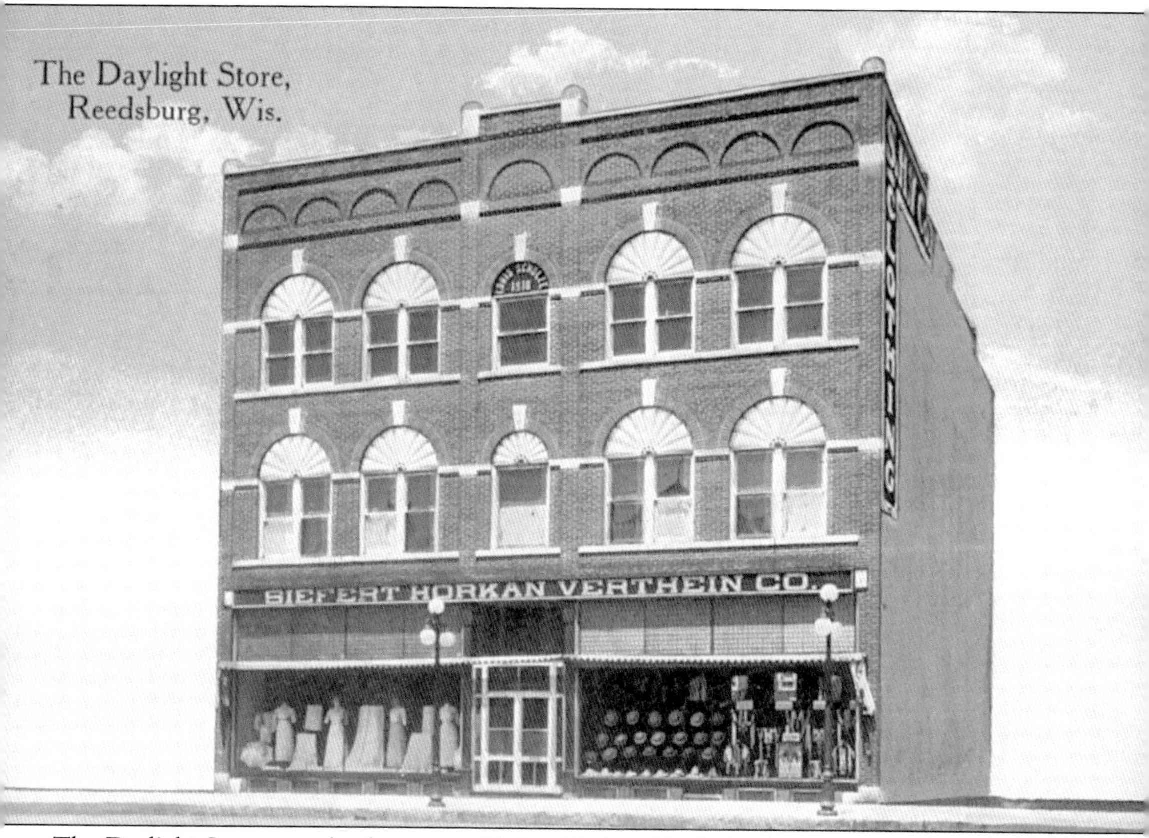

The Daylight Store was also known as Siefert-Horkan-Verthein Company. It was a general merchandise store. Built in 1910, the Louis Schulze building housed many different businesses over the years,. There was a bowling alley and bar in this building. The Modern Woodman Hall was upstairs over the bowling alley. For a few years a garment factory was located on the higher floors of this building when they outgrew their quarters across the street. Eventually, the garment factory also outgrew this site and built a new building on North Dewey Avenue. An automotive store now occupies the building. In the right light, you can see the faint painted sign on the east side of the building, "SHV."

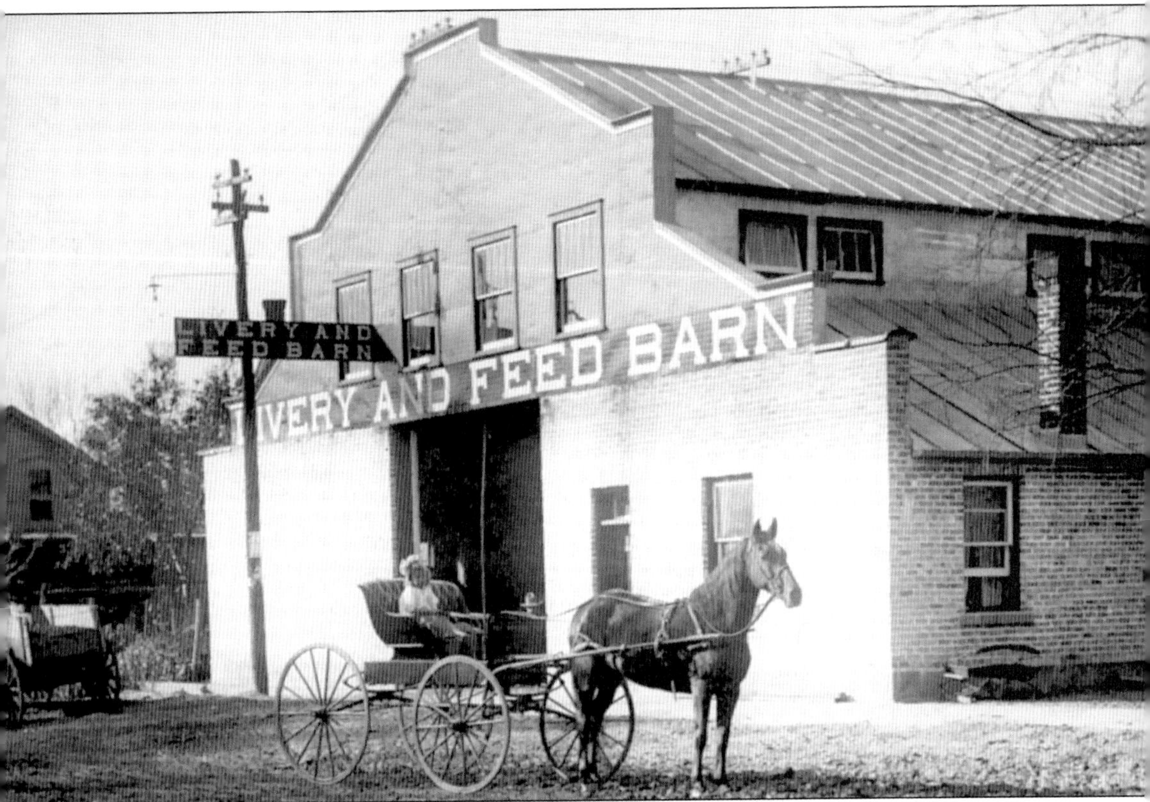

Every town at the beginning of its existence needed a livery and feed barn as much as they needed other businesses. Reedsburg, *c.* 1911, could boast of a very fine facility. A two-story, 160 x 60 foot building, such as this one, was operated by J.W. Corwith. His business could hold about 120 horses. He also had about 19 horses for livery use. This trade business was used not only local, but also in the adjoining states. Mr. Corwith needed the knowledge of every horse in the area to remain as successful as he became. The building remains today and reminds us of the many conversations and meetings that took place here years ago.

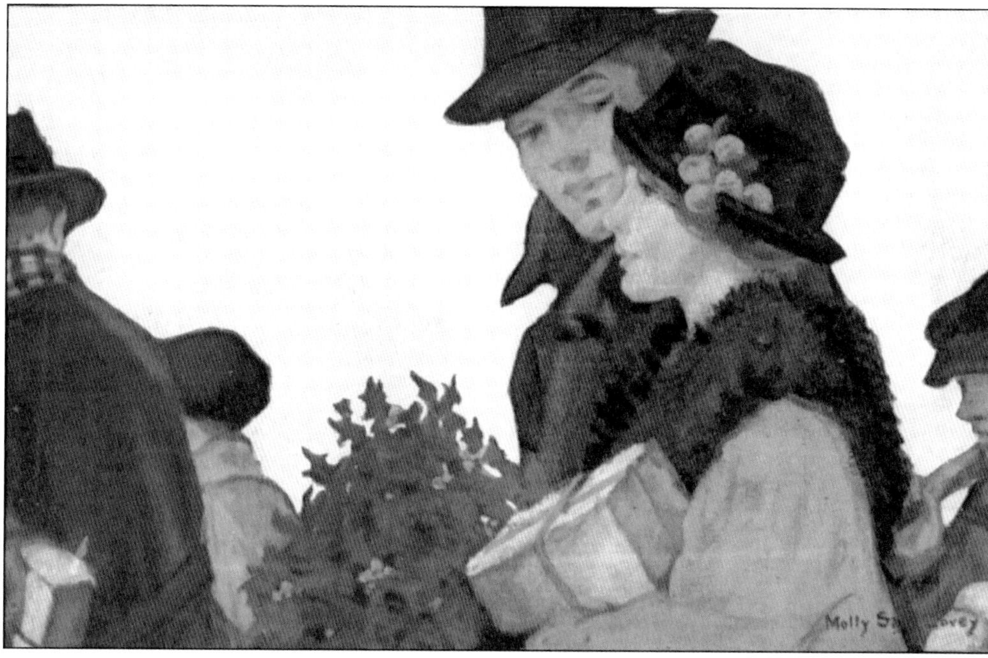

Early in the 20th century, Oehlers and Howland was a prominent business on Main Street. They were a furniture dealer, located in a brick building. This was a prosperous time for Reedsburg, and Oehlers and Howland utilized all three floors of the building. As was custom at the time, they were also in the undertaking and embalming business. This card was used for holiday greetings to their valued customers.

Reedsburg, Wis.

Dear Friend and Patron:

We hope that you have been receiving regularly Farm and Fireside, the National Farm Paper, every other week since we ordered the publishers to send you this magazine for one year at our expense.

Believing that each and every copy will be a constant and persistent reminder of the courteous manner in which we are always prepared to serve you and wishing you a very Merry Xmas and a Prosperous New Year, and hoping that our pleasant relations in the past may be continued in the future, we beg to remain,

Sincerely yours,
OEHLERS AND HOWLAND.

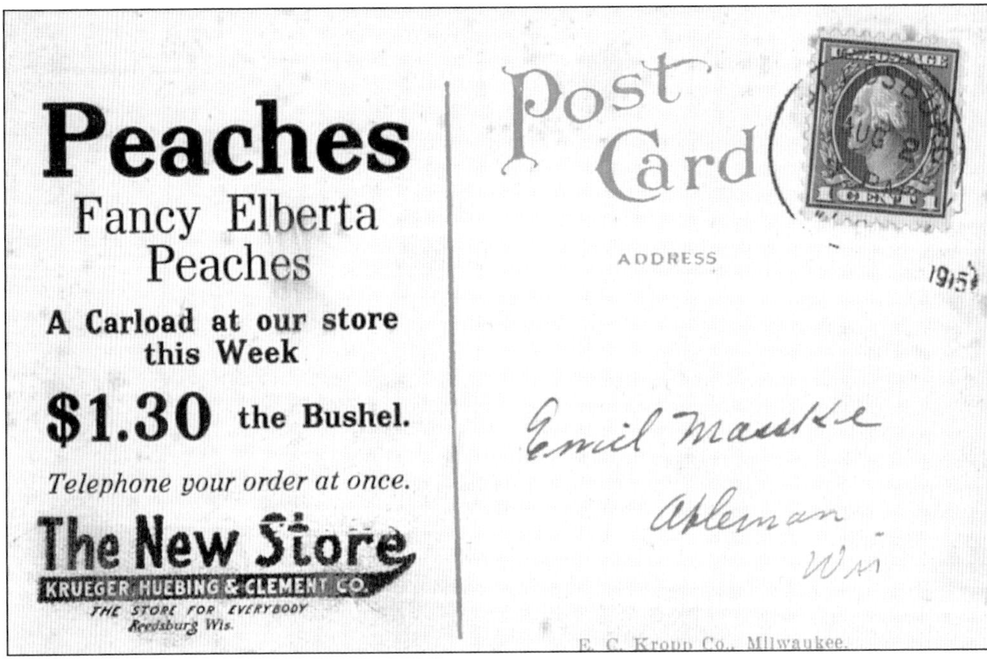

The postcard not only kept family and friends informed of activities and whereabouts, but merchants often used the postcard to stay in touch with his customers. For a penny a businessman could give personal attention to his appreciated customer. On one scenic postcard, a merchant reminded his client that it had been some time since he had been in to purchase a new pair of shoes.

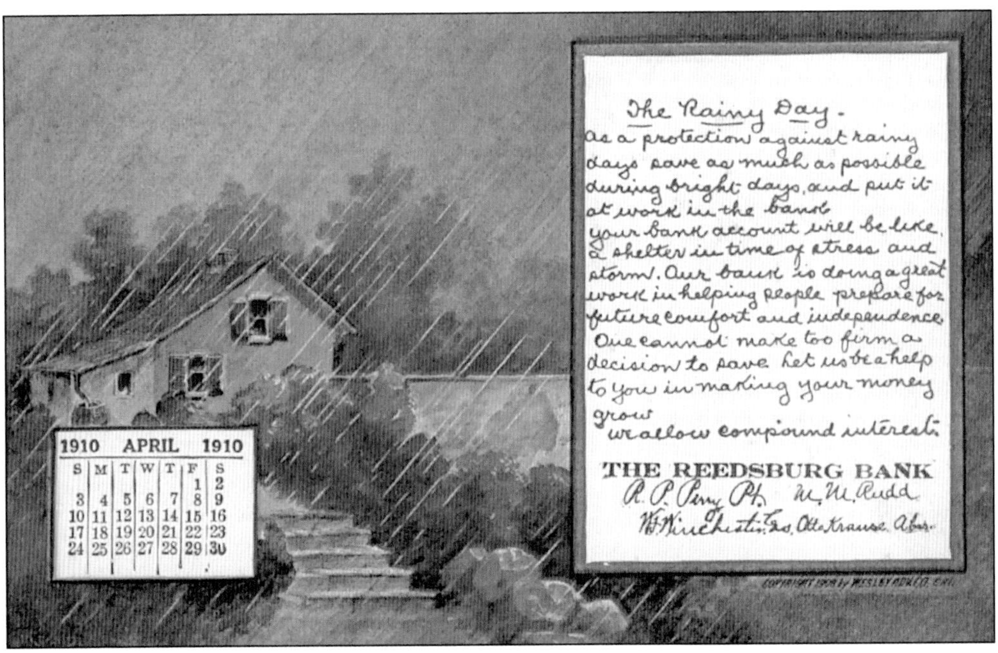

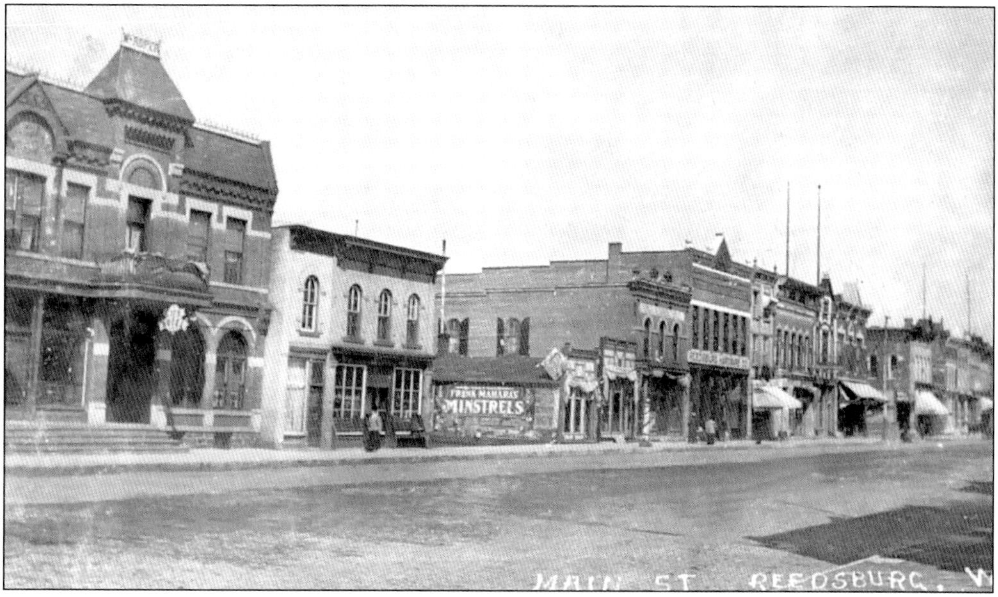

The sign on the side of the building is advertising a Minstrel show coming to town. Could this be the same minstrel show that was in town at the time a little boy drowned in the river? A marker in the cemetery marks the grave of Eugene Brown, buried the same night of the drowning. At midnight on the same day of his drowning, his body was laid to rest at Greenwoods Cemetery to the sounds of the company's band playing "Nearer My God to Thee." A local citizen donated the burial site and also a marker.

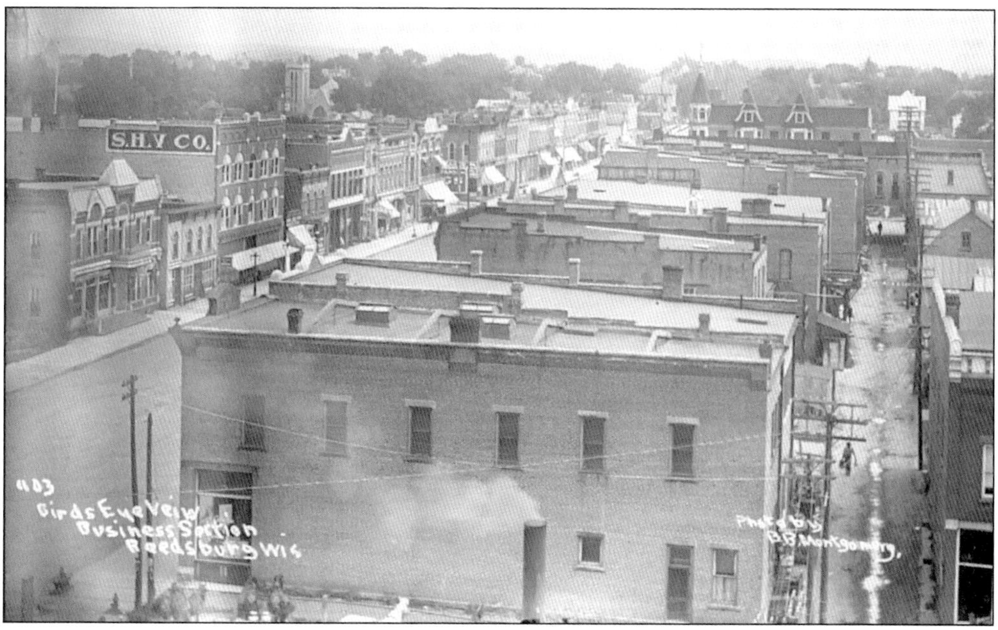

An unusual view of the business district. In the foreground we notice the horses waiting for owners in order to haul cargo to various sites. The utility pole was also becoming predominant.

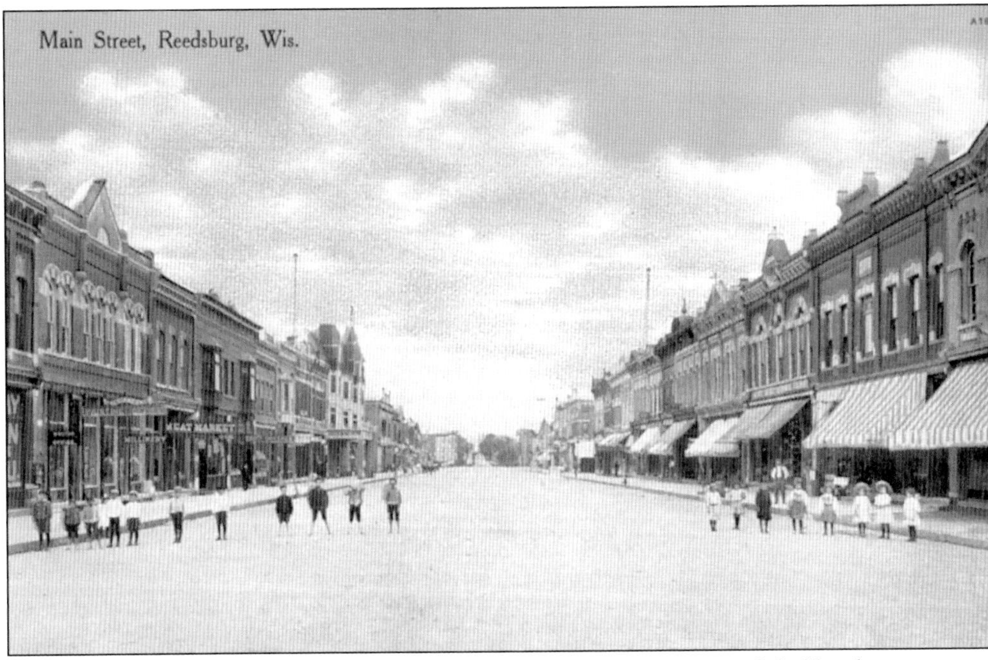

Notice the use of awnings to shelter the merchandise from becoming faded by the sun.

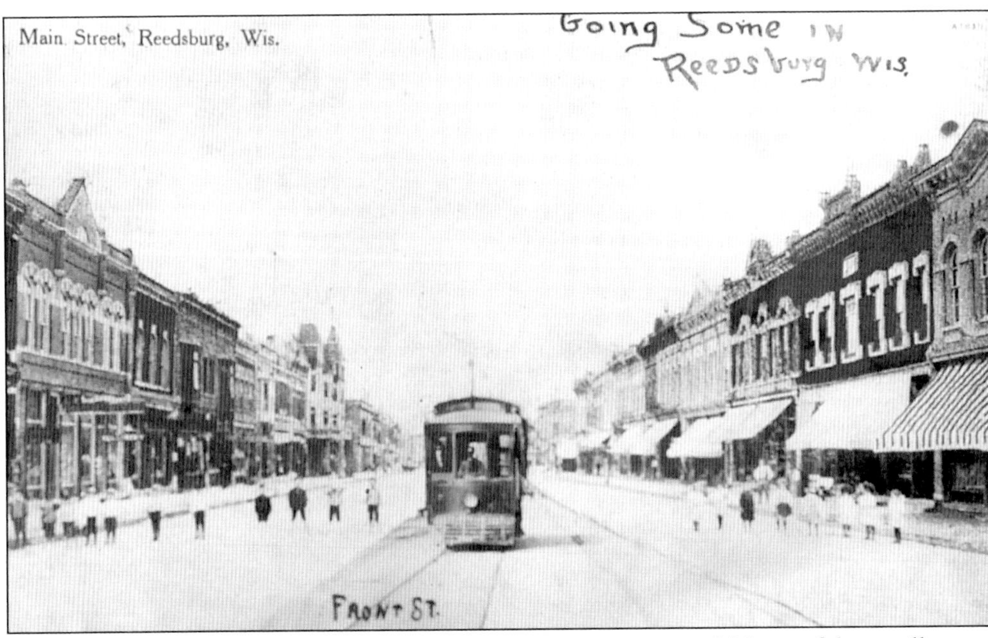

At one time a company promised to put a streetcar in "your town." Many of the small towns at this time only got their streetcar in the picture. Was this the *Streetcar Named Desire* for many small rural towns?

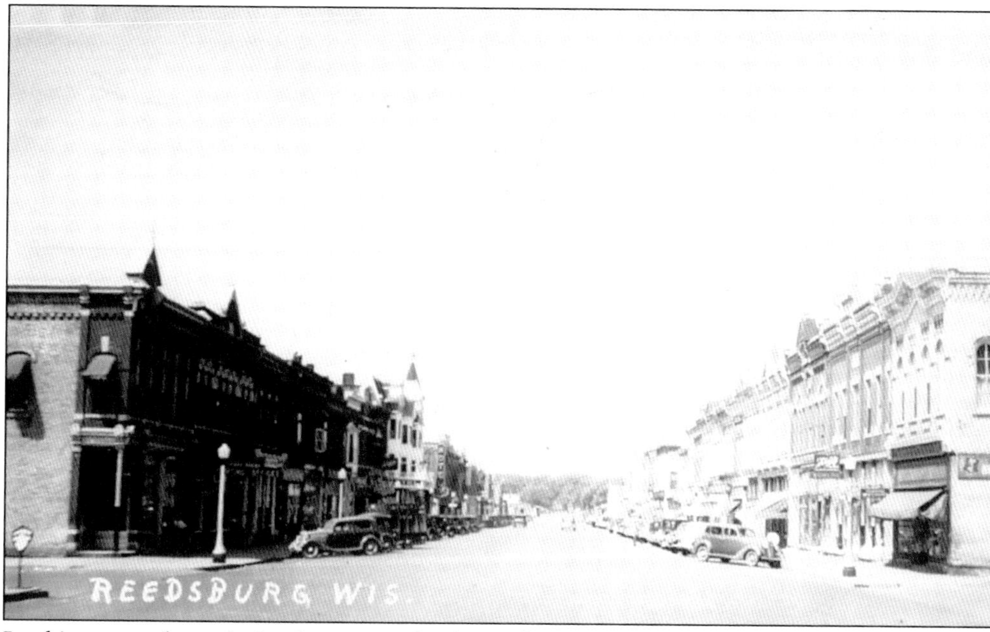

Looking west through the downtown business district toward the bridge. The cars date this image in the 1930s. This was taken at the corner where Park Street meets Main Street.

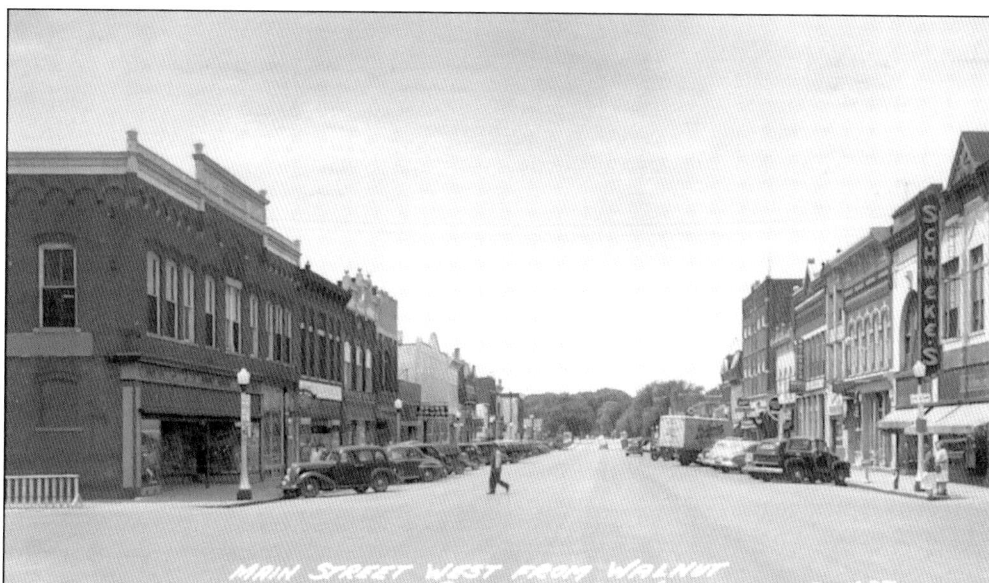

This was taken at the intersection of Walnut Street and Main Street looking west toward the bridge. The bicycle rack stands empty on the corner.

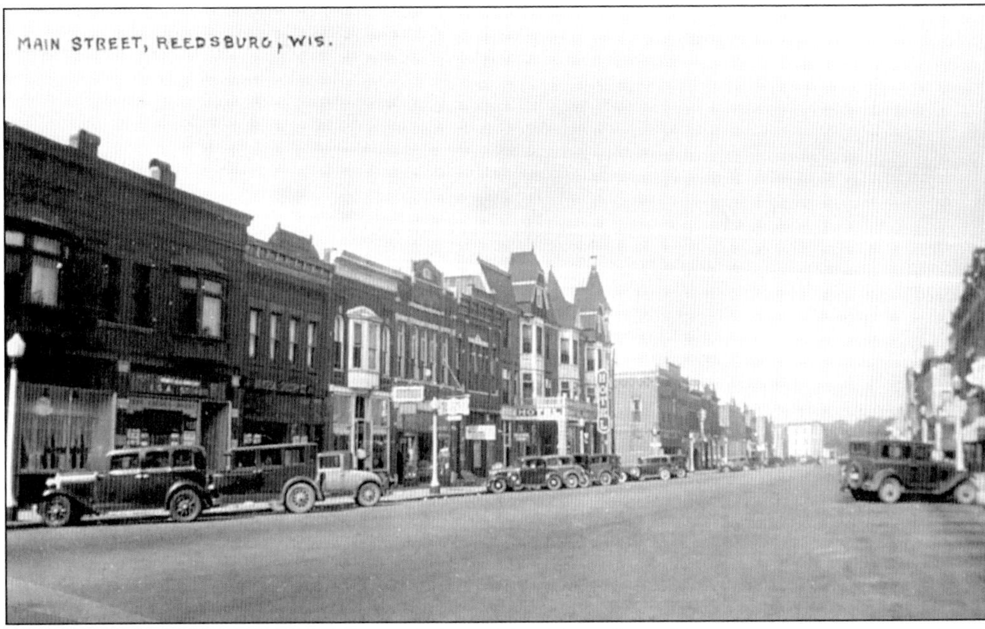

The residents of Reedsburg who trod the wide sidewalks of the town may owe gratitude to a group of young ladies. One day, becoming disgruntled by the swamp and mud, the women donned their bloomers and laid planks from end to end to form the first walk in the town. Apparently, they got their point across, for the town has long been proud of its wide cement sidewalks.

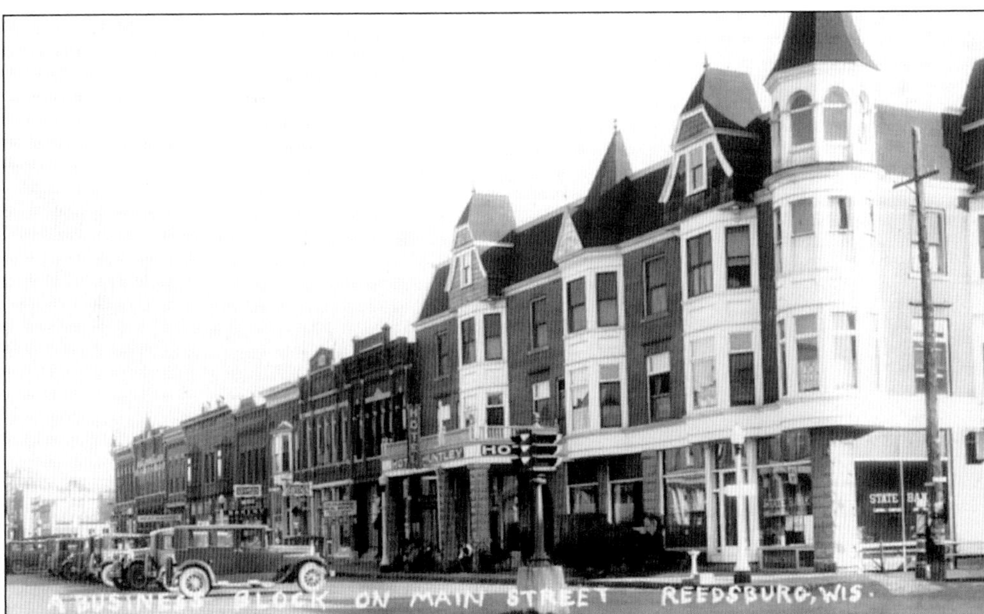

Signals and center-of-the-street parking were tried for a short period of time.

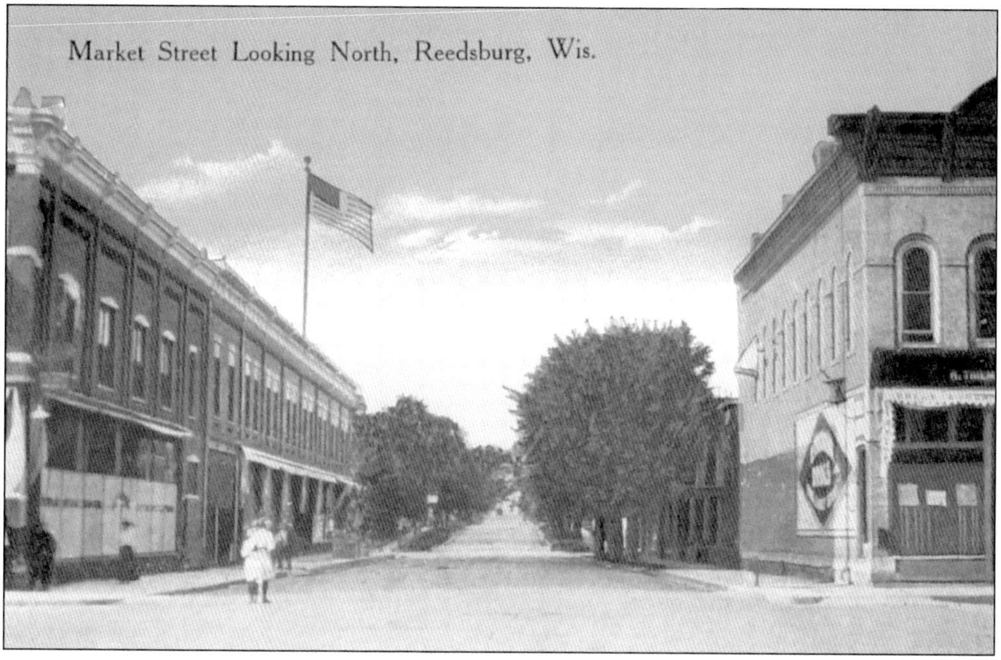

Market Street was active both during the day and at night. The name was eventually changed from Market Street to Walnut Street. On the west side of the street the grandeur of the Big Store can be seen.

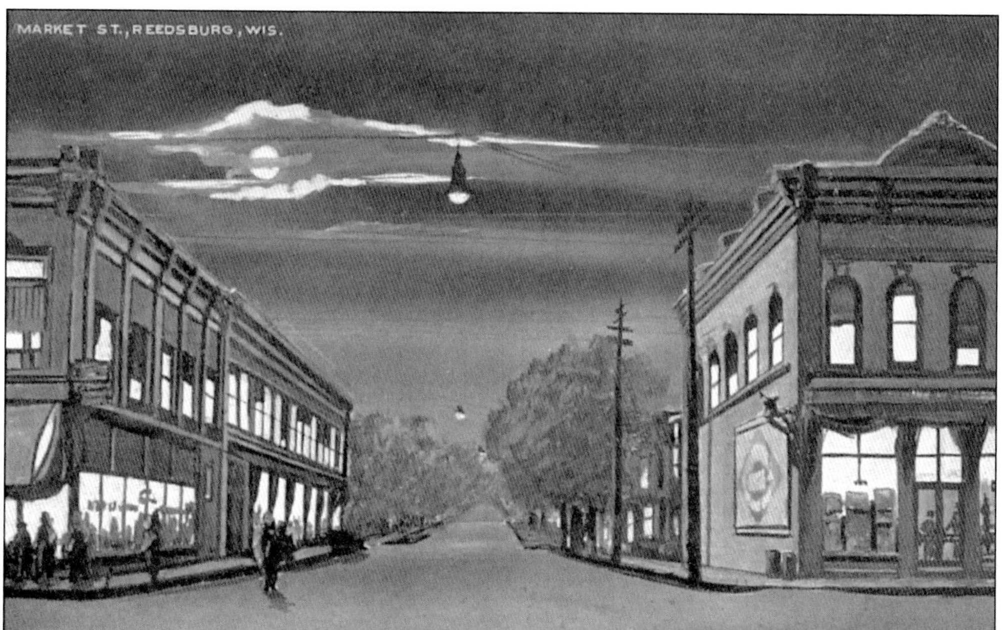

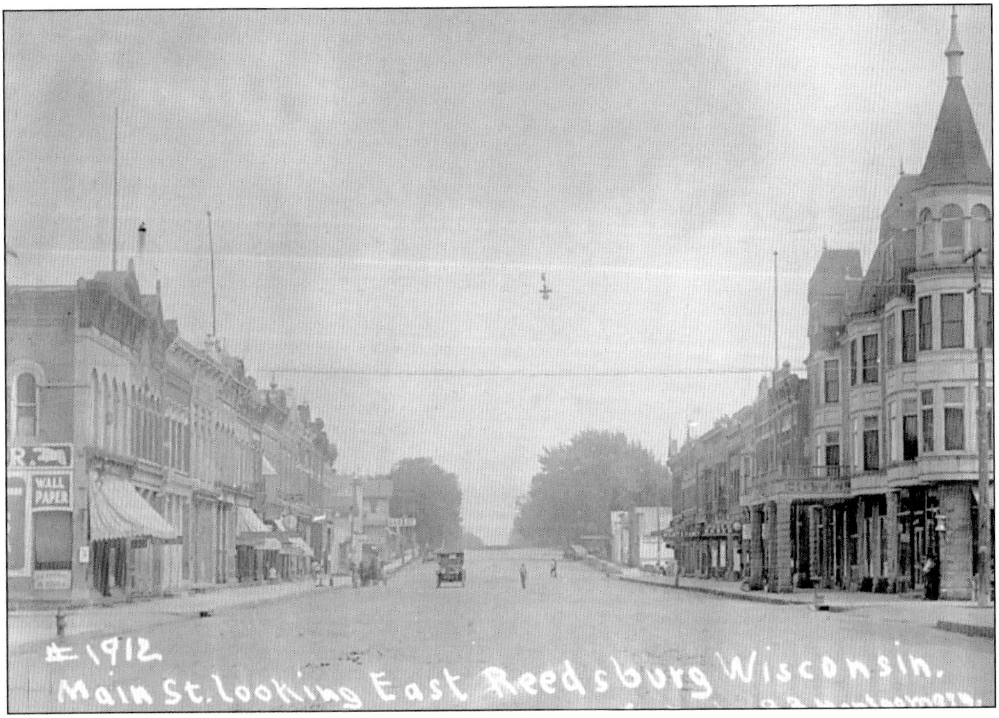

While the Big Store stood sentry on the northwest intersection of Walnut and Main, the Hotel Stolte was the landmark on the southeast side of the same intersection.

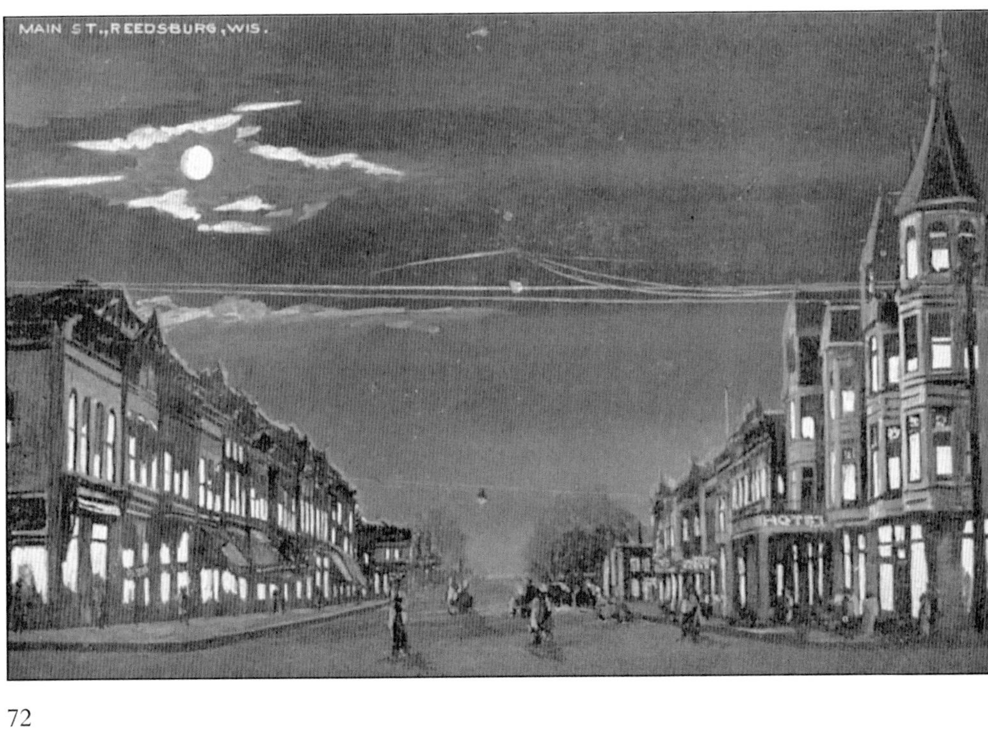

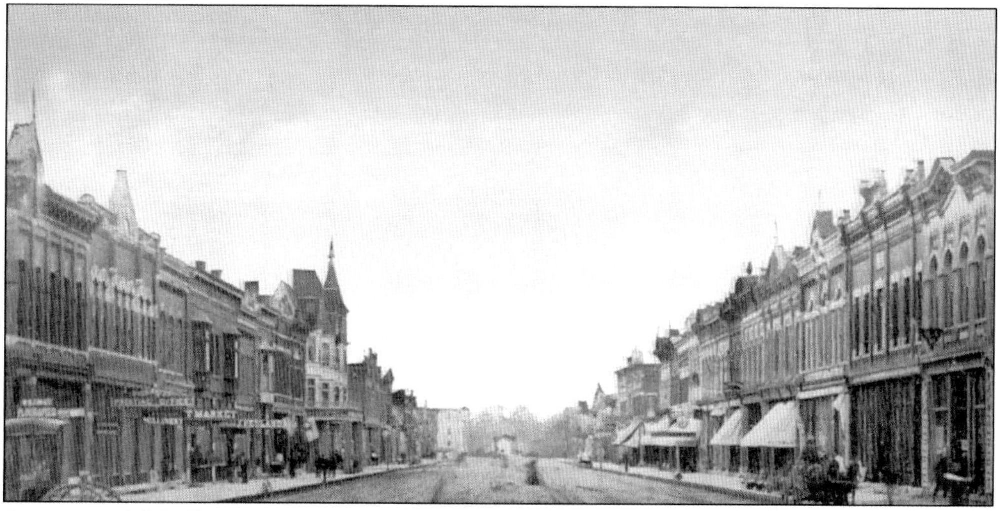

A scene on Main Street previous to automobiles and brick or cement pavement.

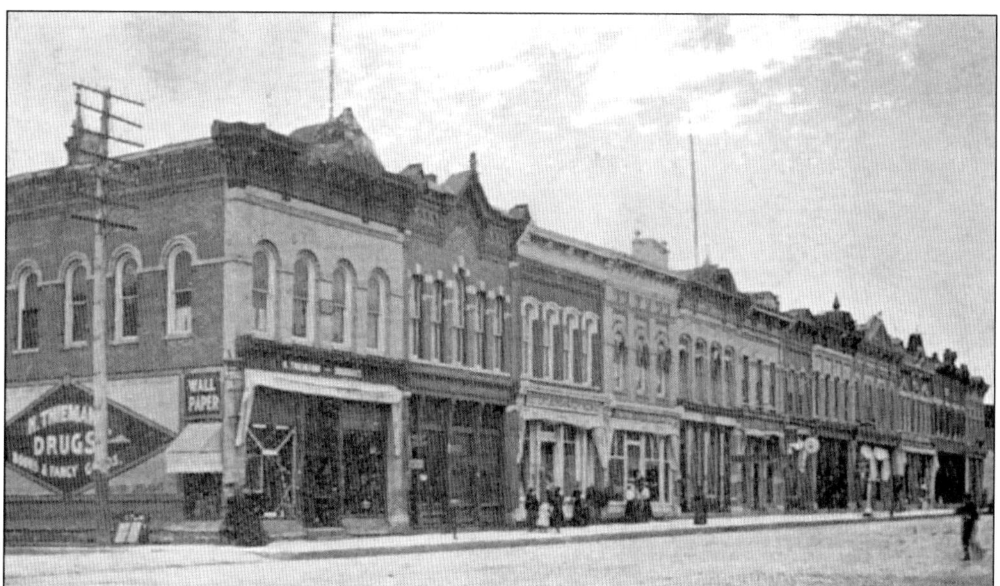

The awnings on the stores are holding the afternoon sun at bay. The old wooden steeple of the Methodist Church is further up the street where the boulevard starts.

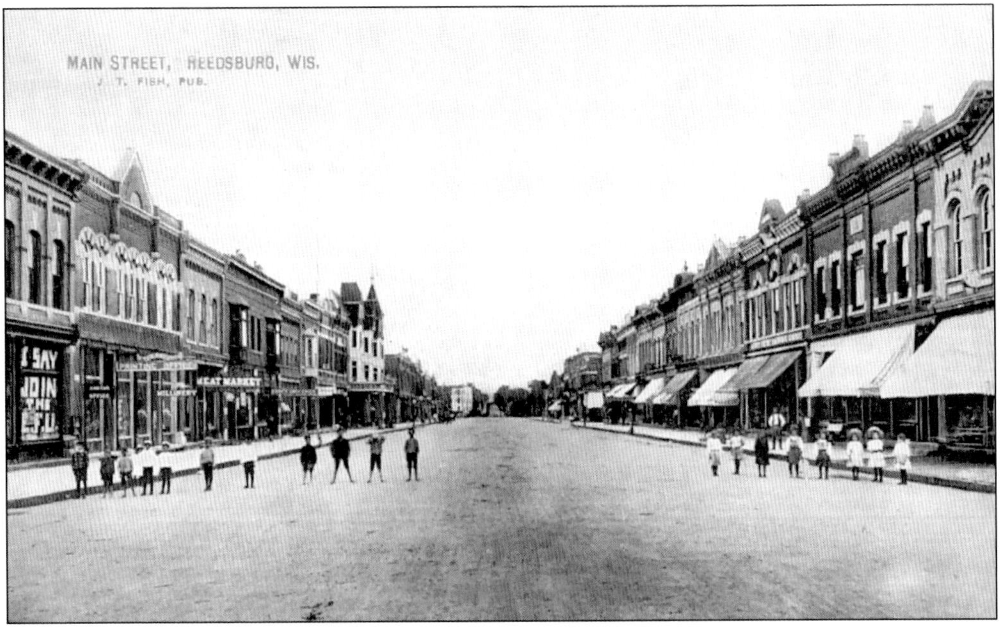

Citizens, both young and old, pose for the photographer's camera.

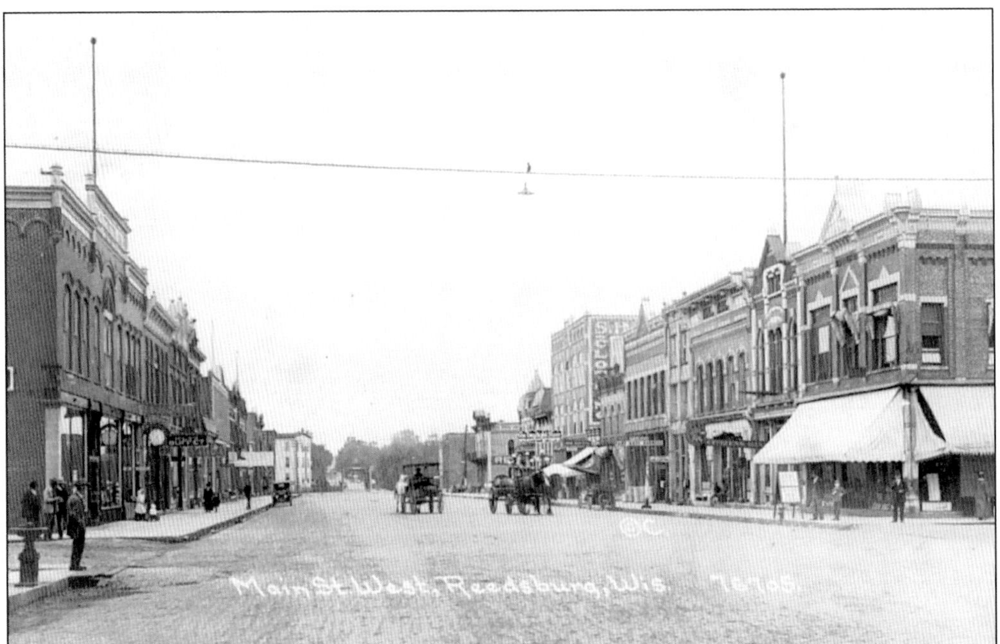

Street lights and pavement replaced the hitching posts and dirt ruts of an earlier day.

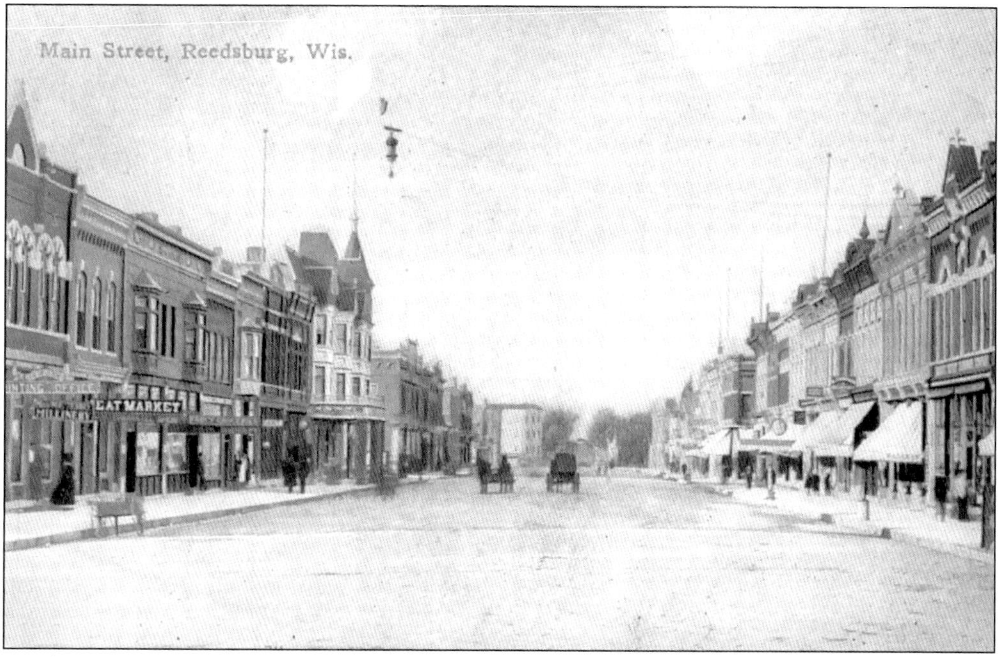

Bricks were laid to improve the quality of travel for both man and horse.

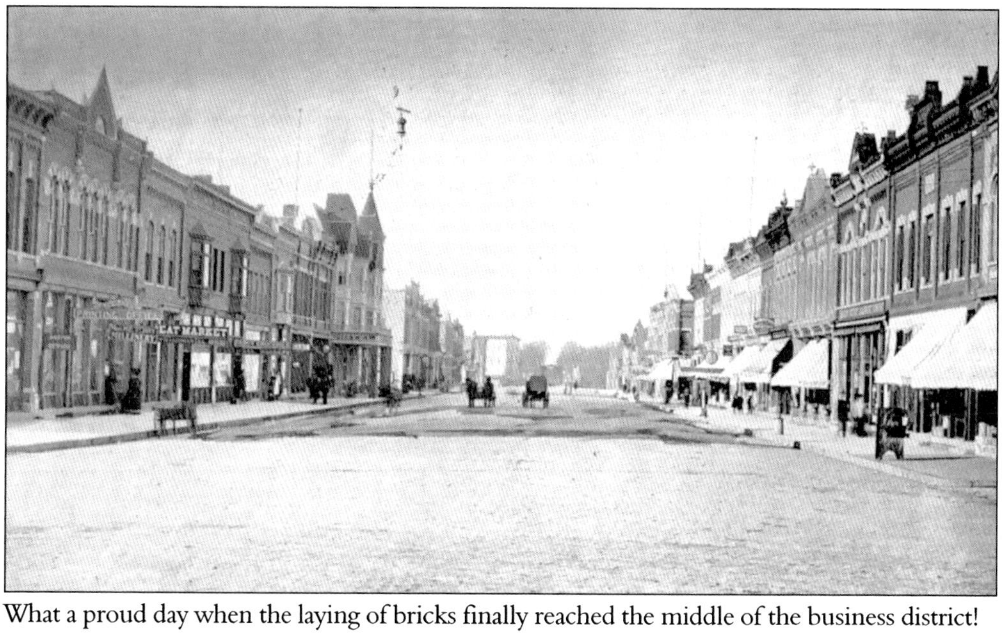

What a proud day when the laying of bricks finally reached the middle of the business district!

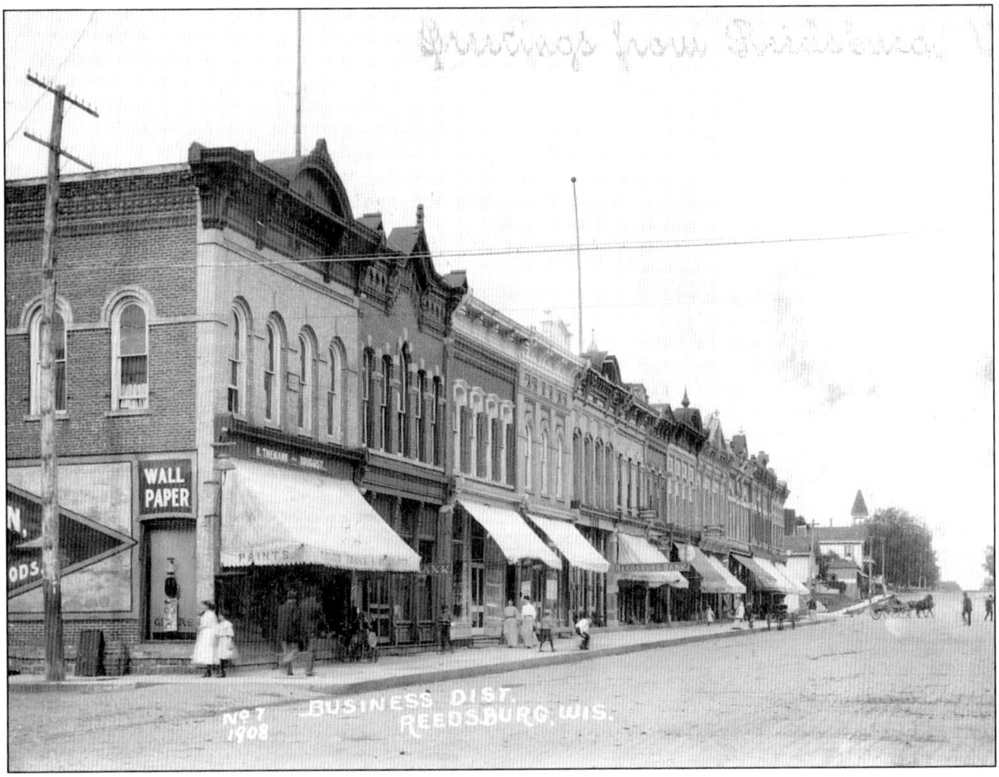

The first businesses of Reedsburg were housed in log structures and then later in frame buildings. In 1877 fire devastated the block of buildings between what is now Walnut and Park Streets, on the north side of Main Street. The proprietors and builders in the community replaced the frame buildings with brick buildings so as to never have a repeat disaster. With pride, the names of the owners or builders were placed at the top of the new buildings, still visible 100 years later.

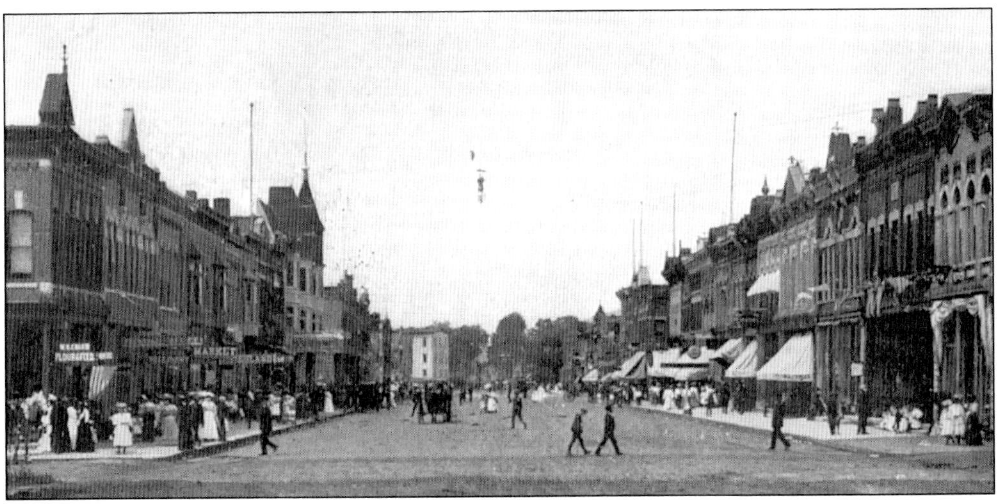

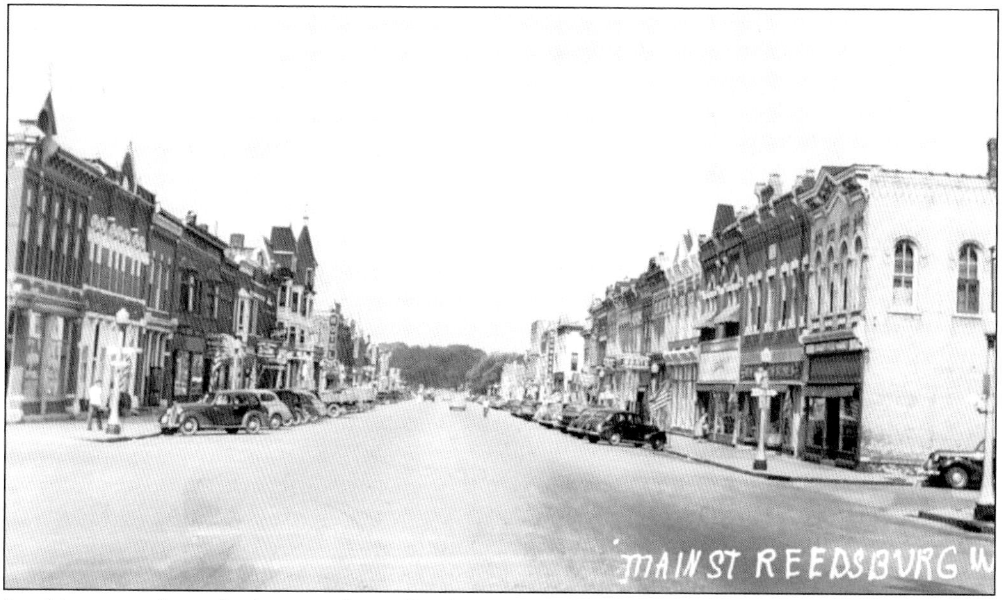

Looking west from the intersection of Park Street and Main Street.

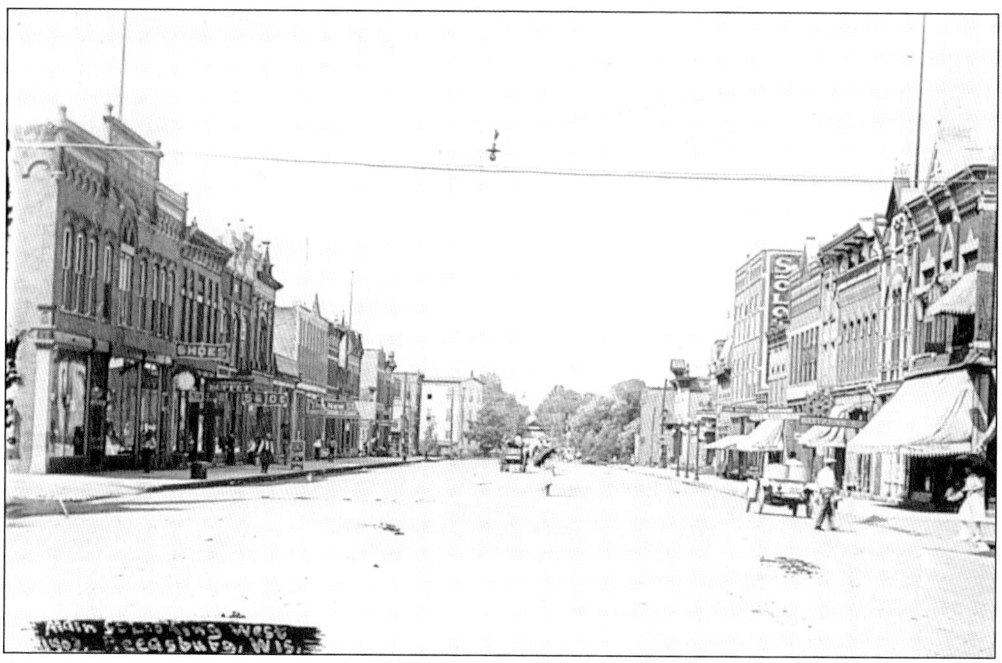

A quiet afternoon on Main Street when only the sound of hoofs and the clinking of a harness disturbed the solitude.

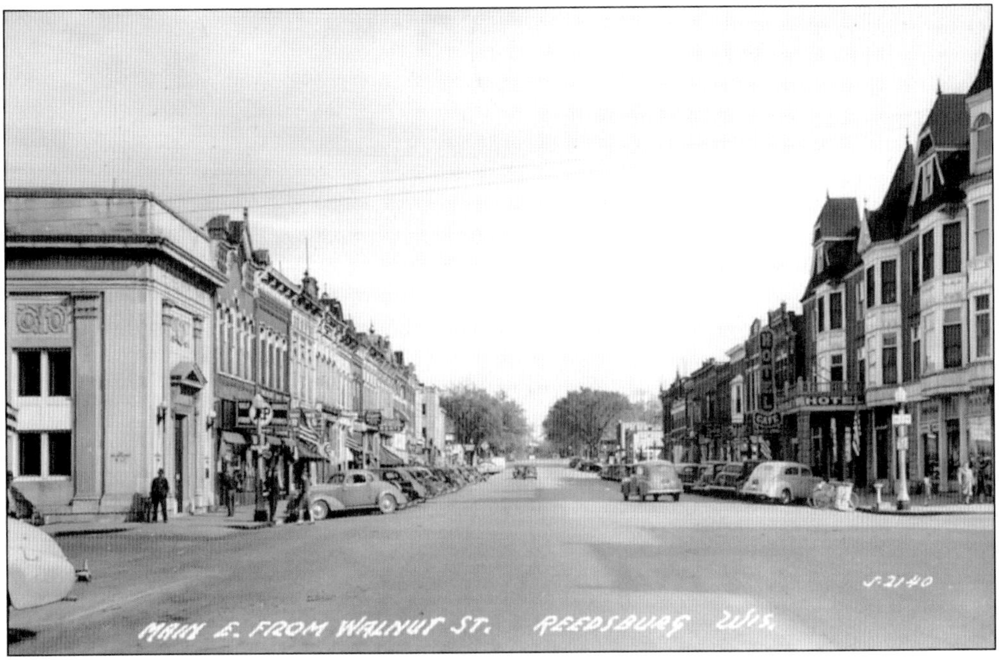

Cars replace the horse and buggy as the main means of travel.

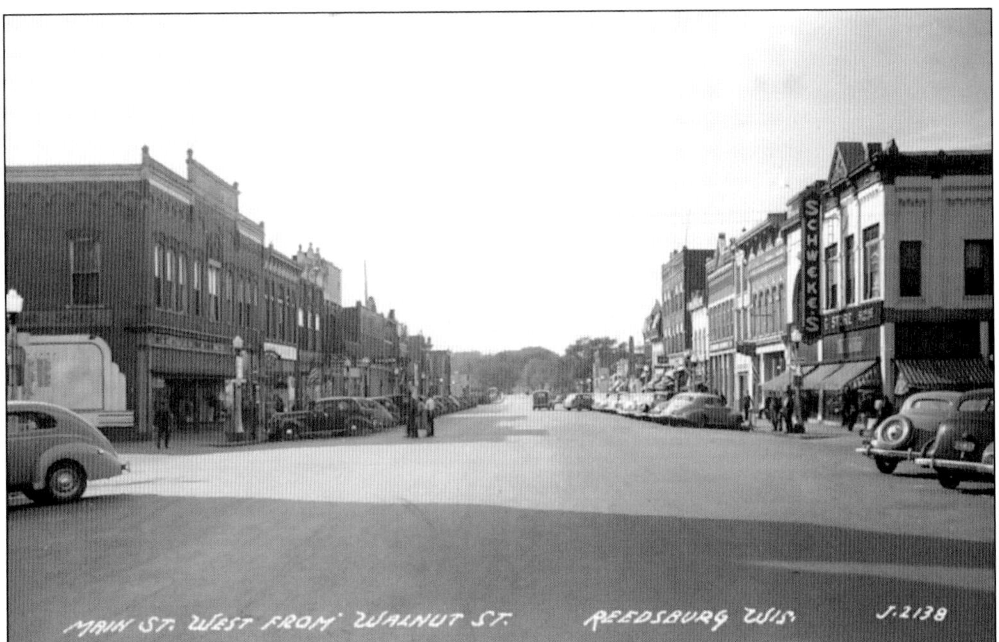

During World War II the Roll of Honor was posted on the side of the old J.C. Penney Company. This is seen on the left side of the postcard.

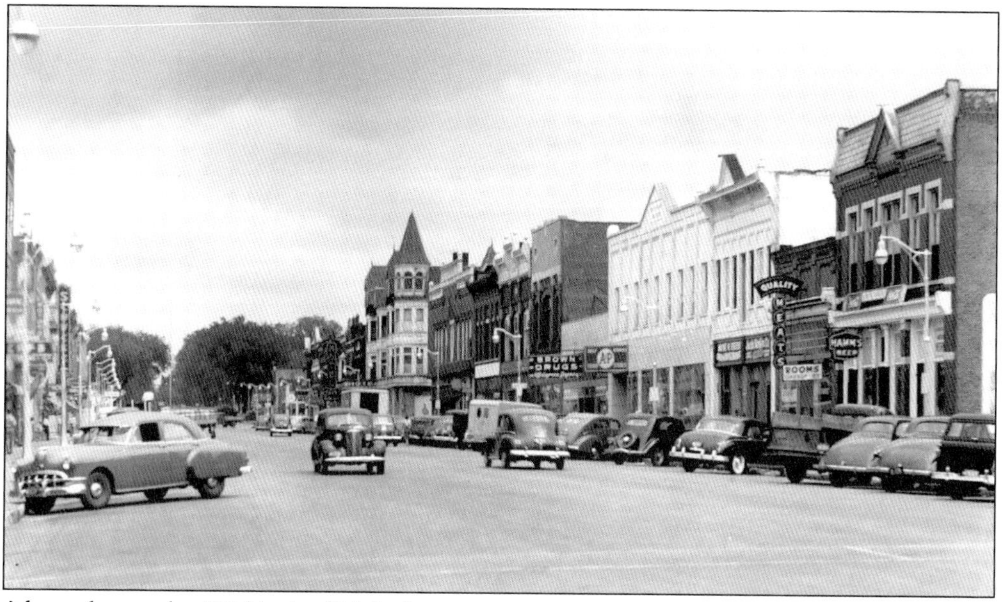

A busy day on the 100 block of Main Street.

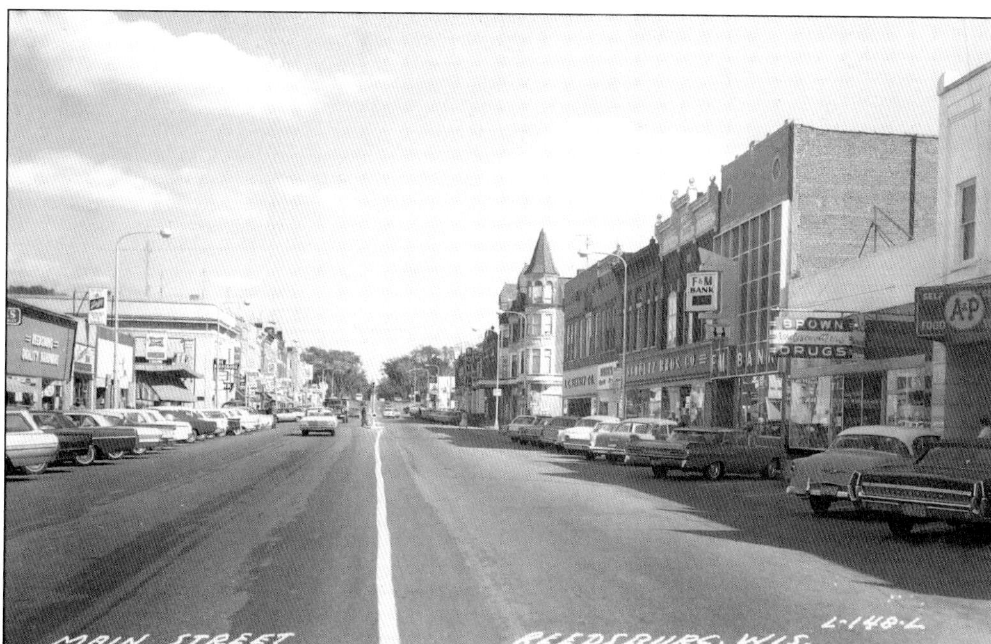

By the time of this photo, the buildings destroyed in the great fire of 1957 had been replaced with new structures and business was again thriving.

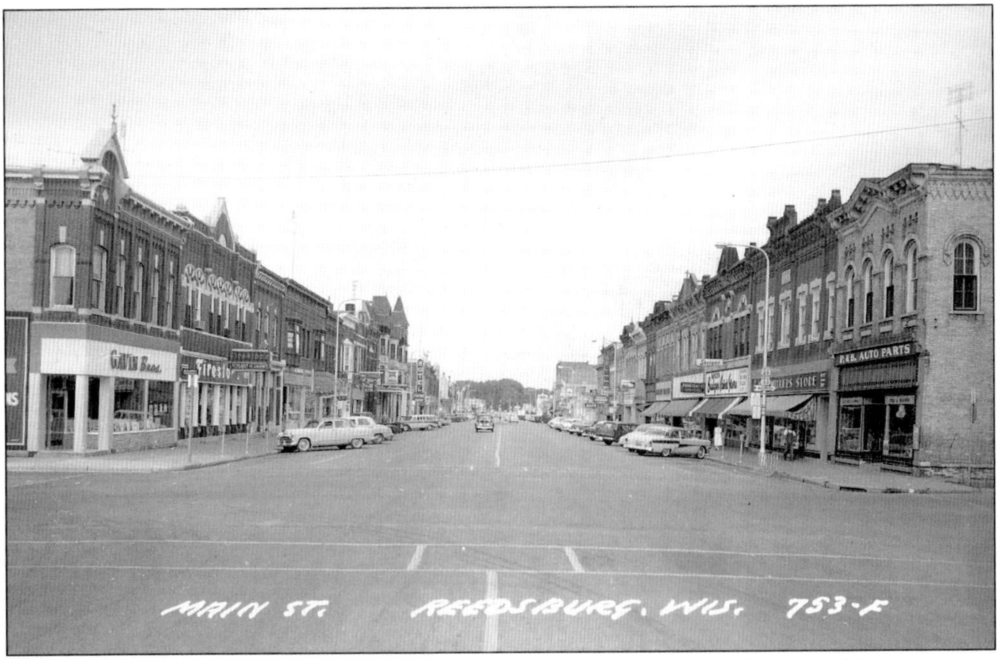

By the time of this postcard, the businesses were replacing their small signs with larger ones to draw attention from potential customers. The activity on Main Street was always lively. The farming community came to town to do their trading and this was also time to meet their friends and neighbors. The sidewalks were filled on many Friday nights with people chatting with their friends. Shopping was combined with social activities and this was a way to keep up on the news in the area.

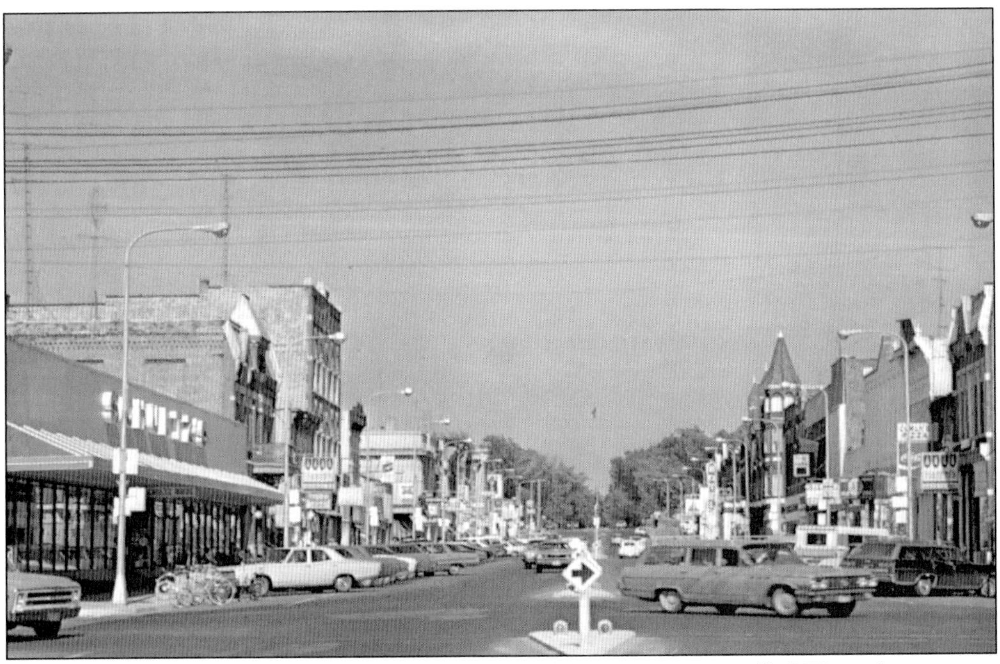

The 100 block of Main Street looking east from Webb Avenue, once called Water Street.

Five

The Churches of Reedsburg

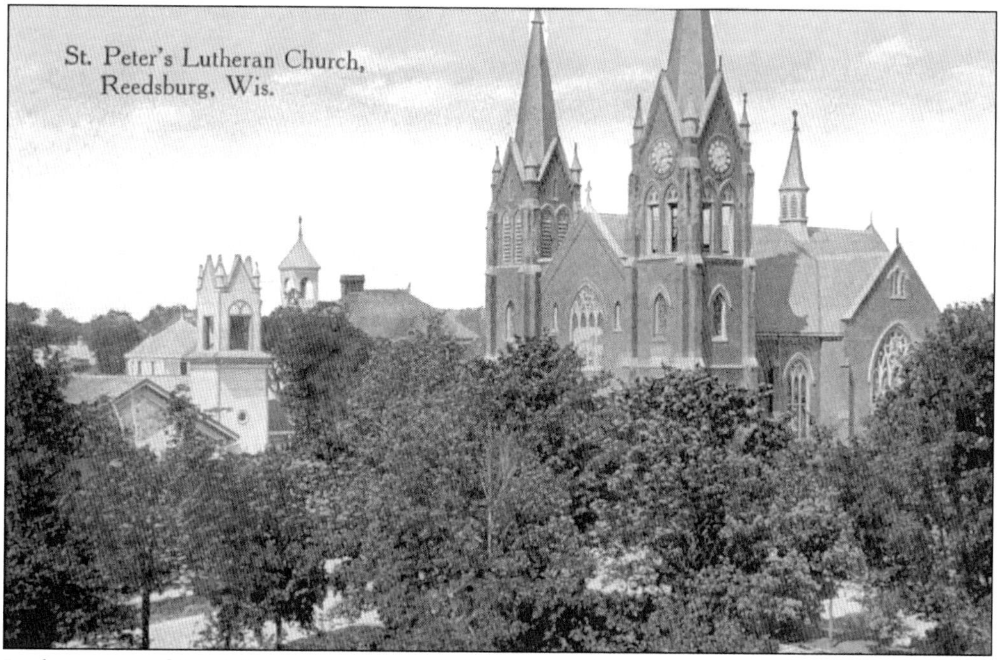

In the center of Reedsburg is the city park. This view shows the park with all of its trees and three of its early church steeples in the background.

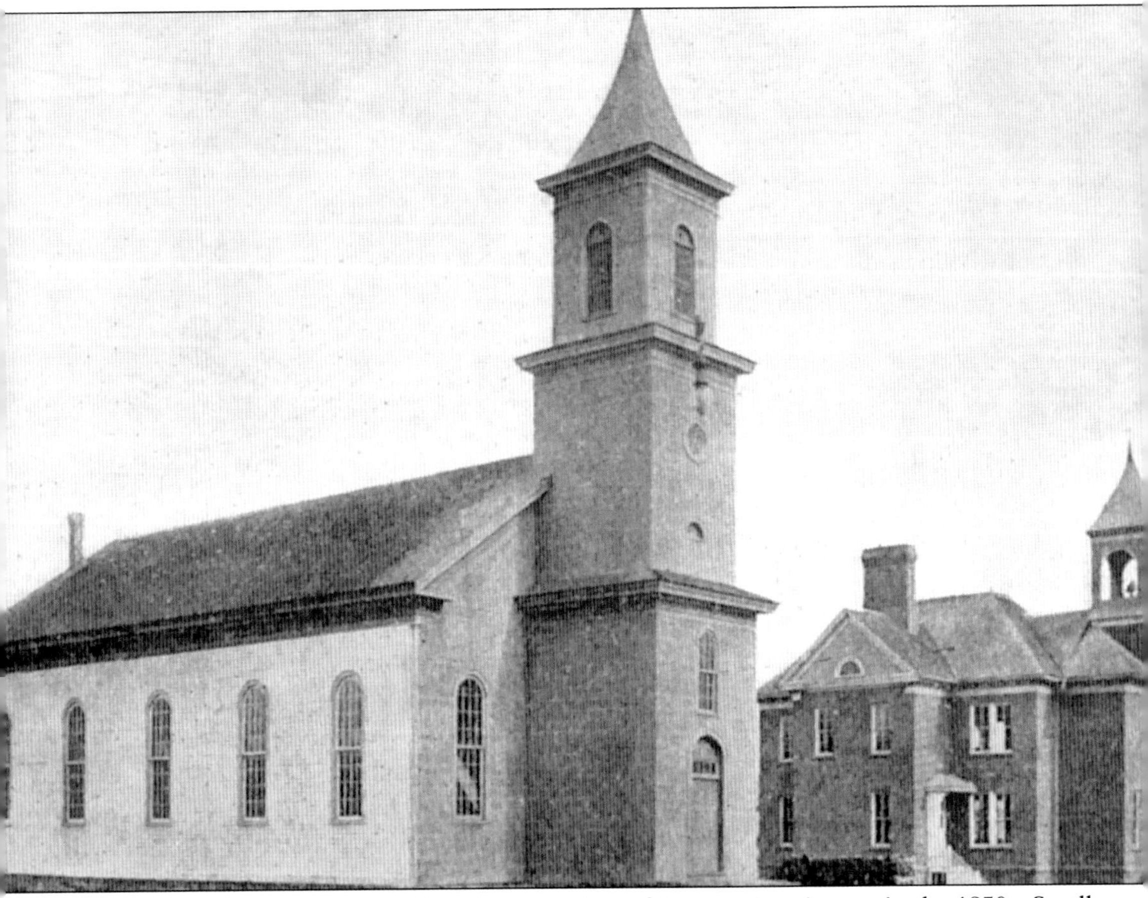

Reedsburg became a magnet for a large number of German immigrants in the 1850s. Small congregations were formed in and around the village. The first Missouri Synod Lutheran church was founded about two-and-a-half miles northeast of Loganville. In 1867, members formed and met in a one-room country school known as the County Farm School. Because the congregation was growing, and more and more people resided in and near Reedsburg, there was a deep desire to have a place of worship of their own in town. An entire city block was purchased and a frame building erected on the northwest corner of the block. Lumber was hauled from Necedah by a team, over a distance of 42 miles. The bell for the steeple was purchased and moved here from Kilbourn. Because of the growth of the congregation, balconies were added to both sides of the church. This building served the congregation for nearly 40 years. By 1907, because of needed repairs and a still growing congregation, a decision was made to construct a new building. The group had already provided a brick school building for the education of their children.

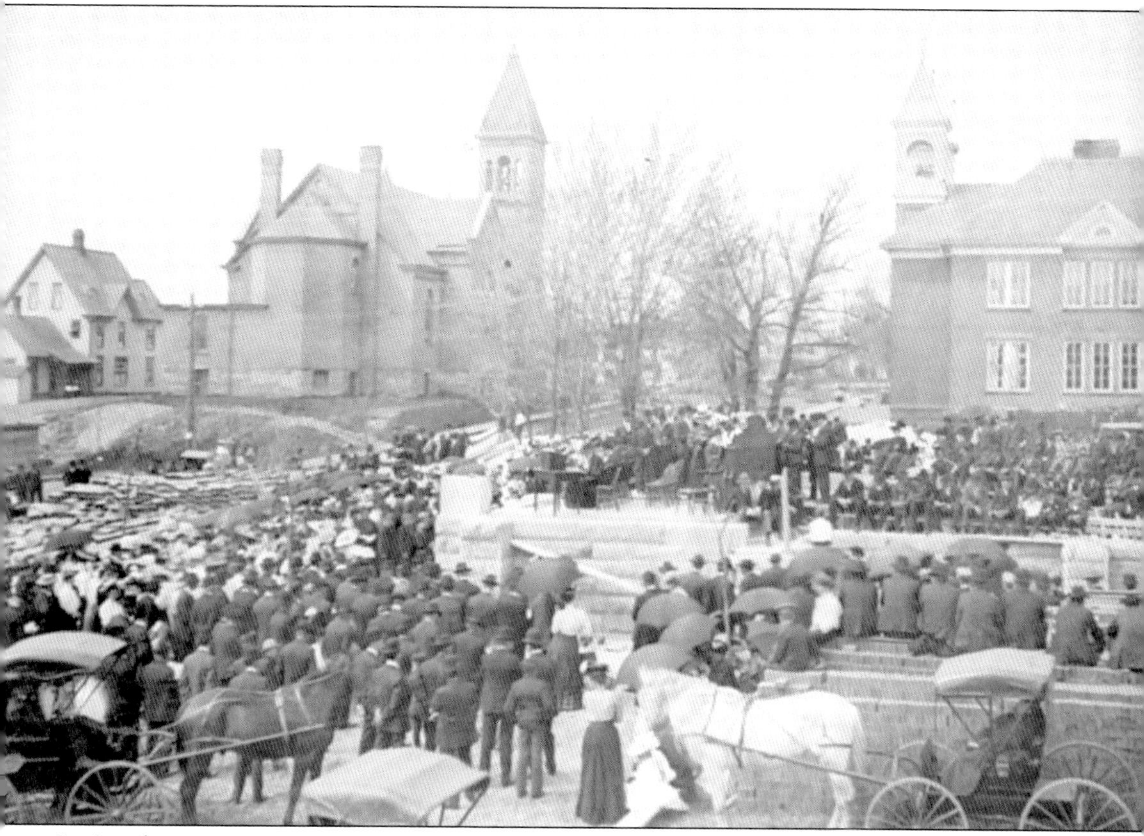

Laying the corner stone in May 1908. In September of 1907, construction of the new church was underway. The height of the nave was to be 40 feet. Two steeples were planned for this new building. The tallest steeple was to be 136 feet tall and hold the bell and a clock, 7 feet in diameter, with a face in each direction. The shorter steeple was to be 116 feet high. Notice in the background the large Catholic church and rectory.

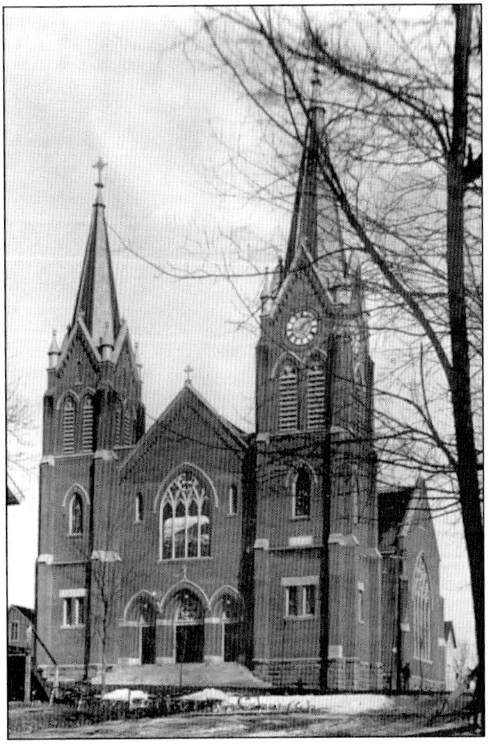

On March 14, 1909, a new brick church was dedicated for St. Peter's Lutheran Church. Three stained glass windows grace the north, east, and west sides of the church. By 1915 the congregation finished the basement of the church to be used for meetings. All other churches dispensed for that day, so pastors and members of other denominations could attend the dedication if they so wished.

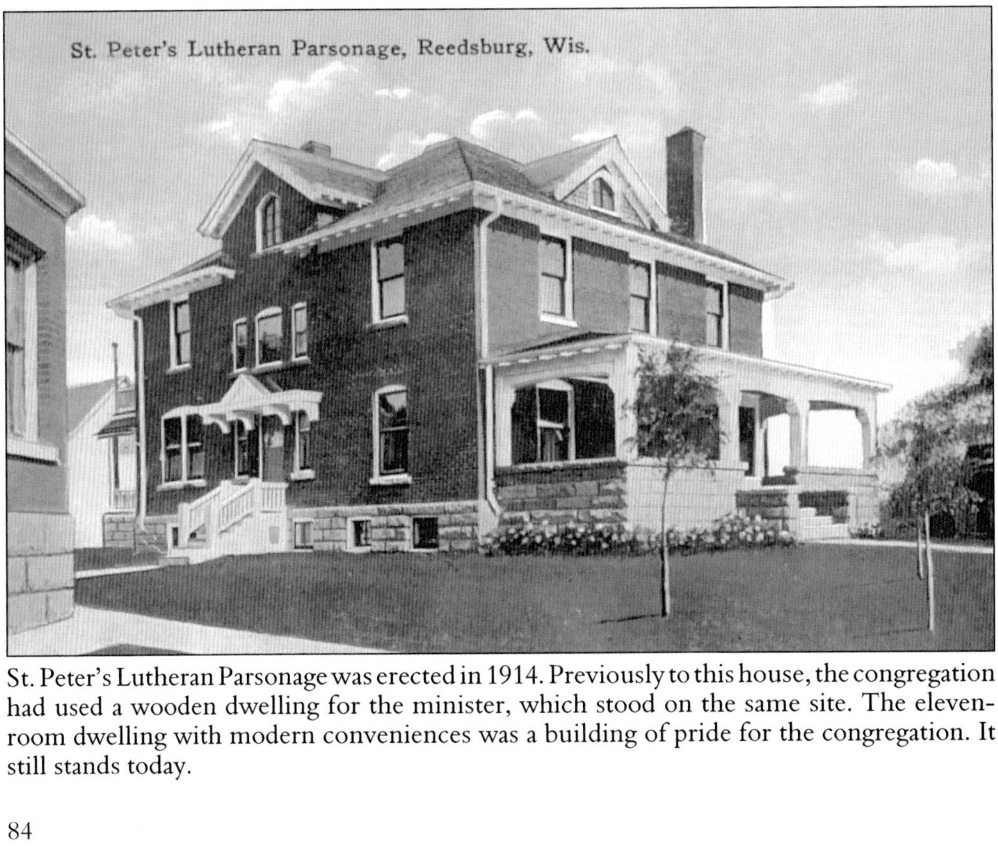

St. Peter's Lutheran Parsonage was erected in 1914. Previously to this house, the congregation had used a wooden dwelling for the minister, which stood on the same site. The eleven-room dwelling with modern conveniences was a building of pride for the congregation. It still stands today.

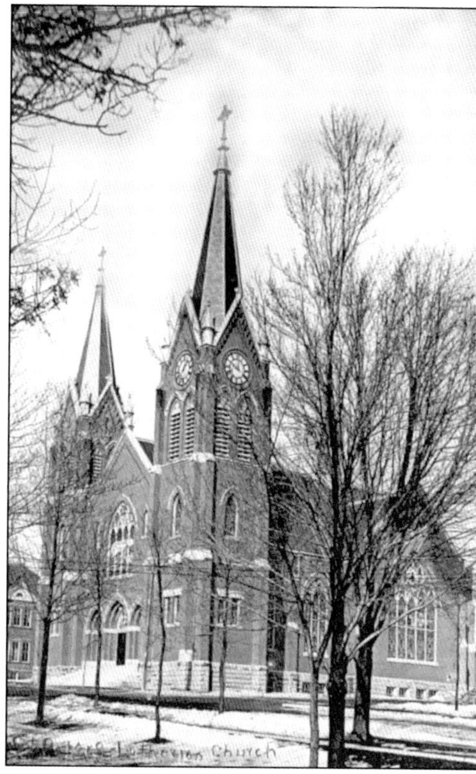

St. Peter's stands on a high knoll near the city park. This church with its high steeples graces the skyline from each direction as you enter the city of Reedsburg. The clock chimes and the bell can be heard throughout the area yet today.

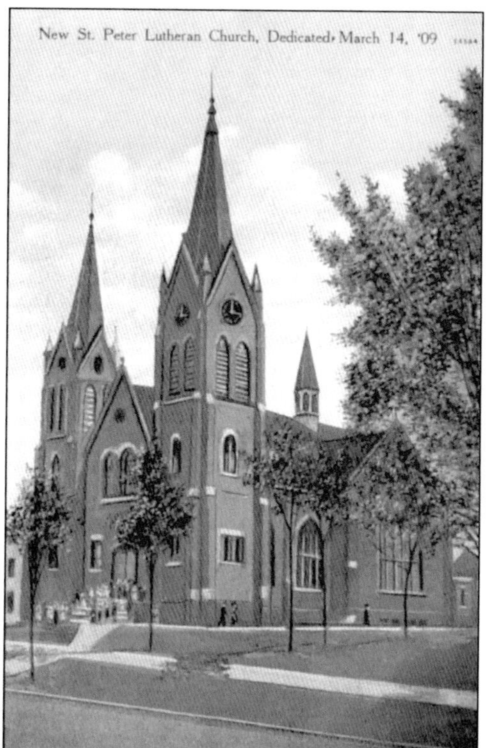

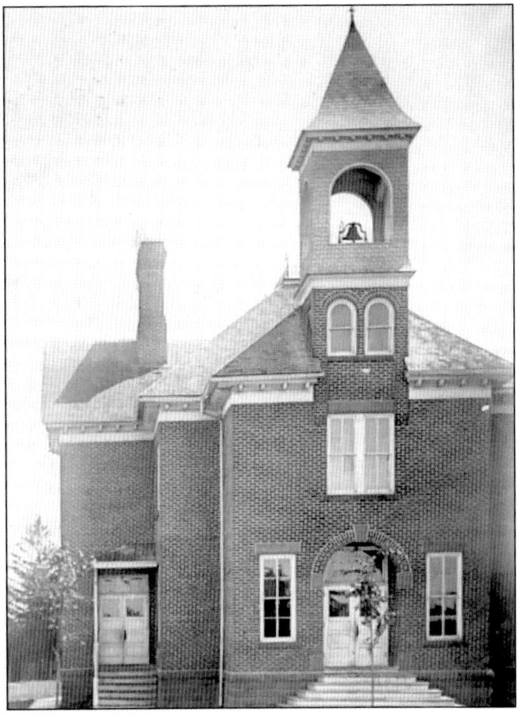

In 1898, a new two-story brick building was constructed for St. Peter's Lutheran School, just south of the church, but still on the same block. Previously, the school had been in a wooden frame building in the parsonage and at one time in the home of a parishioner.

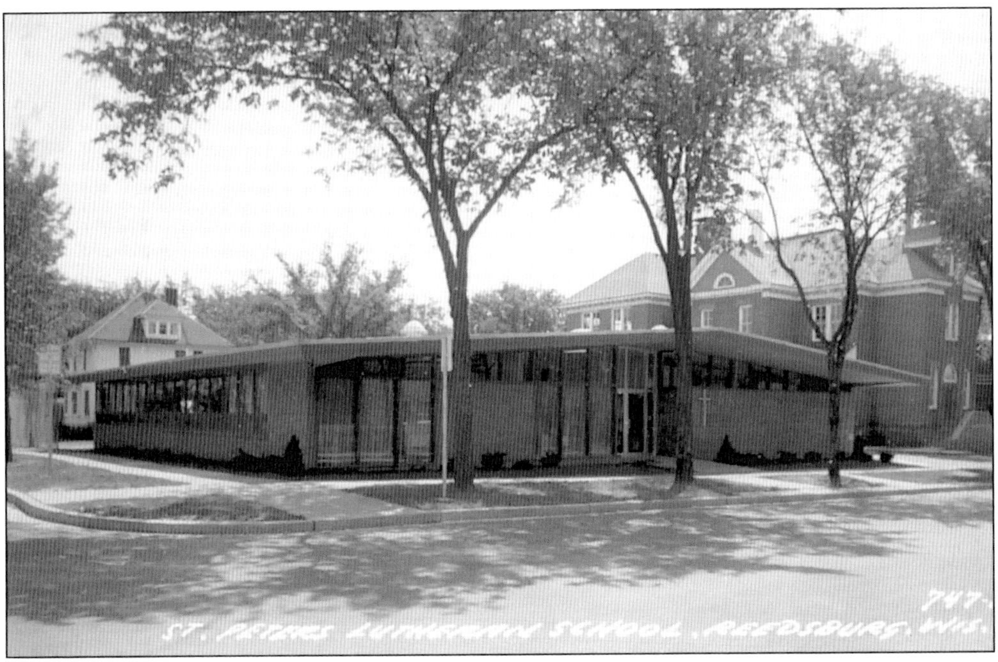

By 1956, the enrollment outgrew the school building and a new four-classroom building was erected on the northwest corner of the block. In 1965 the congregation continued to improve and enlarge the school and proceeded to complete the structure with four additional classrooms, a gymnasium, locker room, as well as offices and a meeting room for the pastors and church secretary.

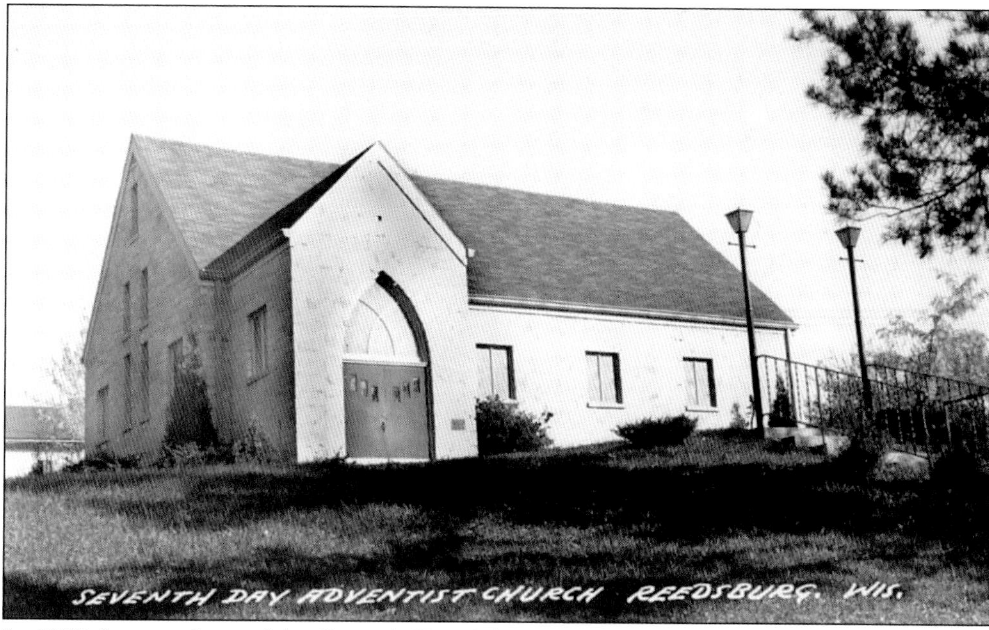

In 1952 the members of the Seventh Day Adventist Church built this fine structure at the corner of East Main Street and South Oak Street. It sits high on a bank overlooking East Main Street. The Seventh Day Adventist congregation has been in existence since the turn of the 20th century. Through their generosity, other congregations have used this building for their own services until arrangements could be made for them to have a building of their own.

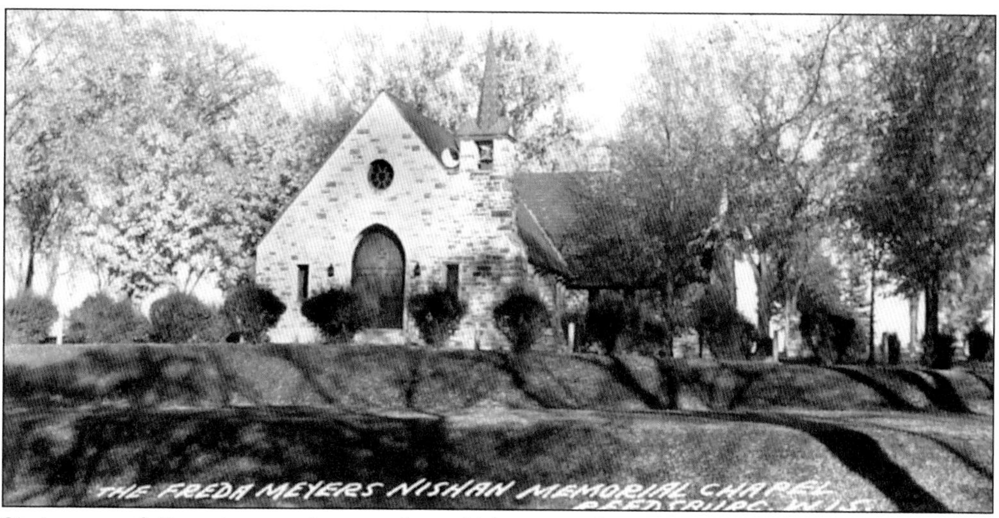

Sitting gracefully at the top of a natural amphitheater at the Greenwood Cemetery is the Freda Meyers Nishan Memorial Chapel. Due to the generous donation of Freda Meyers Nishan, this chapel was built in the 1930s for the people of the area. This was a non-denominational chapel to be used for funerals during inclement weather. There are four crypts in the east end of the basement. The Greenwood Cemetery Association acts as the trustees of this structure and is responsible for maintenance and discretion as to the use of this chapel. The 31-by-60 foot building, with an 18-by-28 wing is built from hand-cut hard stone, which was quarried near Richland Center, Wisconsin.

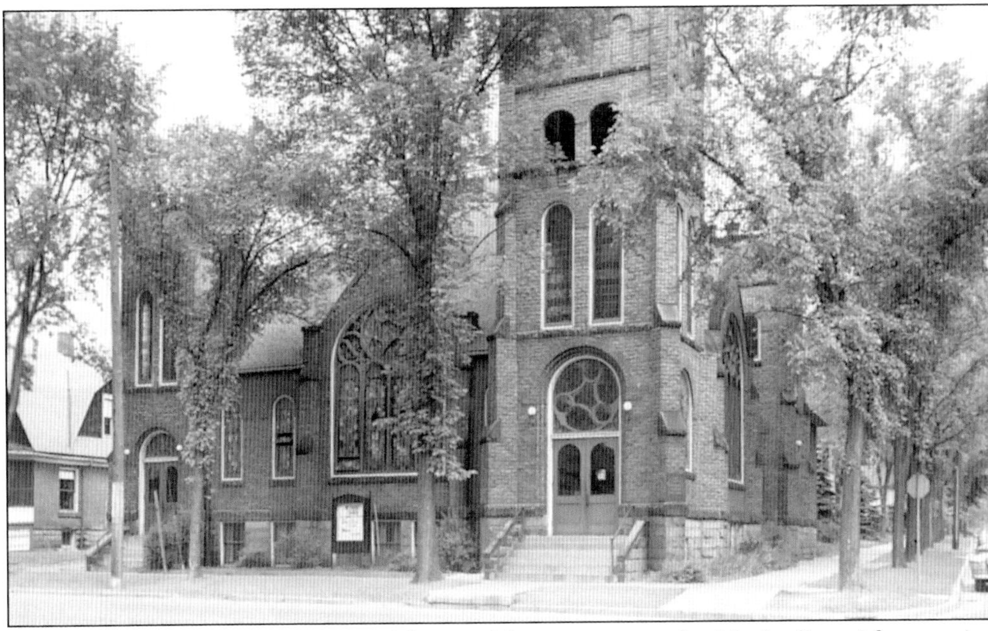

One of the earliest congregations of the Reedsburg area were the Methodists. After moving around to several locations, construction of a beautiful brick church was started in 1907. In 1908, at a cost of $15,000, the new church and parsonage was completed at the corner of Pine and Main Streets, facing the lovely boulevard of East Main. This parsonage and church were used until, in need of repairs, the church was abandoned for a new building and a new location. The parsonage was sold and moved to a new location on Mary Avenue and is still in use today as a private home.

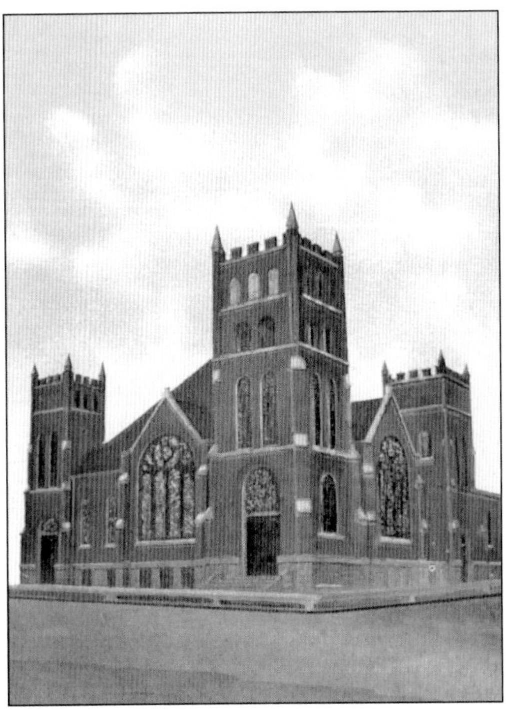

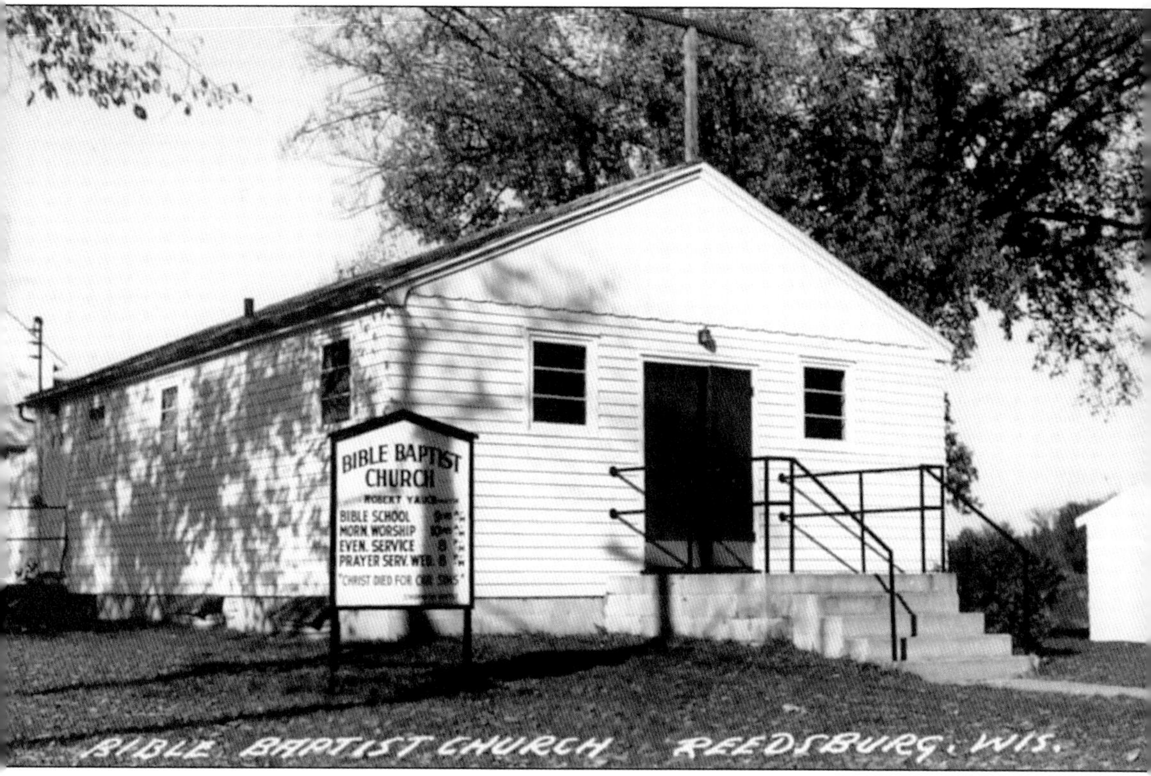

The Bible Baptists founded their first congregation in this building on Third Street and Oak Street in 1951. Eventually the congregation outgrew this building and moved to a larger building on West Main Street. In later years this structure was rehabbed into a house.

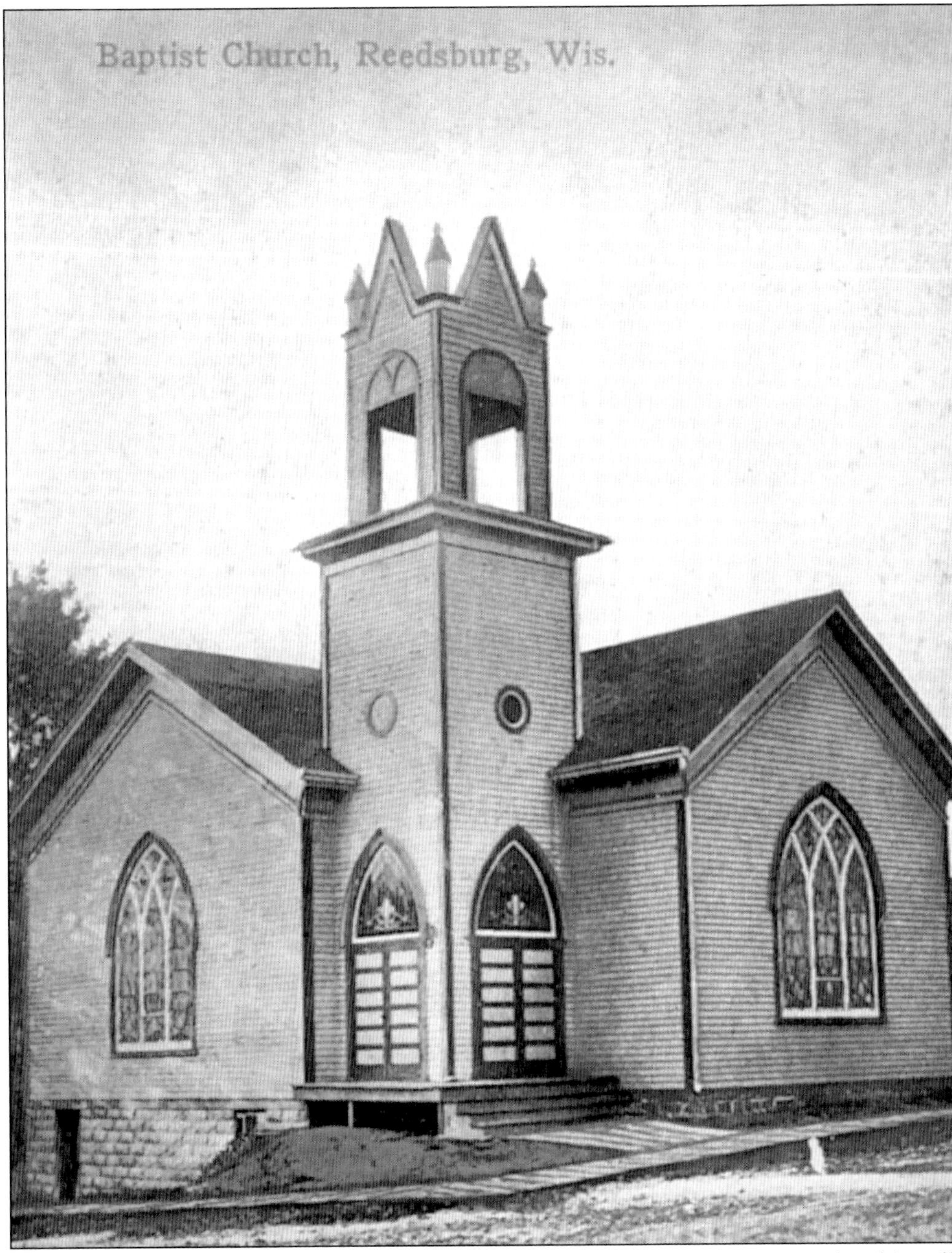

In 1852, 11 brothers and sisters of the Baptist faith signed their names to a membership roll, thus becoming the First Baptist Church of Reedsburg. By 1872 the congregation decided to build their church. The wood for the sills and floor joists came from Carver's Wood about three miles from the village. The rest of the finished lumber was hauled from Kilbourn. All the work was done by having building bees. Building bees, much like quilting bees, are a day everyone set aside from their usual work and donated their time and talents to the benefit of getting a job done all at once. On October 12, 1873, the hardworking members of this early congregation dedicated their new church.

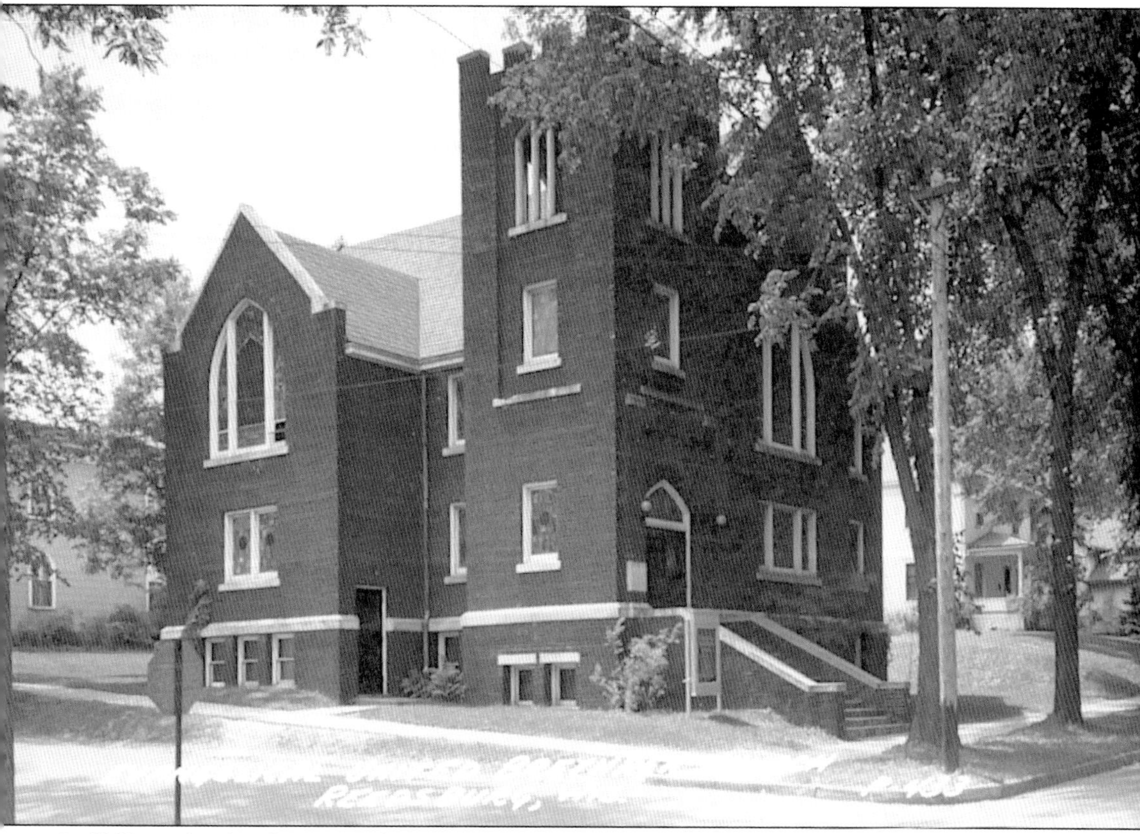

In 1922, under the direction of E.C. Miller and Will Townsend, the United Brethren Church became a reality. The beautiful windows of the church were donated by members of the congregation. The big window overlooking Main Street was put in by the congregation and the dedication read, "In Memory of Our Country's Defenders" (the soldiers of World War I). This building has been the home of different denominations, currently the Church of the Nazarene is using it as their place of worship. Much remains as it was at the date of construction.

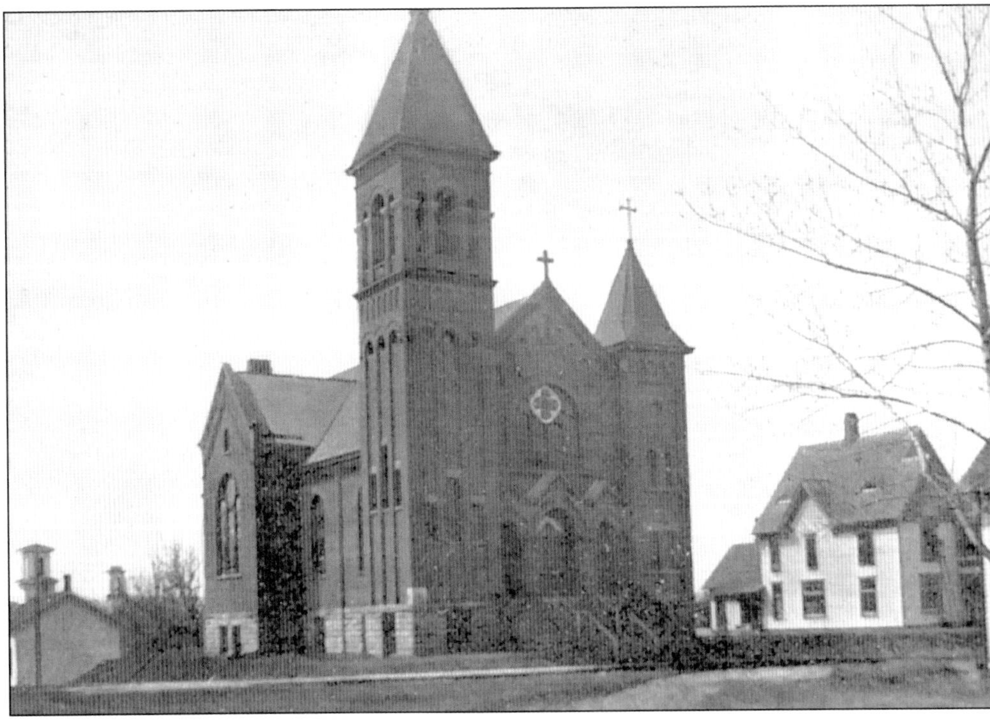

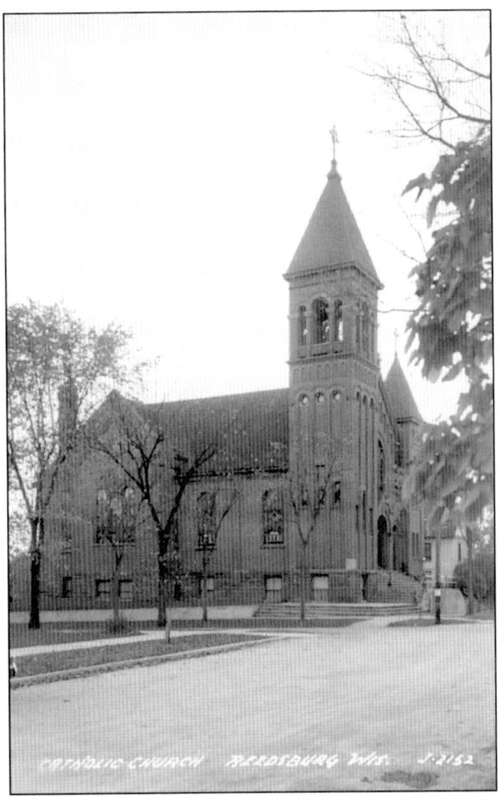

Among the first immigrants to come to this area of Sauk County were the Irish. A place to worship became one of the first concerns of these early settlers. Before there was a parish in the city, the early settlers built their churches in the townships of Dellona and Windfield. By 1878 a few people pursued to build a church within the city. A wooden church and rectory were built at the corner of Fourth and Locust Streets. In 1902 the church was burned to the ground and almost immediately the cornerstone was laid for a new brick building. That structure was dedicated in the spring of 1903. This structure was used by the growing congregation until a new building near their school was erected and dedicated in 1969. The bell from the brick church was moved to a bell tower at the new church. In the entrance of the new building is the cornerstone of the old brick church, which was torn down in 1971.

The Old Sacred Heart Church on Fourth and North Locust.

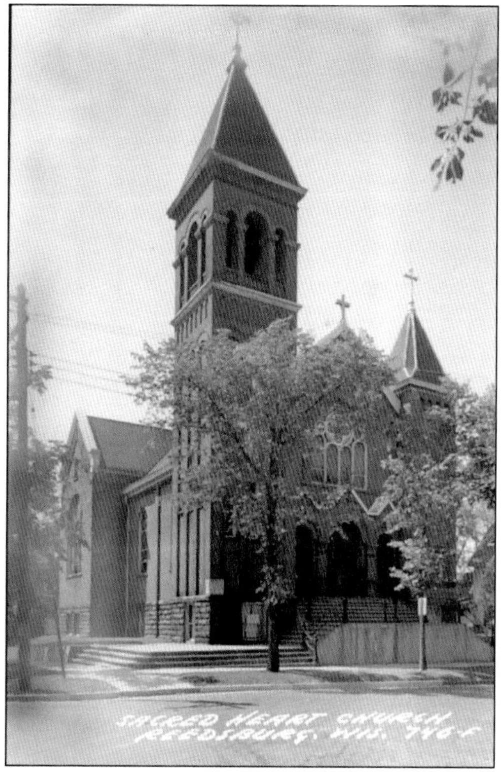

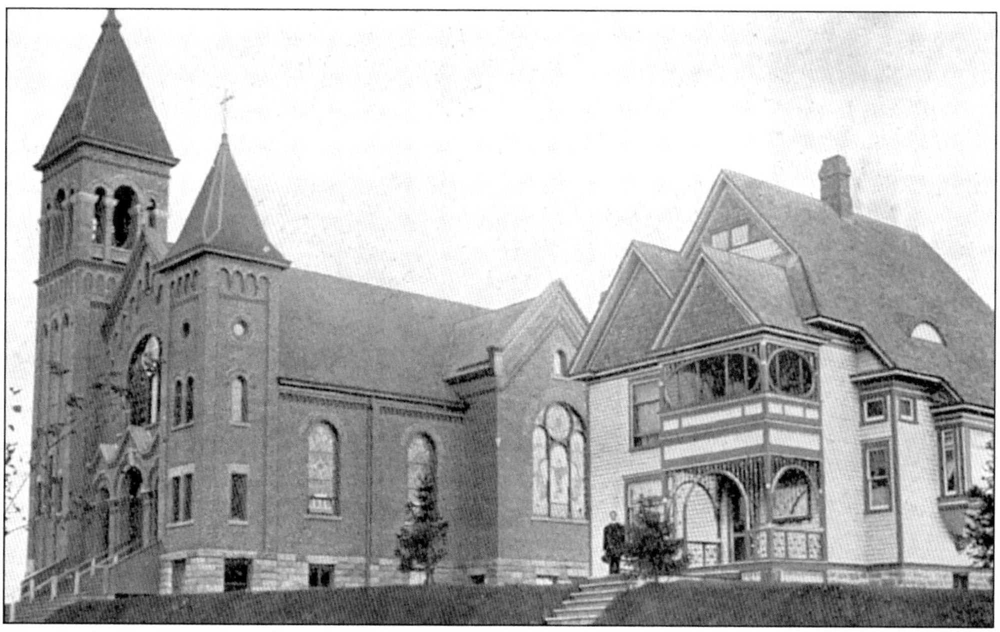

The Catholic Church and Rectory, Reedsburg, Wisconsin.

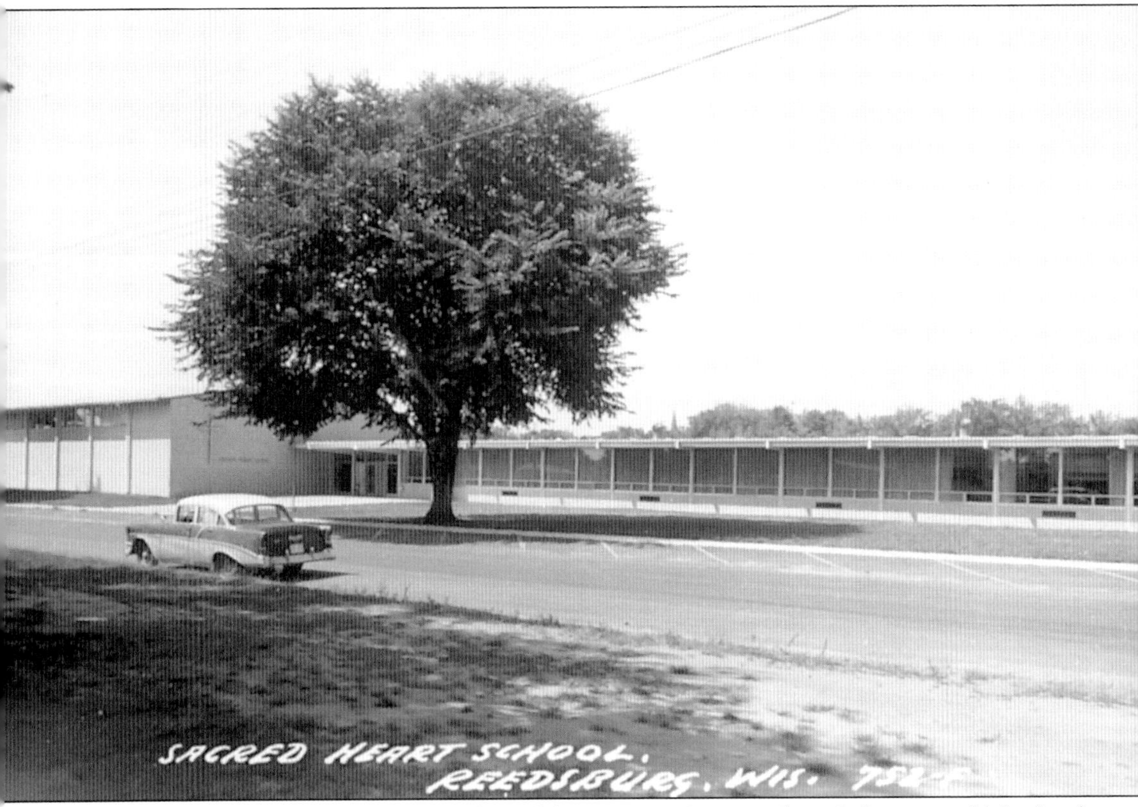

As early as 1935, the Catholic churches of the community started work for a parochial school. A building committee was selected in 1940. After the Dominican Sisters of Sinsinawa agreed to staff the school, a site was selected and purchased. Ground was broken in 1954 and the school and auditorium were completed and opened for enrollment in 1955.

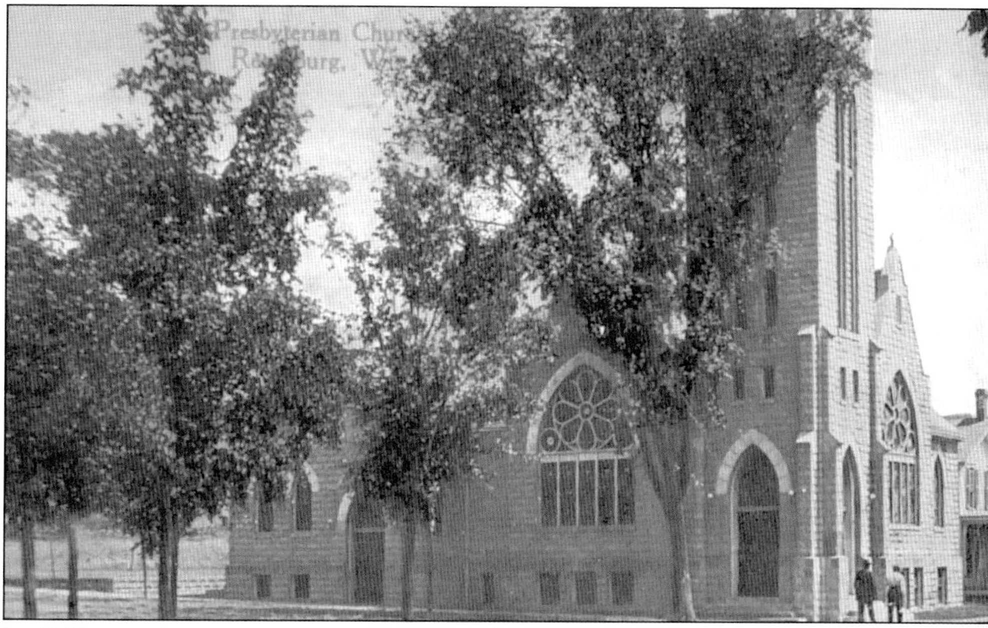

In 1857, a petition was presented to the Columbus Presbytery to form a congregation in Reedsburg. In 1871, a wooden building just east of the present building was constructed to house the First Presbyterian Church. By 1905 plans were made to build a cement block building. The blocks were made to look like stone and done by local contractors on site. A granite cornerstone was laid in 1906 and by January 1907 the building was ready to be used. The arched windows have green opalescent glass. The roof is gabled with parapets and has an irregular roof line. In the bell tower is a carillon bell system still heard on occasion. The people who chose this method of building the church did so because it was so durable. This is where Rev. John Moorehead, father of Agnes, served as minister for many years.

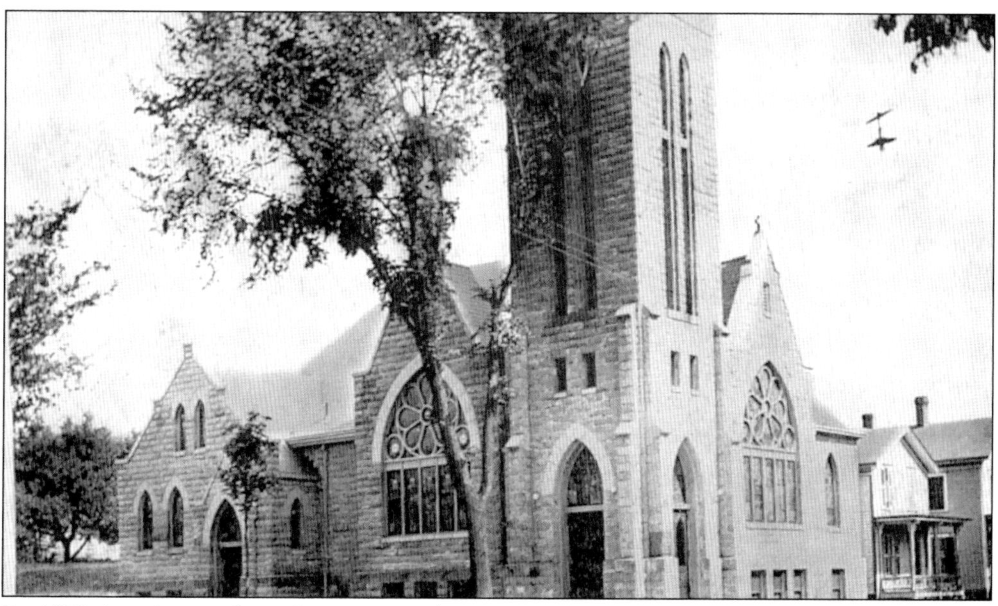

By 1870, immigrants from Germany made up more than half of Sauk County's population.

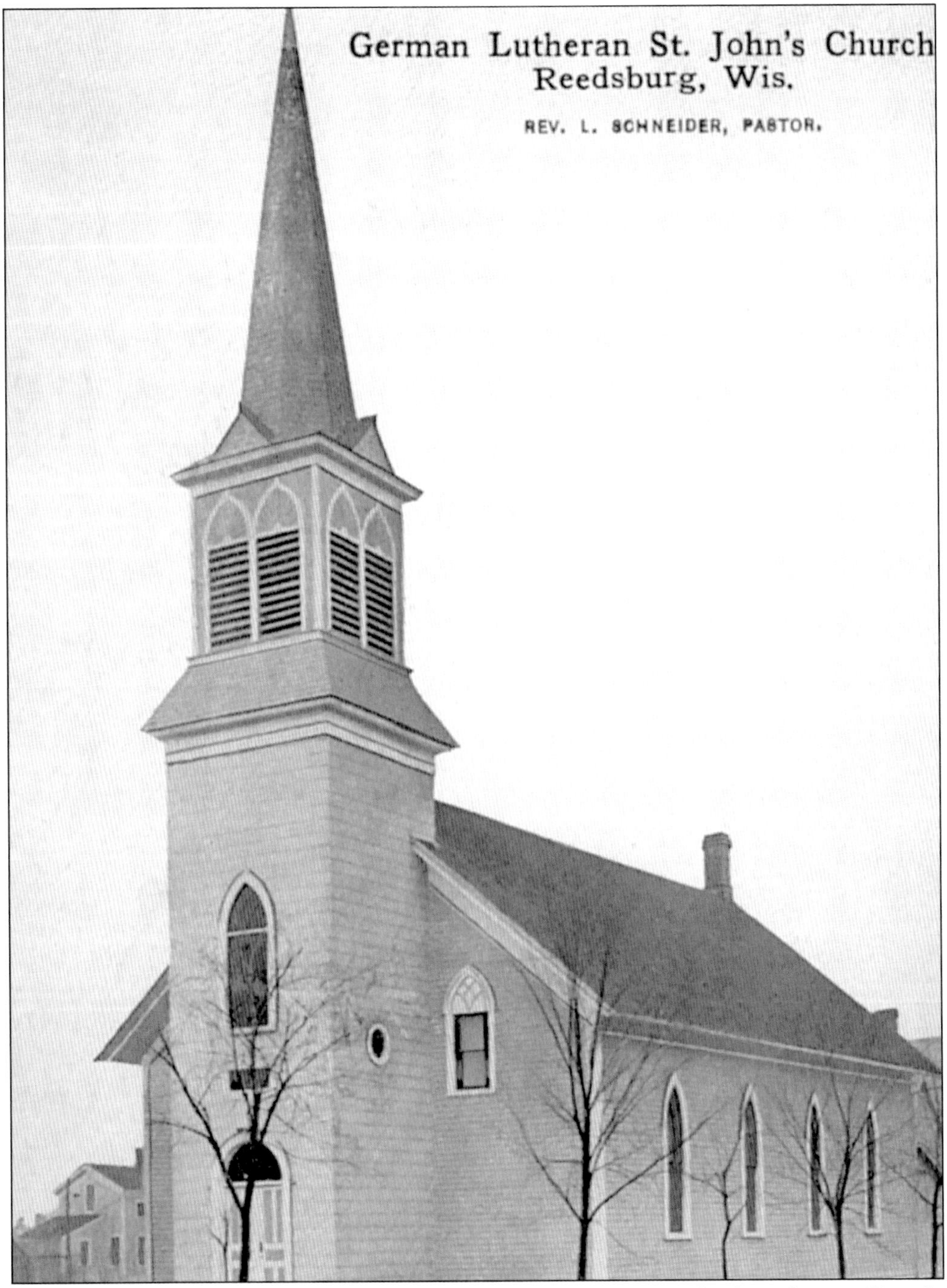

In August of 1878, 26 members formed the St. John's Evangelical Lutheran Church. Throughout the years improvement were made to the wooden structure. In 1916, English services were introduced in the church services to benefit the younger people of the congregation. Early one Sunday morning, January 10, 1937, the entire building was burned to the ground. While plans were being made to construct a larger church building, parishioners met at the Badger Theatre.

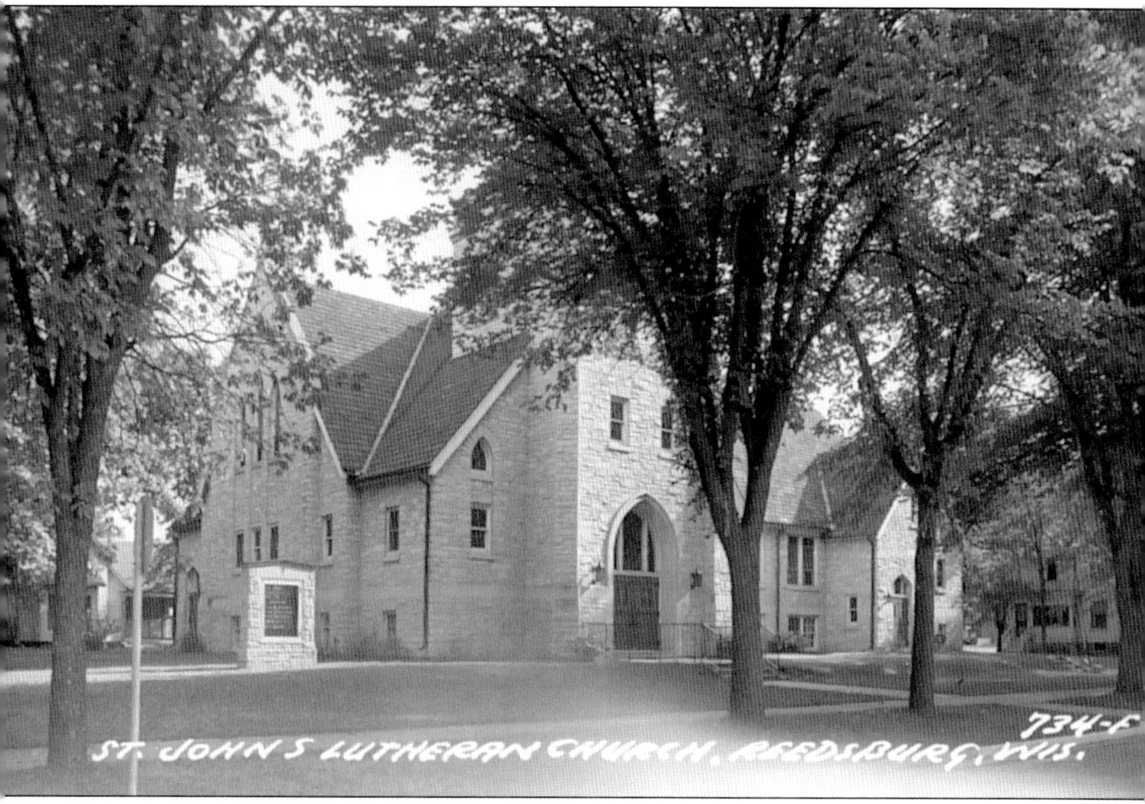

The cornerstone for this lanonstone edifice was laid in 1937 and the St. John's Lutheran Church was dedicated in 1938.

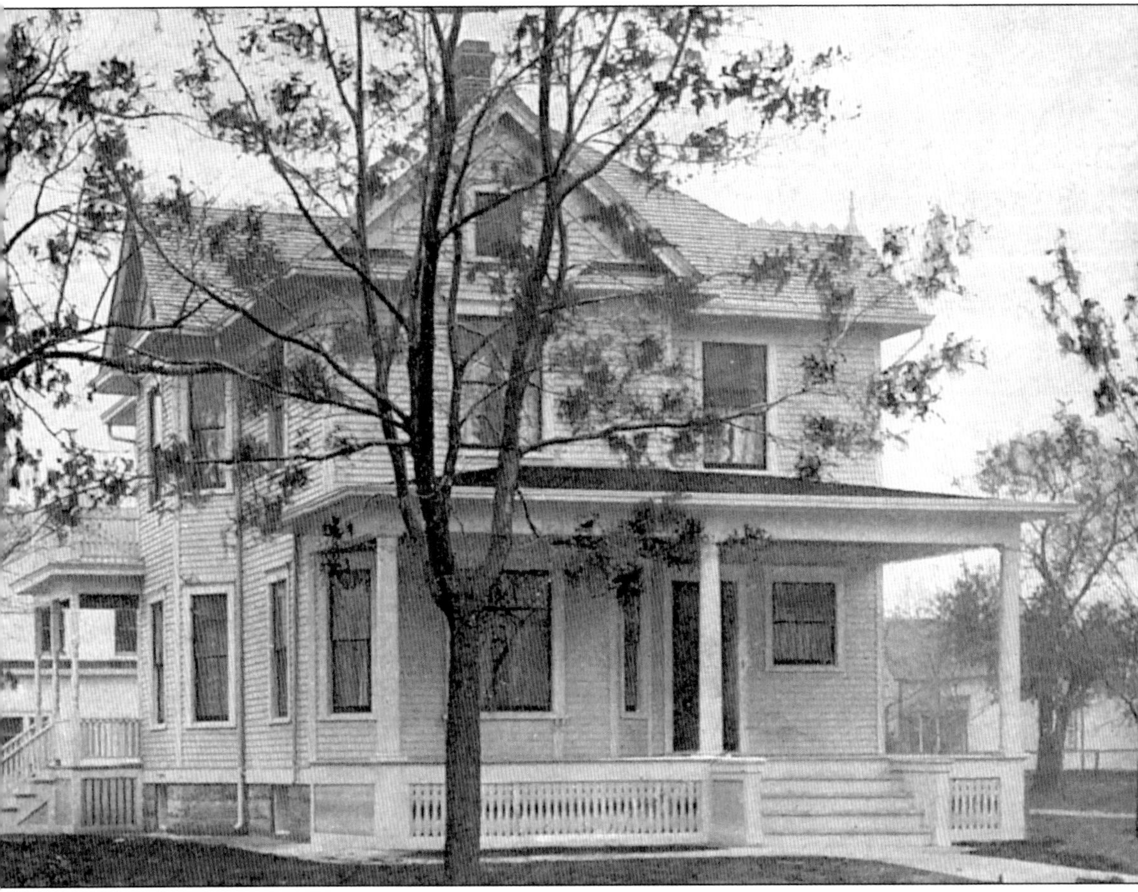

The congregation of St. John's Lutheran Church built a lovely new parsonage on Sixth Street in 1911. In 1989 this parsonage was torn down and the educational unit was added to the existing church. A new parsonage was acquired, after the removal of the big square house, at a location on Eighth Street.

Six

Schools of Reedsburg

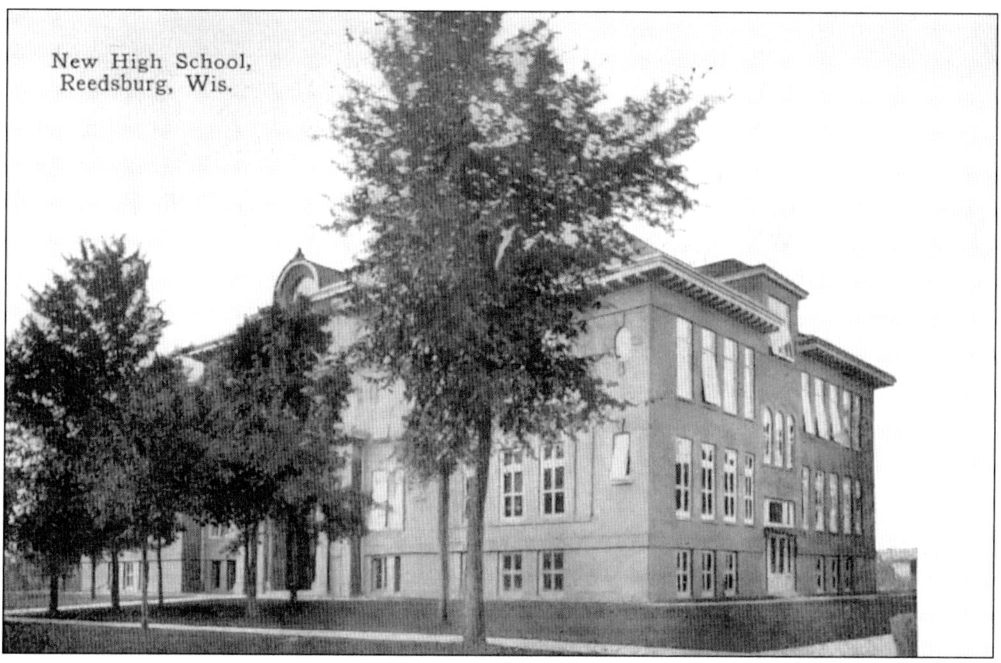

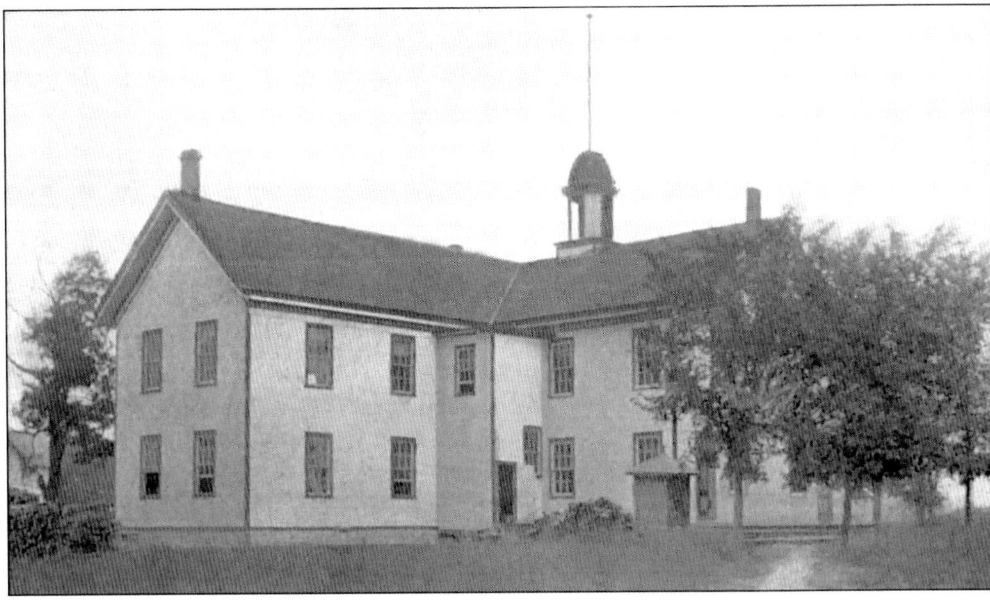

The Original High School. From the earliest days of settlement, the people of Reedsburg were very eager to have the young ones of the settlement receive a good education. In the winter of 1849, school was held in a shanty, which measured 12 feet square. There were seven children enrolled and a single window was the source of light. The following year Miss Saxby relinquished her job to Miss Amanda Wheeler, who held class for 20 pupils in a wing of the millhouse. By the fall of 1868, the students had a new structure after having had classes at two other sites. A movement was made to have a high school in town, and by 1875 the first group of seven received their high school diplomas. By 1879 an addition was necessary and built on to the existing school. Enrollment increased to 100 and the old wooden high school was no longer able to accommodate the educational needs of the students of the area. A portion of the building was moved to another part of town and used as a house. The rest of the building was torn down to make room for a new brick building in 1903.

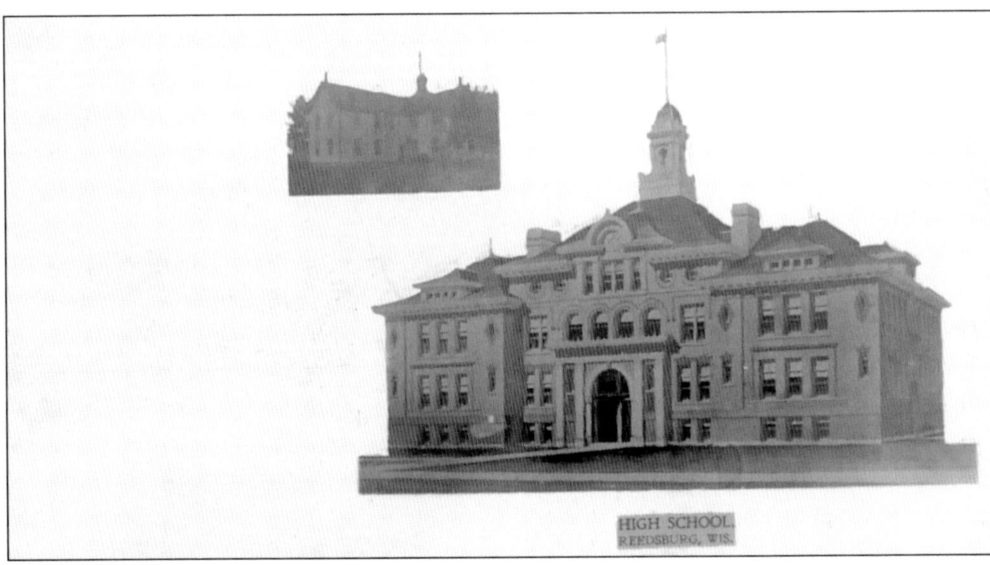

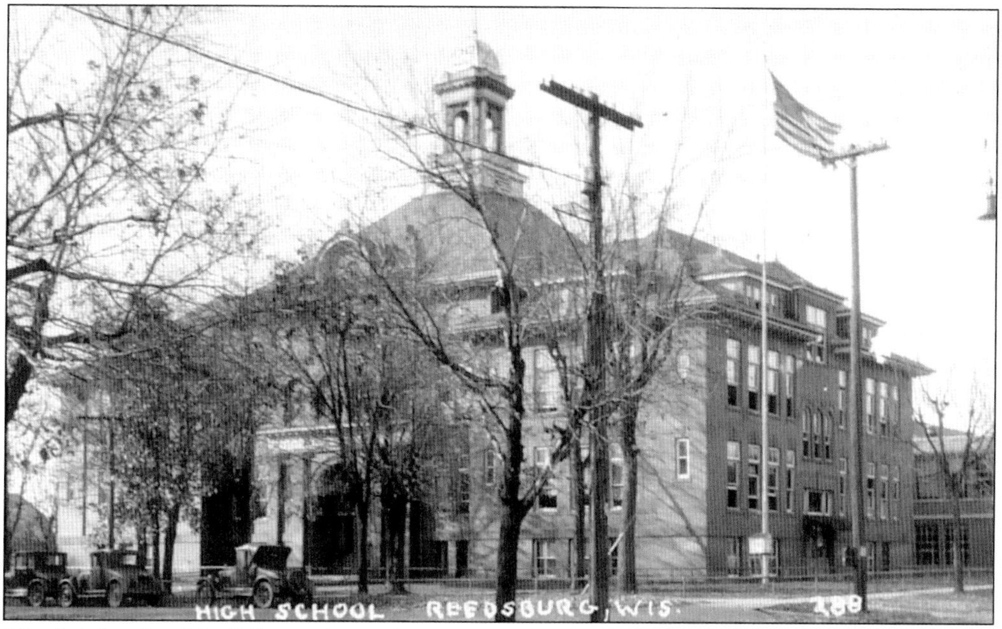

The brick school building educated many pupils. Among them was Mary Joyce, born in Reedsburg in 1909. She attended three years of high school here before moving to Milwaukee. Mary was a nurse, stewardess, pilot, dog musher, and an Alaskan homesteader. The local newspaper kept track of her 1,000-mile trek by dog sled between Taku and Fairbanks, Alaska. Because she did not arrive at Fairbanks for the Miss Alaska beauty contest, in which she was a participant, many feared she was lost. In the 1970s, word reached the Reedsburg community of Miss Joyce's death in Alaska.

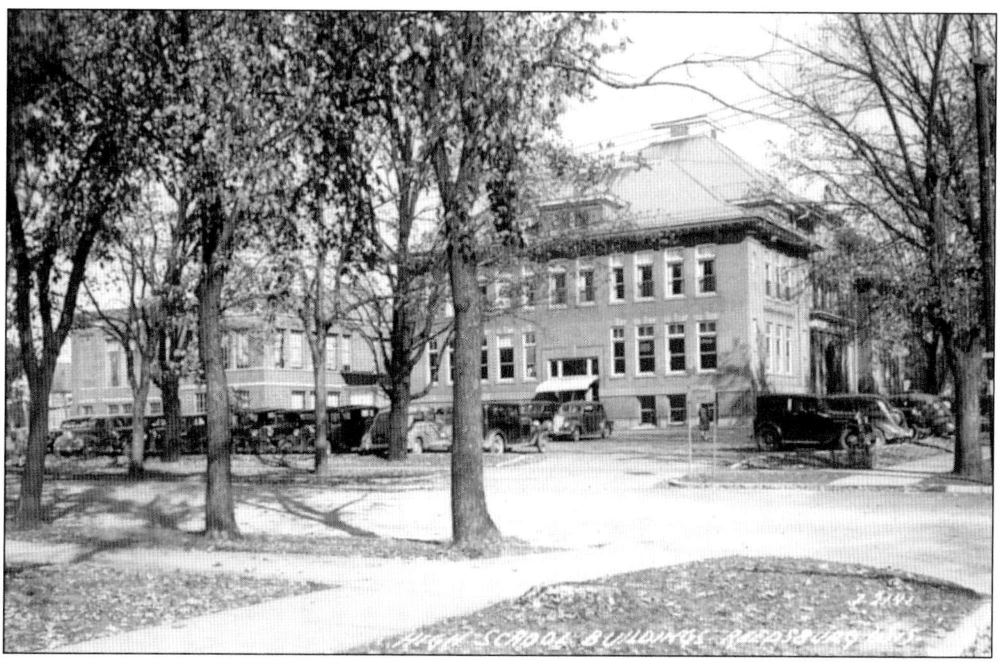

Cars have always been seen surrounding the high school , even in the 1930s and earlier.

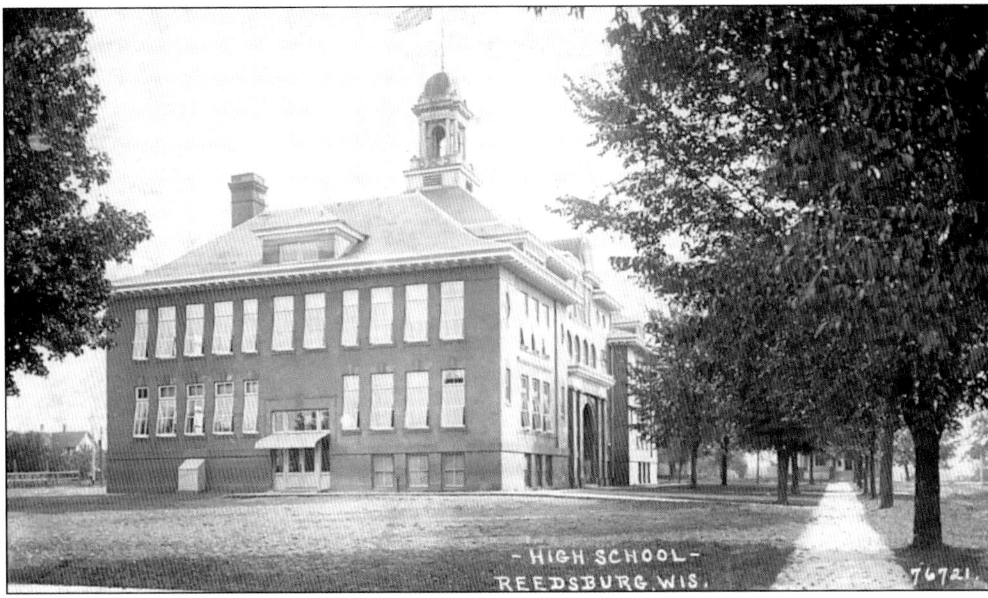

At a cost of about $50,000 the community built a new brick high school. For a time the teachers training school was located on the third floor. The building was constructed with the welfare of the students in mind. There were showers, a running track, and a very large assembly room. The gymnasium made it possible to have basketball teams compete locally with other high schools in the area. Students from outlying areas that had no high school attended Reedsburg by either staying with relatives or renting rooms in available homes. By 1923 there was a need to add on to the north side of the school's structure. There were always lovely shade trees on the school property. The student population kept growing until by 1951 the state was insisting that a better, safer school building had to be built. The students would no longer be able to sit two to a seat at general assembly. Also, a heating facility and other equipment needed for a quality education were missing. Therefore, the planning for a new high school at a new location got underway.

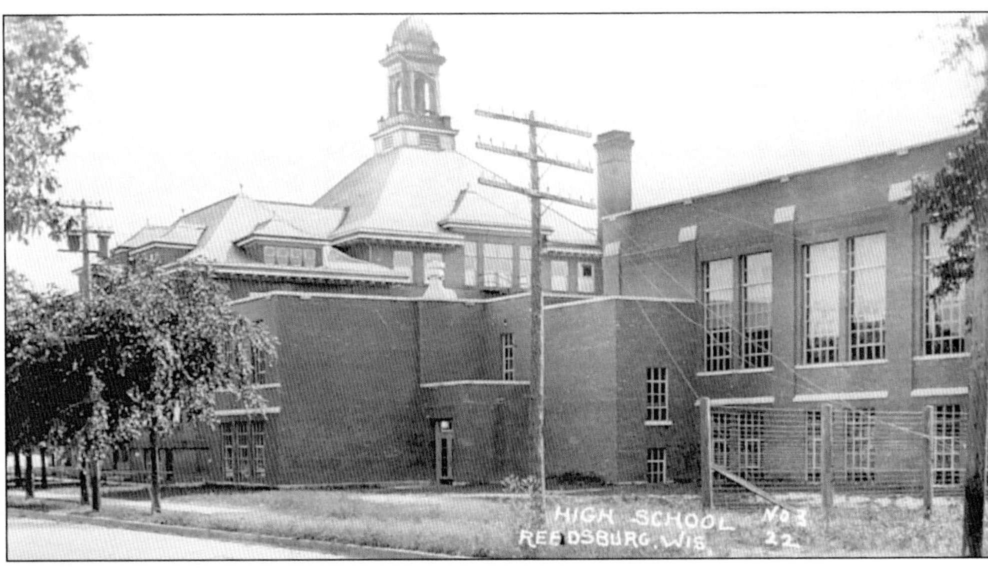

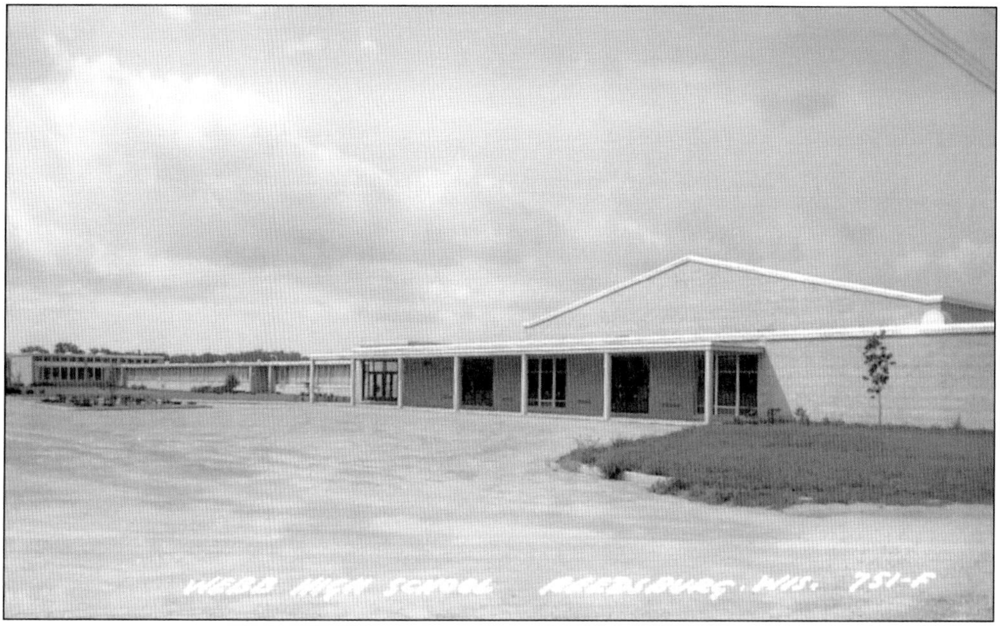

Due to a large donation by Herbert Webb, the school board followed his suggestion of building a new high school which adjoined the park which he had previously donated. During construction of Webb High School, many people recall walking between the building on Sixth Street and the one on Webb Avenue. Can you imagine the chaos as the students trudged between the two buildings? As well as the fact that hot lunches were served at the South School, another few blocks to the south. Finally, by 1957 the high school students had a new building complete with a gym, lunchroom, music room, and classrooms all under one roof. The athletic field was just to the north of the building. When the weather was favorable, many students received their diplomas at a ceremony held on the athletic field.

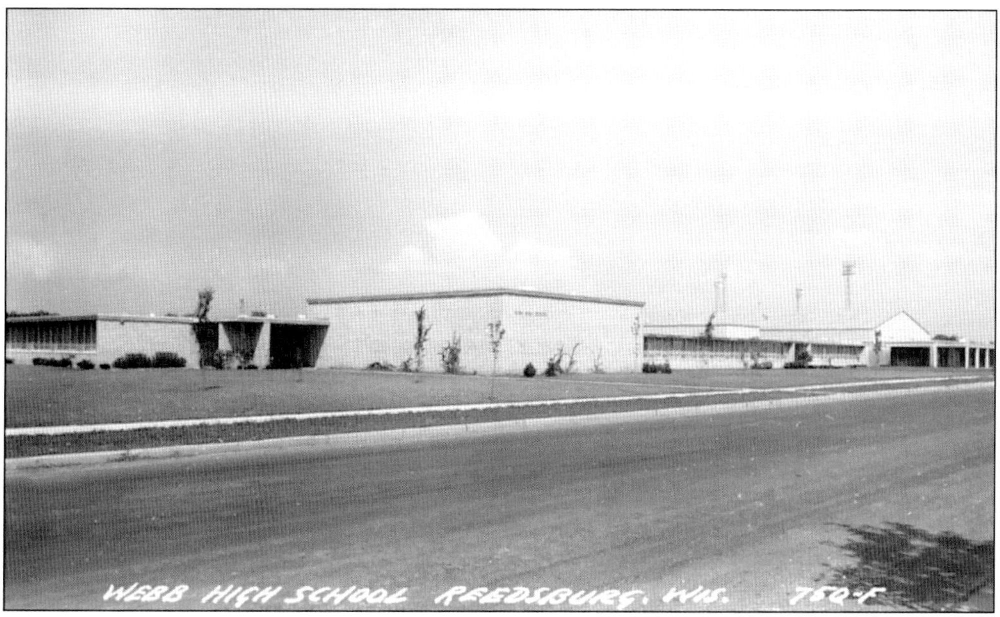

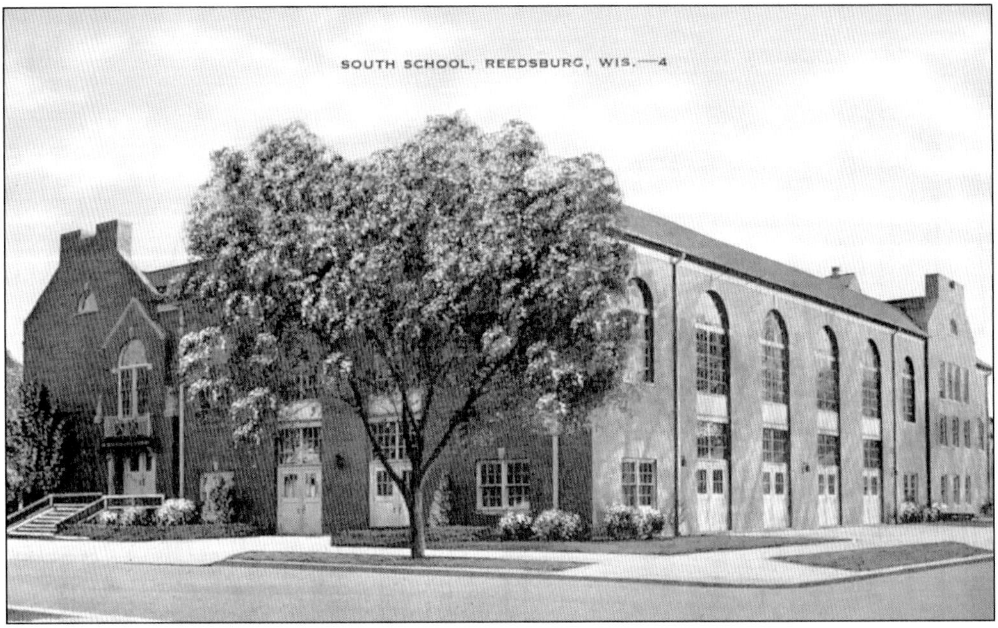

The new South School was built in 1936 with WPA funds. The planners for this school were the members of the school board itself, as they found other bids to be too high. A large auditorium was included in the building, which was used for many civic functions. For many years the Old Settlers Association held their annual day at the South School. It was also the site of Miss Wisconsin Pageants, John Deere Days, and other social events which required a large auditorium. A room known as the Pine Room was used for many civic meetings. One of the last meetings in the Pine Room was the citizens efforts to save the South School from being razed and replaced by a new building.

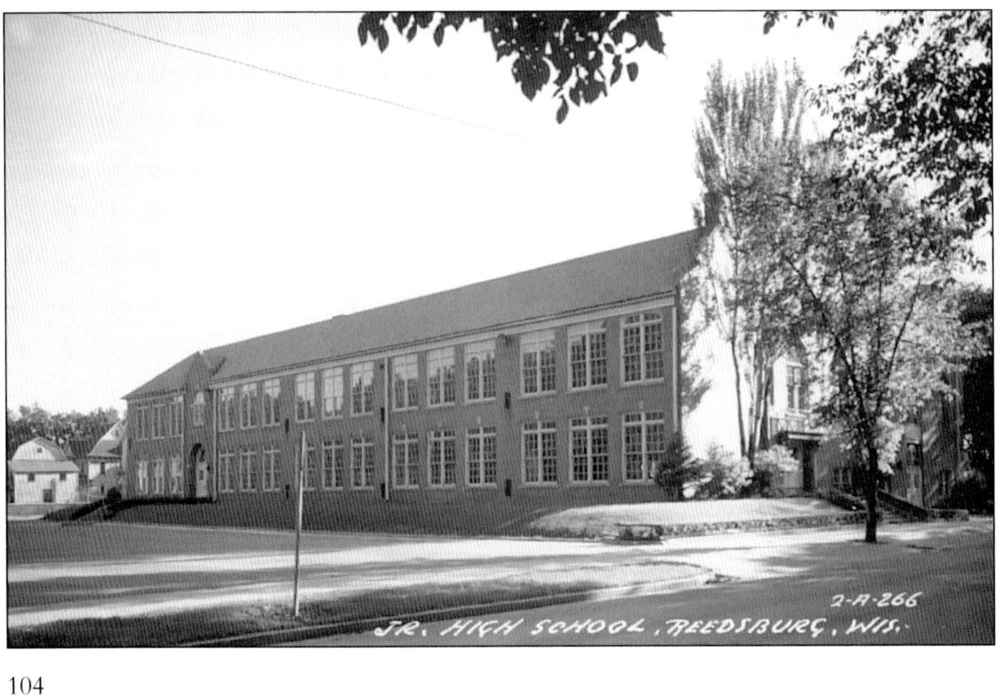

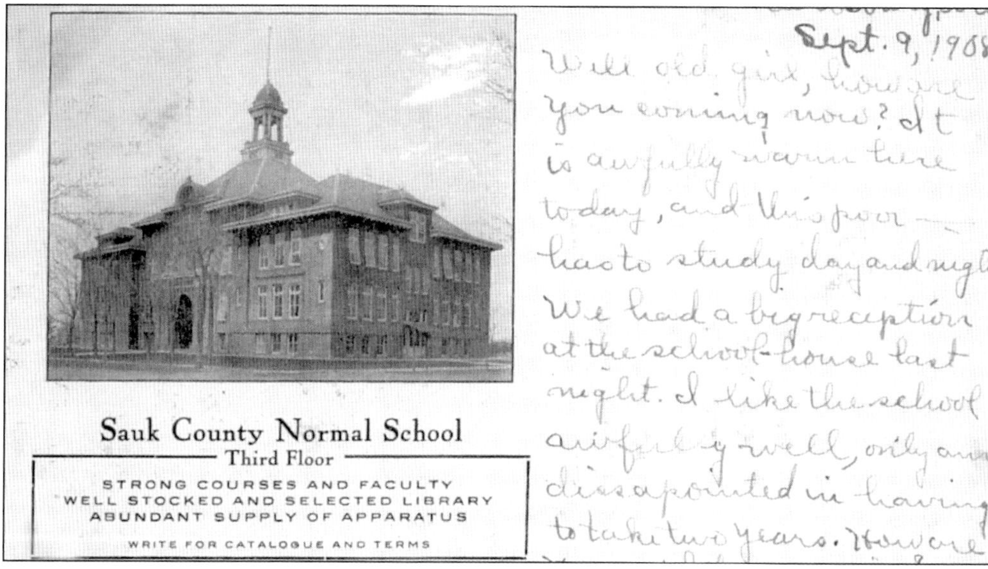

Sauk County Training School. In 1905, men with foresight saw the need for a training school to educate persons to teach at one of the many rural schools in Sauk County. Local citizens saw the benefits of locating such a school in the city of Reedsburg. Arrangements were made to establish the new Sauk County Training School on the top floor of the Reedsburg High School. There were 21 people enrolled, of which only 11 had a high school diploma. Students from around this and neighboring counties found housing within the city. The school was very popular and grew to such a size that it soon became apparent to the county board that the training school needed a building of its own. James Stone, a local attorney, worked diligently to have the school remain in Reedsburg. Mr. Stone donated land on the west side of Reedsburg and the city council promised to extend city water and a sewage system to the site. The land was deeded to the city of Reedsburg and Sauk County as long as the building was a school for training county teachers. If the time came when the building was no longer used for educational training of teachers the building would be reverted to the city of Reedsburg as sole owners.

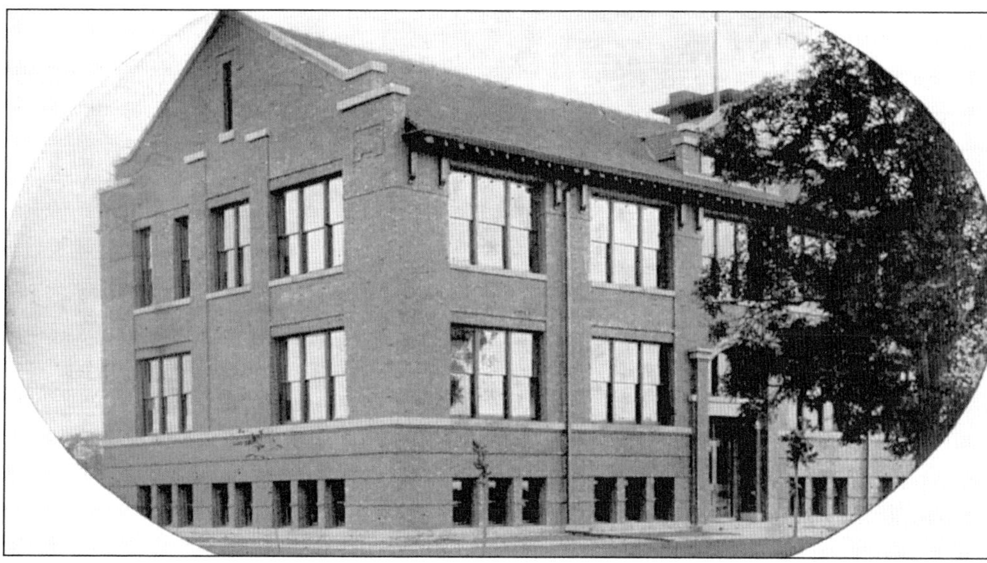

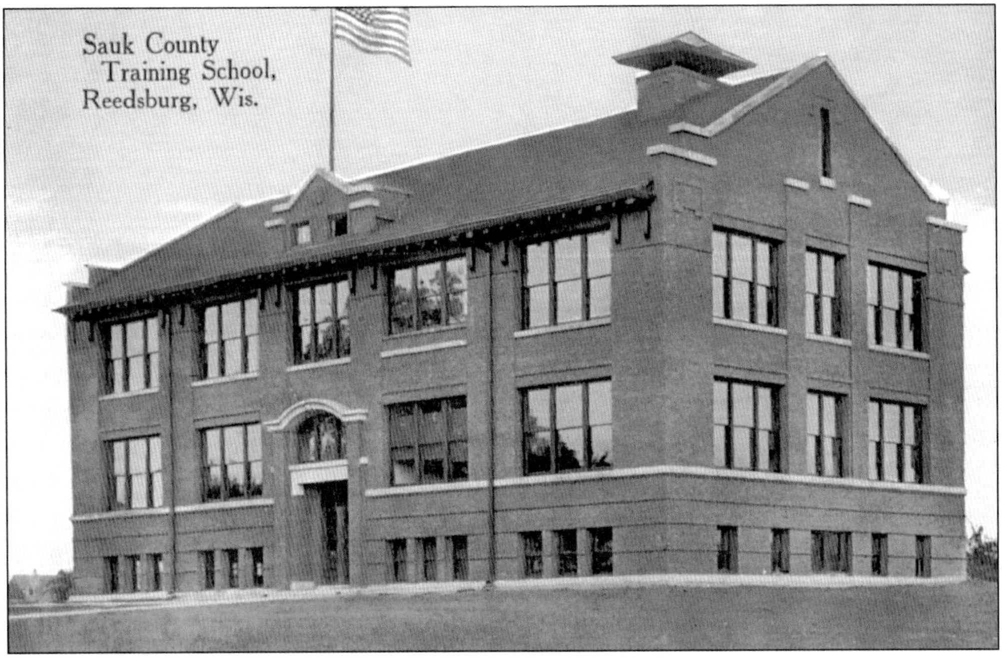

In 1927 the training school started a model for practice classes within the Sauk County Normal School. At first only children from first through fourth grades were admitted to the school. Later all the children of grade school age who lived west of the river were allowed enrollment. Eventually kindergarten classes were held in this building. Before the school closed its doors as a training school in 1969, many second generation teachers were trained at this facility.

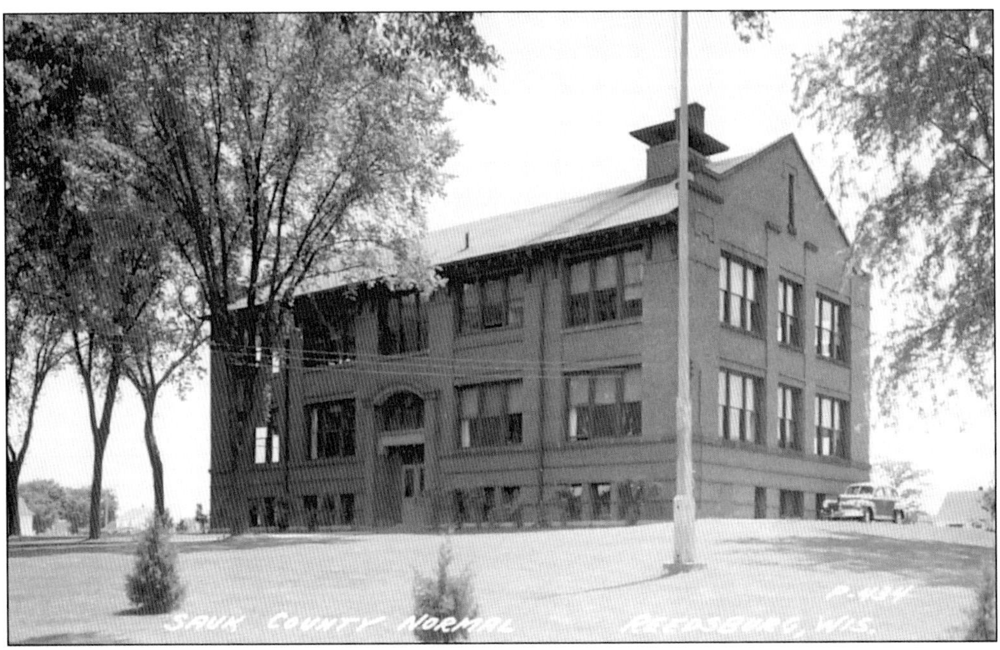

Seven

Industry

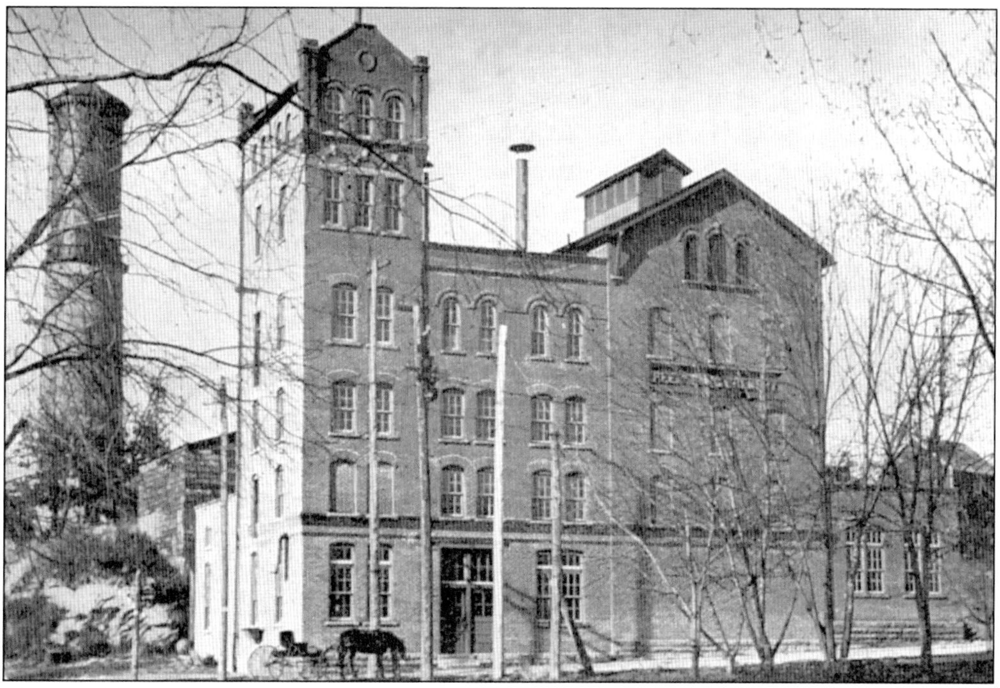

The Reedsburg Brewery's *c.* 1904 building replaced an earlier wooden structure, built in the 1870s that was destroyed by fire around the turn of the 20th century. For a few short years Sauk County was a great producer of hops. Many growers made and lost their fortunes during the boom and bust of the hop industry. This brewery had the capability of producing 6,000 barrels of beer per year. Prohibition was the downfall of the brewery. The business reopened under new ownership in 1933. It produced Old Gold, Badger Brew, Champion, and Blue Wing in its heyday. Blue Wing was the name of a Native American Chief who lived in this area for many years. In 1947 the brewery closed its doors as a brewery for good. It is now home to several people who live in cozy apartments and once again the "Old Brewery" is an asset to Reedsburg and its neighbors on North Walnut Street.

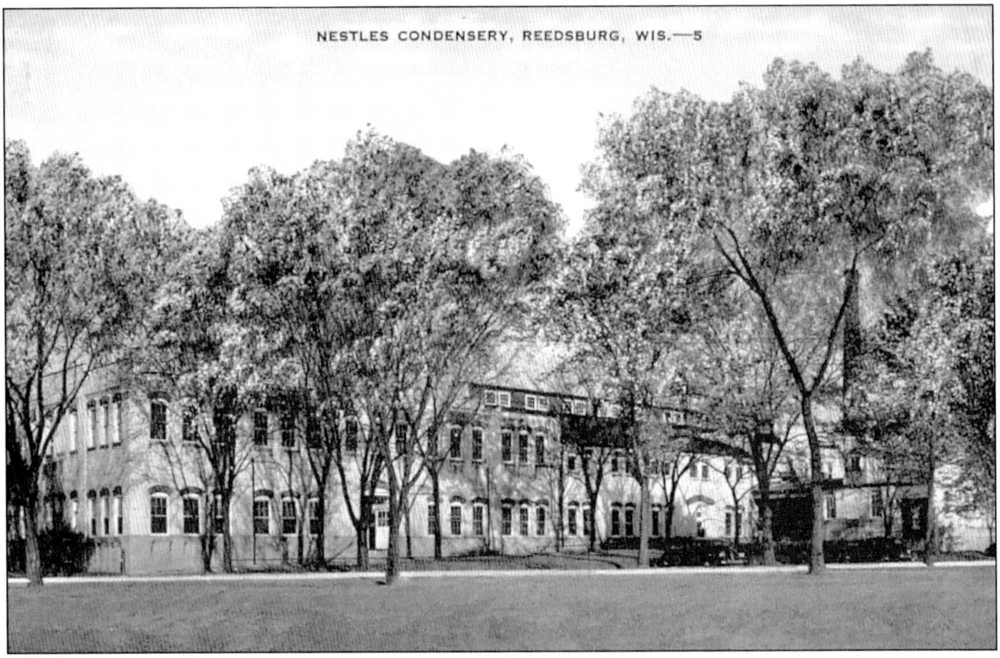

Nestle Food Condensory. In 1914 the Valecia Condensed Milk Company of Madison built an $85,000 to $100,000 plant in Reedsburg. The original condensory suffered a few financial pitfalls and around 1918 Nestle Foods bought the company. The Nestle Food Condensory had cold storage, ice machine, receiving, sterilizing, wrapping, and shipping rooms. In about 1924 it was said to have the biggest payroll in Reedsburg. The railroad constructed a sidetrack to the condensory.

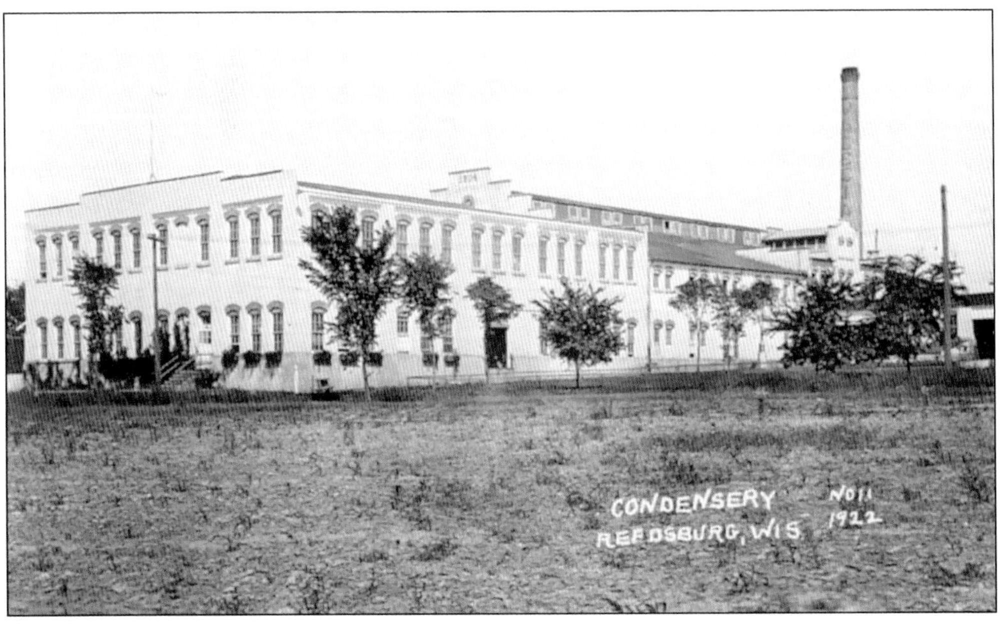

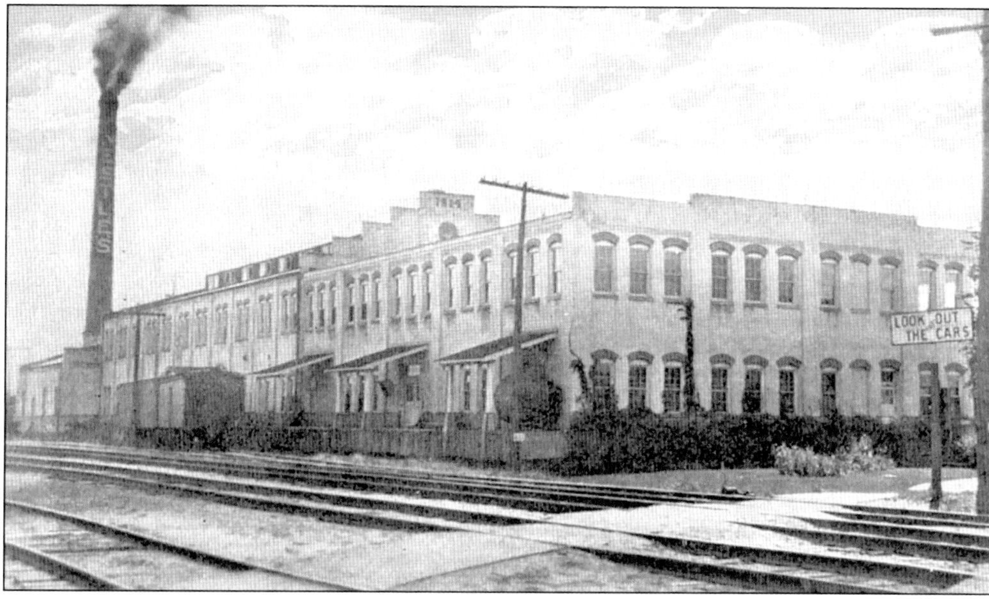

Caution was needed at the railroad crossing on South Pine Street as vehicles traveling south had to cross several sets of tracks instead of the one set that is there today.

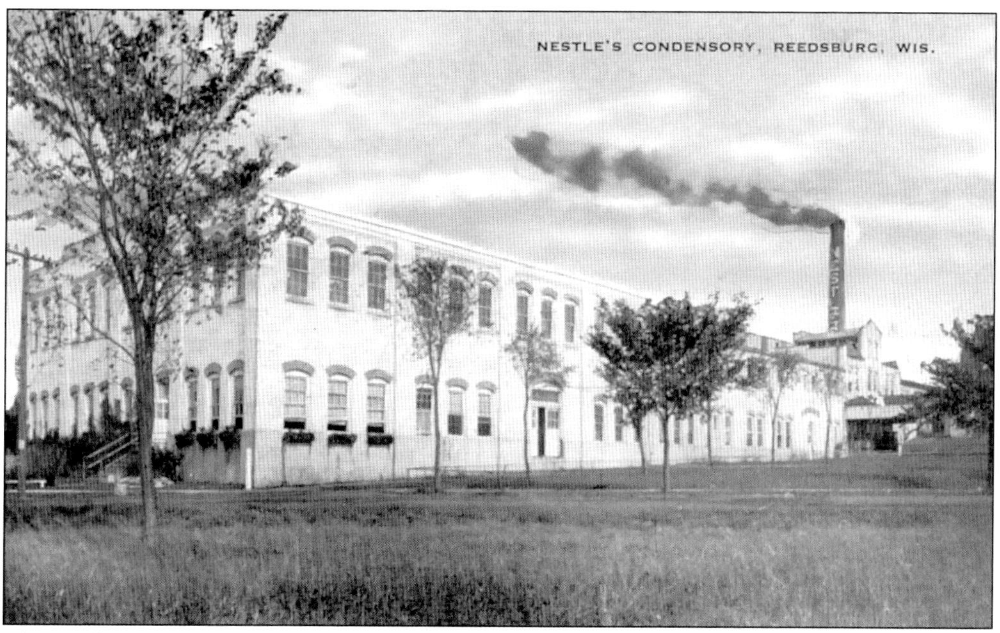

The smoke stack towered over the Nestle Plant in a much earlier day.

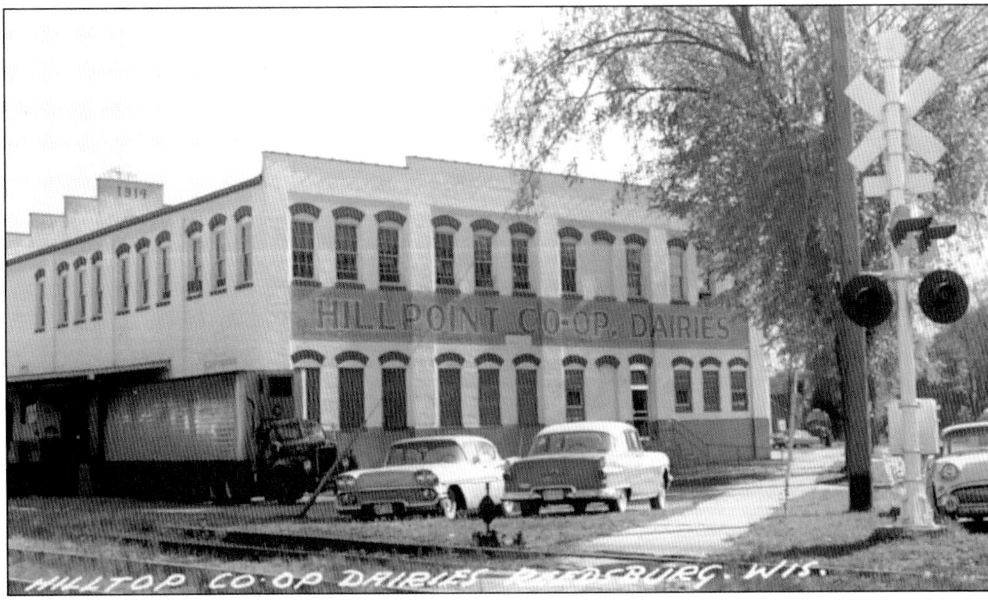

Hillpoint Co-op Dairies. Hillpoint Dairies bought the Nestle Condensory in 1946, affiliating with Wisconsin Dairies in about 1947. The Hillpoint Co-op Dairies was and still is a major employer in Reedsburg. At one time only one plant in New Zealand had a greater volume. The company produced about 50 million pounds of butter in 1983. This was when Reedsburg flouted itself as "Butter Capital of America." The summer festival, called the Butter Festival, was started and still exists today. Butter was packaged under Land O' Lakes label.

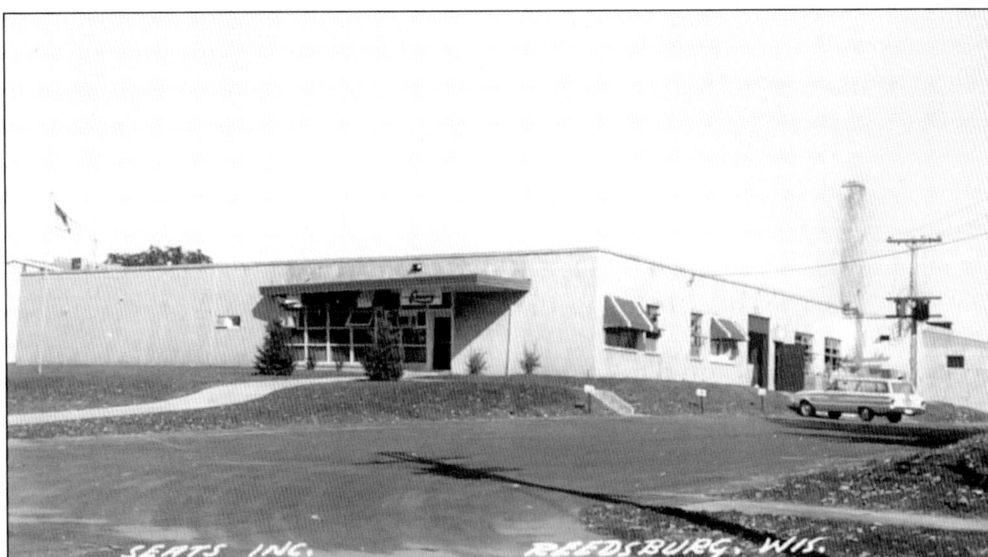

Seats Inc. was established in 1952. Initially this factory employed seven people. Through many expansions and moves the factory gained more than 300 employees. The company produces seats for heavy vehicles that travel nationwide from east to west and north to south. Many of the seats ordered to be made in the plant at Reedsburg are custom-made. Seats has moved to a larger facility in the Industrial Park and the building in the photo is now the home of Columbia Par Car.

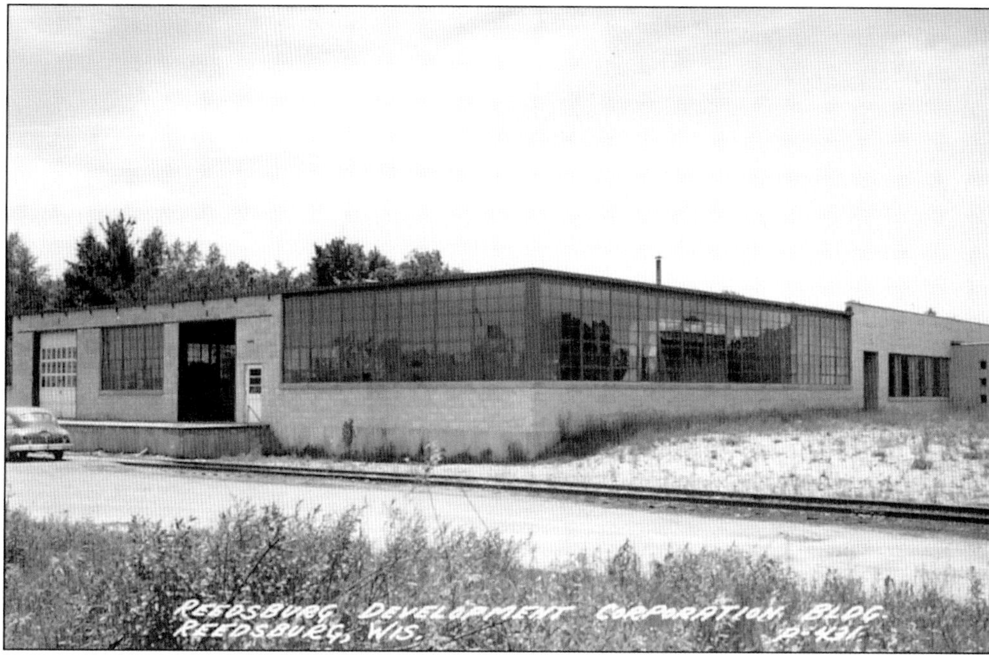

The Reedsburg Foundry opened in 1947 and was in operation until 1951. Grede Foundries Inc. purchased the facility in 1951.

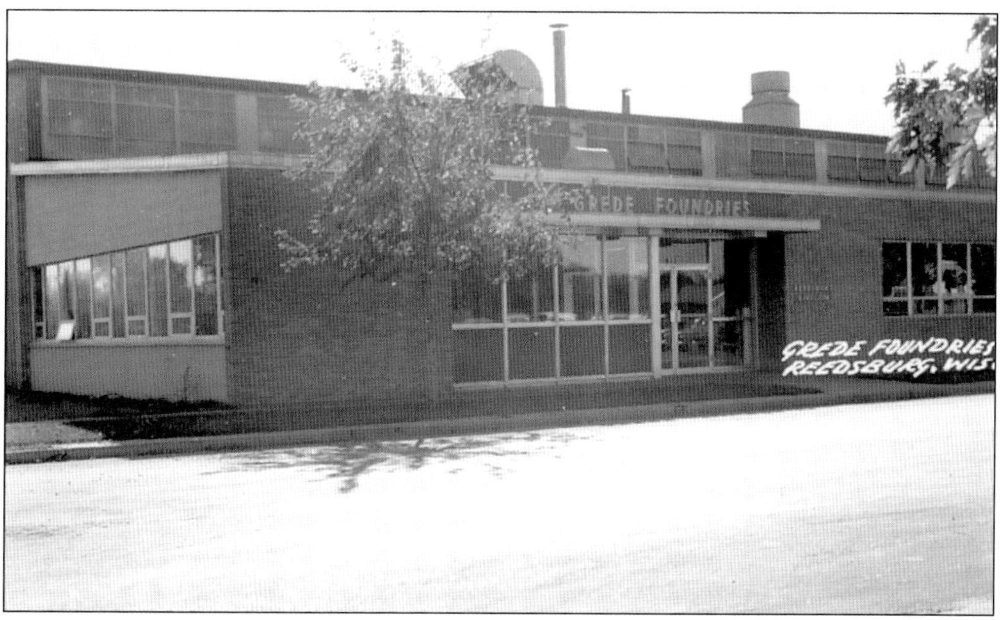

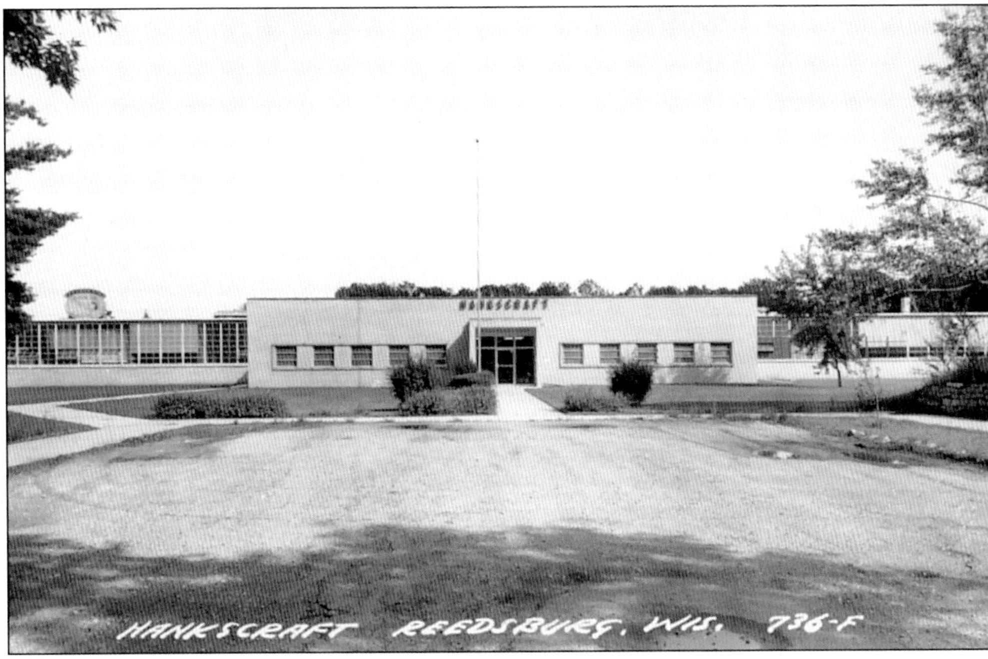

Early in the 20th century, M.W. Hanks invented and patented a basic heating unit, which was the foundation for his first product, an electric egg cooker. After several moves within the city of Madison, Hankscraft responded to a bid from an industrial search group and moved his manufacture to Reedsburg in 1949. By 1970 the company was purchased by Gerber Products of Freemont, Michigan. Hankscraft also became a leader in production of point of purchase motorized displays.

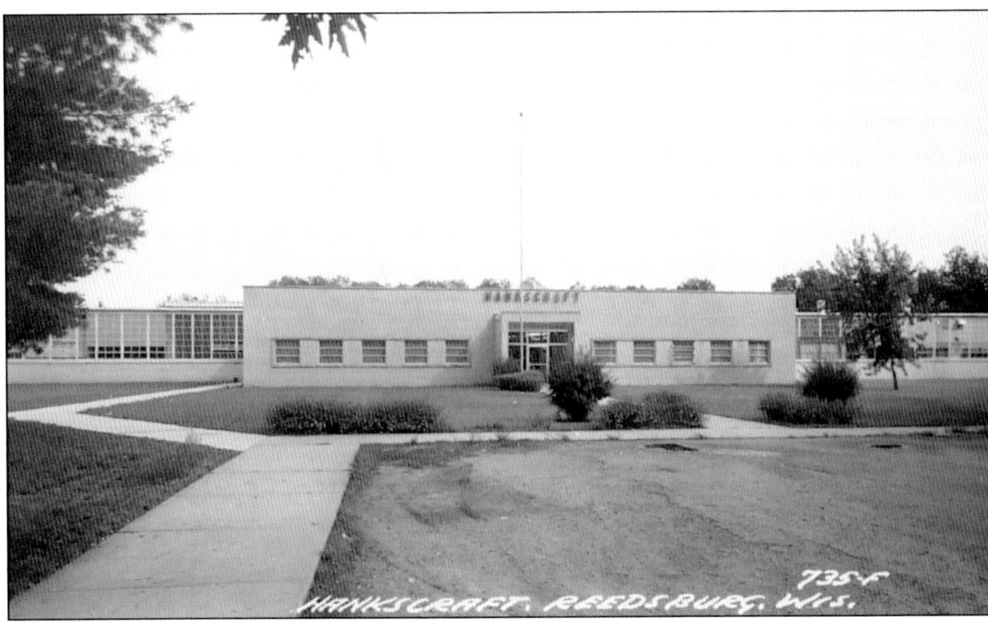

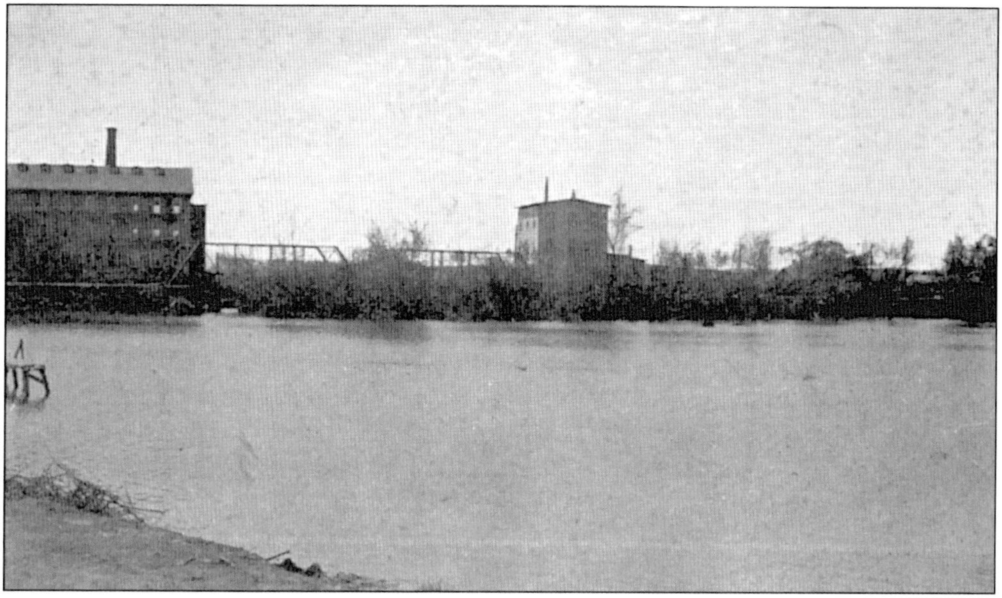

Reedsburg Flour Mill. Previous to the building of the Reedsburg Flour Mill, the local farmers took their grain to Baraboo or Lake Delton to be milled. One of the big market places for the flour was Milwaukee. The mill was located on the west bank of the Baraboo River, on Main Street. It shared the power of the river with the woolen mills built on the east bank of the river. Bella French noted a flour mill in her *History of Reedsburg–1875*. In the 1902–03 edition of the *Reedsburg Directory* there was also a stave factory which perhaps provided the barrels needed to ship the flour to sites beyond.

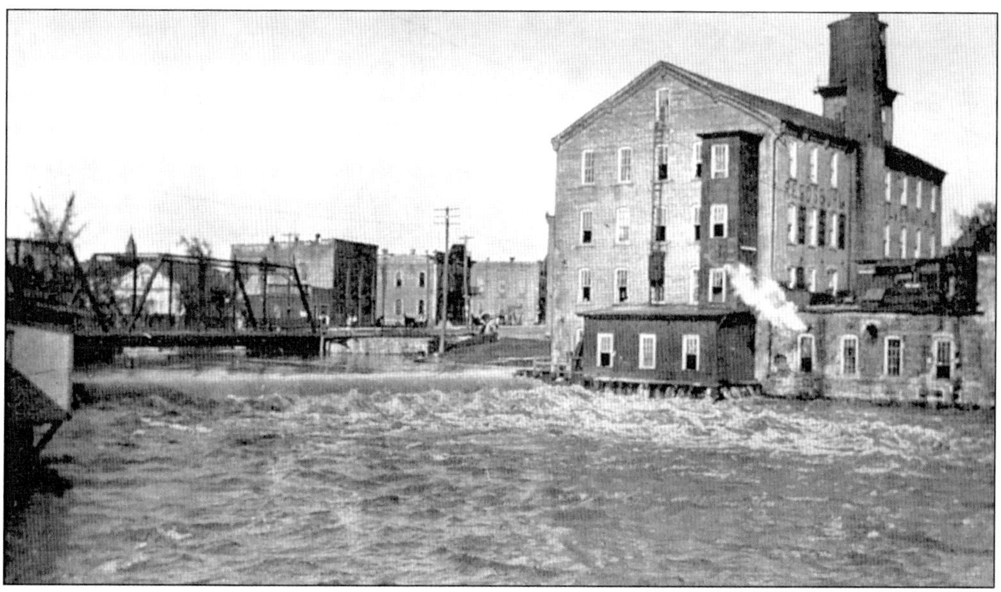

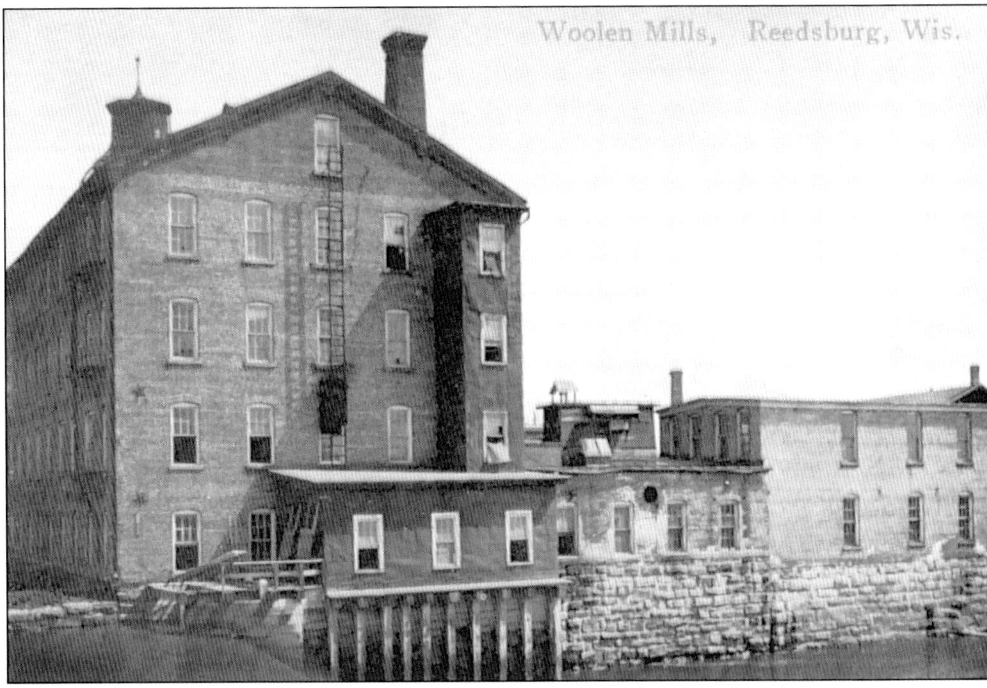

The Woolen Mills made up one of the oldest industries in the city.

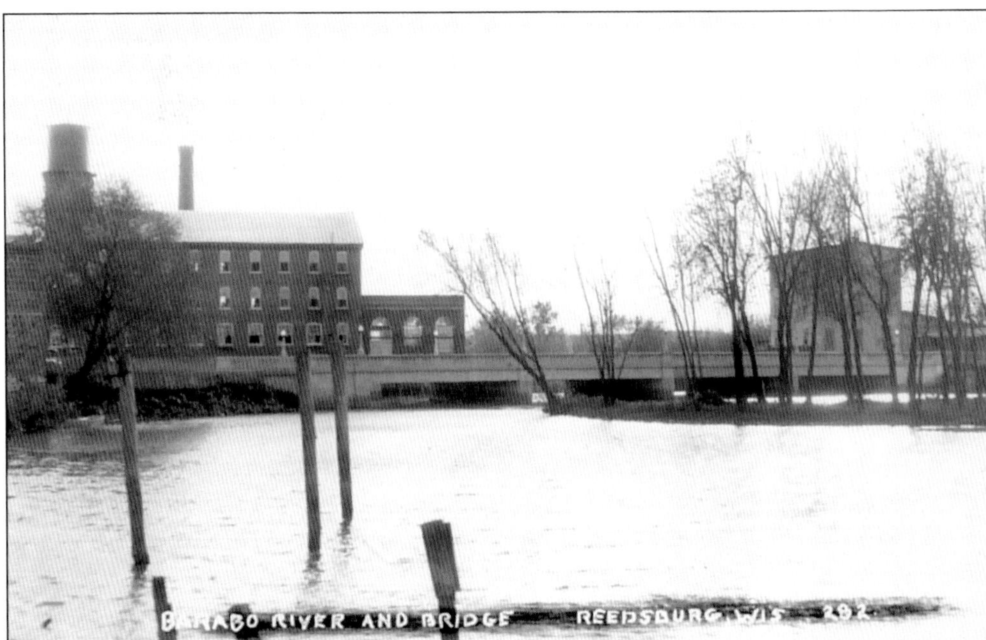

Looking south from a boat on the Baraboo River, one could see the Reedsburg Woolen Mills on the left, and to the right, across the bridge, was the flour mill.

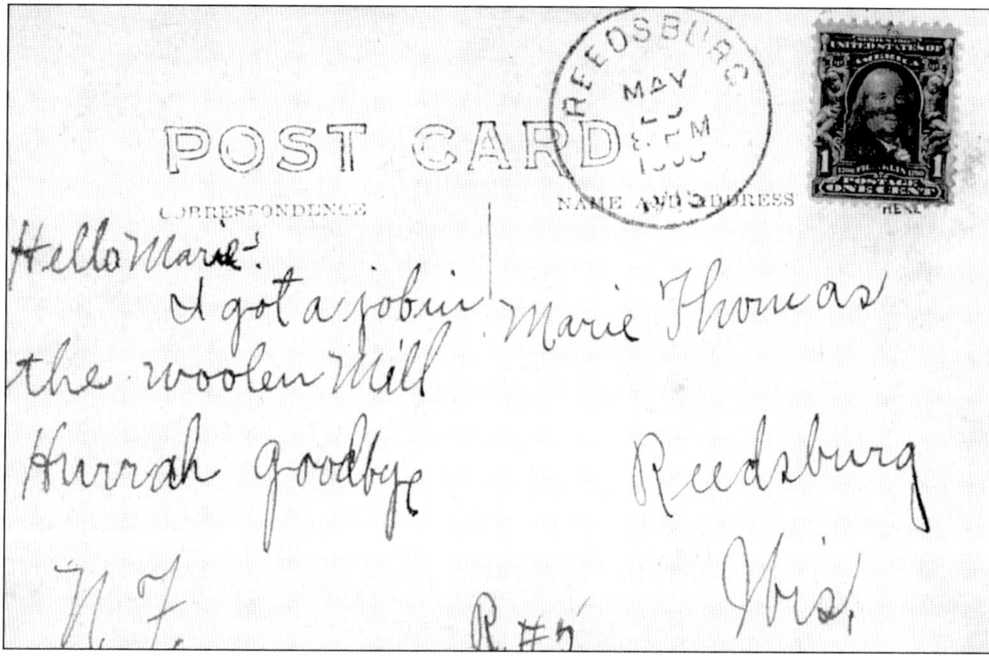
POST CARD

CORRESPONDENCE

NAME AND ADDRESS

REEDSBURG MAY PM

Hello Marie:
I got a job in
the woolen Mill
Hurrah goodbye
N. Z.

Marie Thomas
Reedsburg
Wis.
R.#5

The Woolen Mill was one of the early industries of Reedsburg. The Stolte Hotel, built in 1896, ordered their blankets from the mill. During World War II designer blankets were discontinued and only the manufacturing of army blankets was pursued. There was a mill store in the office building that was located just to the east of the mill property. Many families were affected by the closure of the mill in the late 1960s.

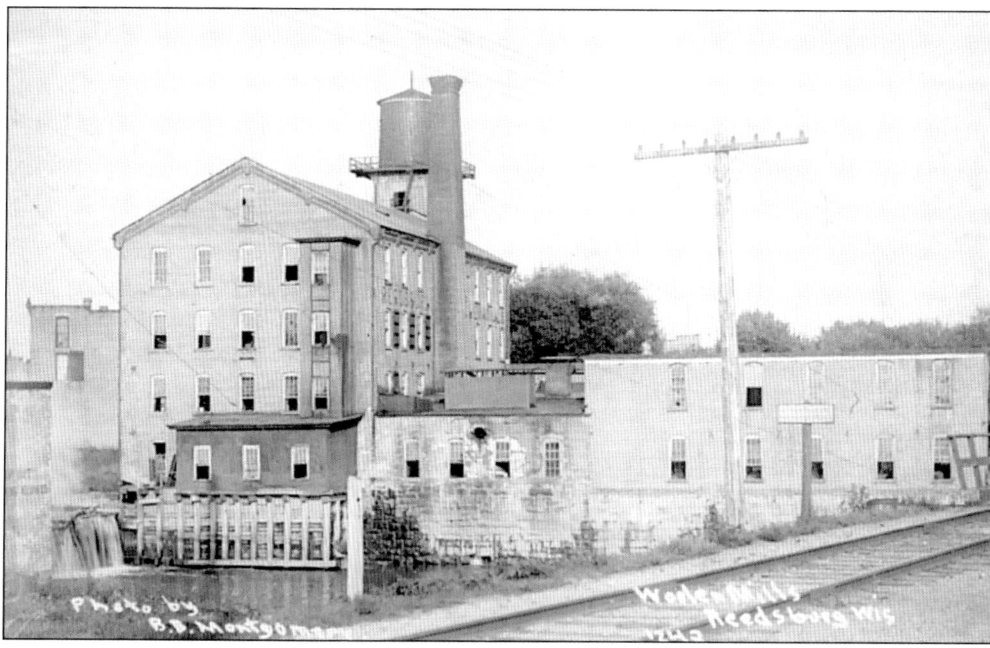

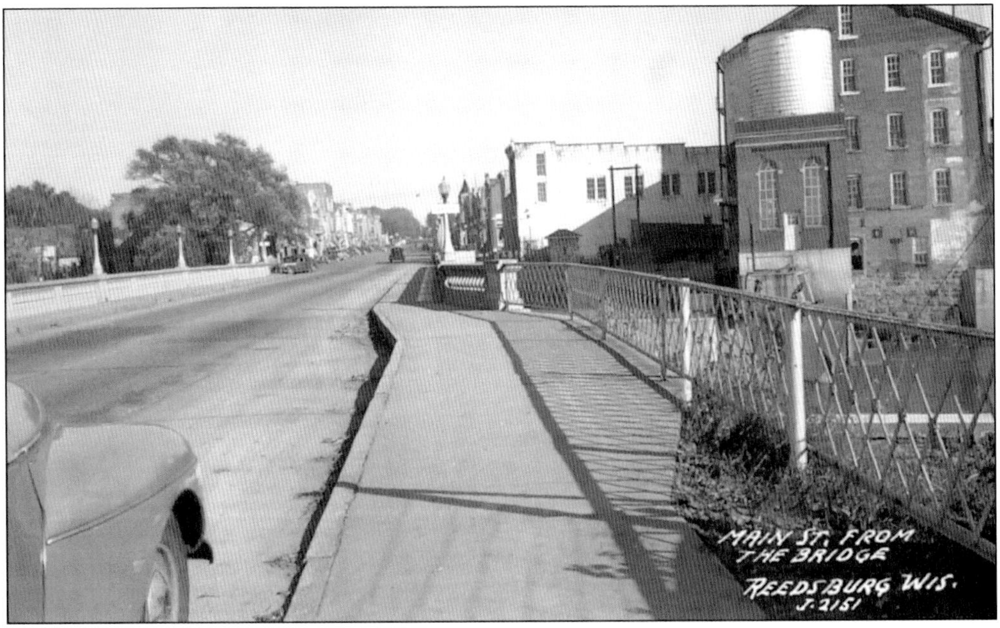

The Woolen Mill had a whistle that blew at 5 p.m. each day.

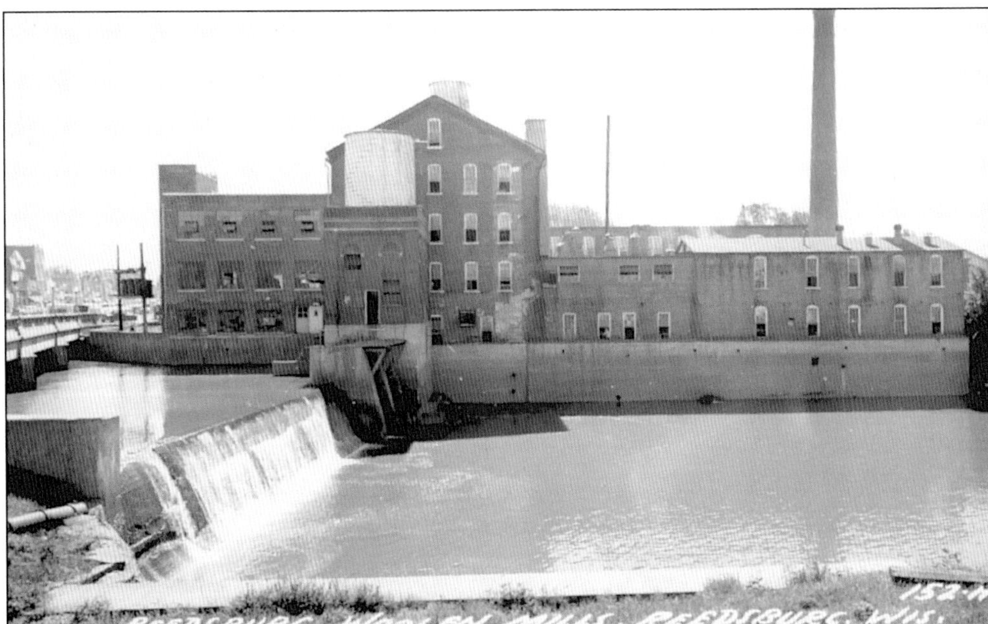

At one time, although it was the business streets that kept the town growing, it was the residential areas where the community bonded together. These shaded streets are where the druggist, bankers, builders, and liverymen called home. Each family took pride in their homes and found security and serenity on the side streets of Reedsburg. Children grew up and perhaps left the town for greater cities, but a large majority of these children remained and contributed to the town's growth and prosperity. The Woolen Mill was one of the largest employers in the city of Reedsburg.

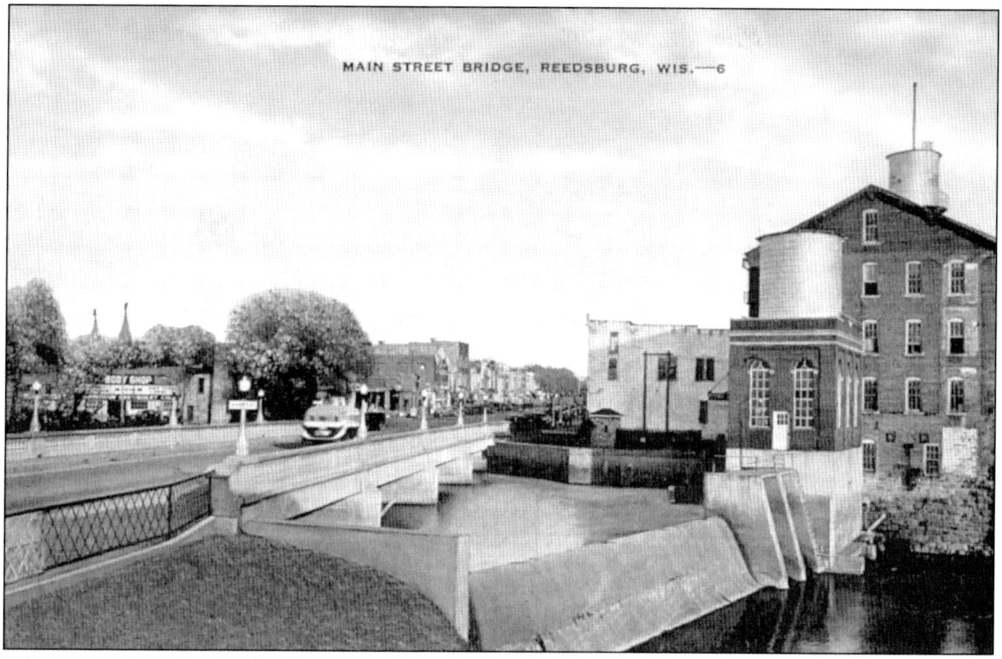

When crossing the Main Street Bridge, The Reedsburg Woolen Mill was almost the first thing you would see.

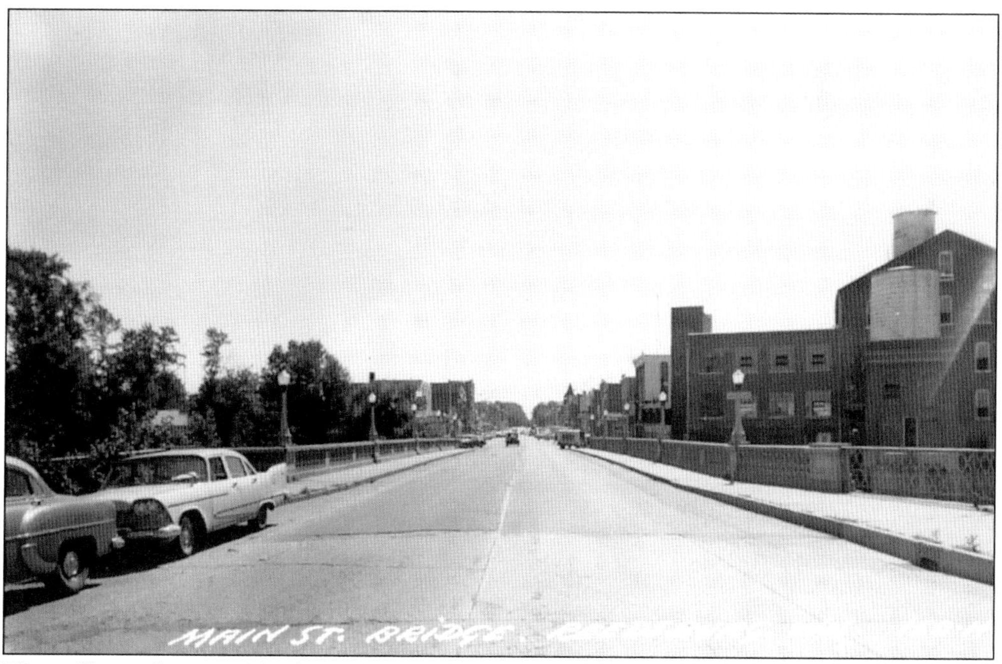
The mill was destroyed by fire on April 9, 1968.

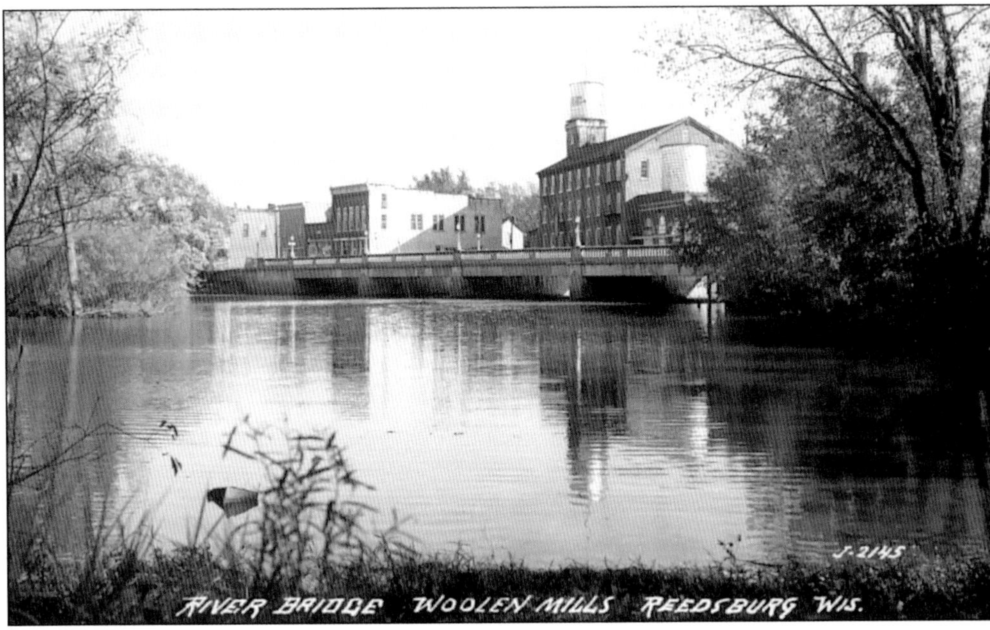

When the dam was on the river, it created a lovely pond on the north side of the bridge.

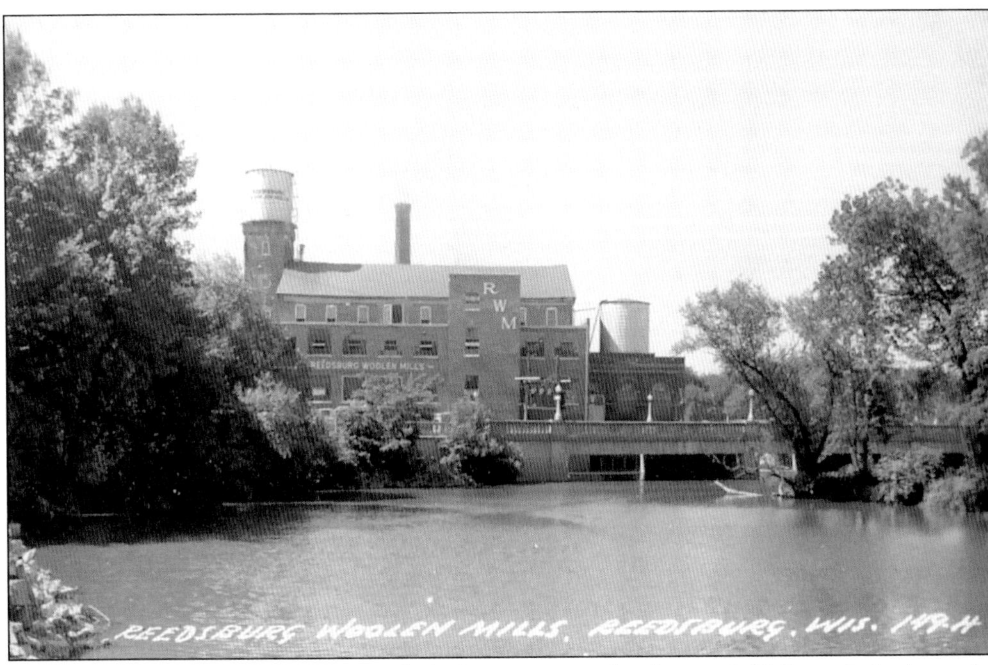

The north side of the bridge was an ideal place to canoe the river to LaValle and picnic on the west side of Reedsburg.

Eight

Residential Streets

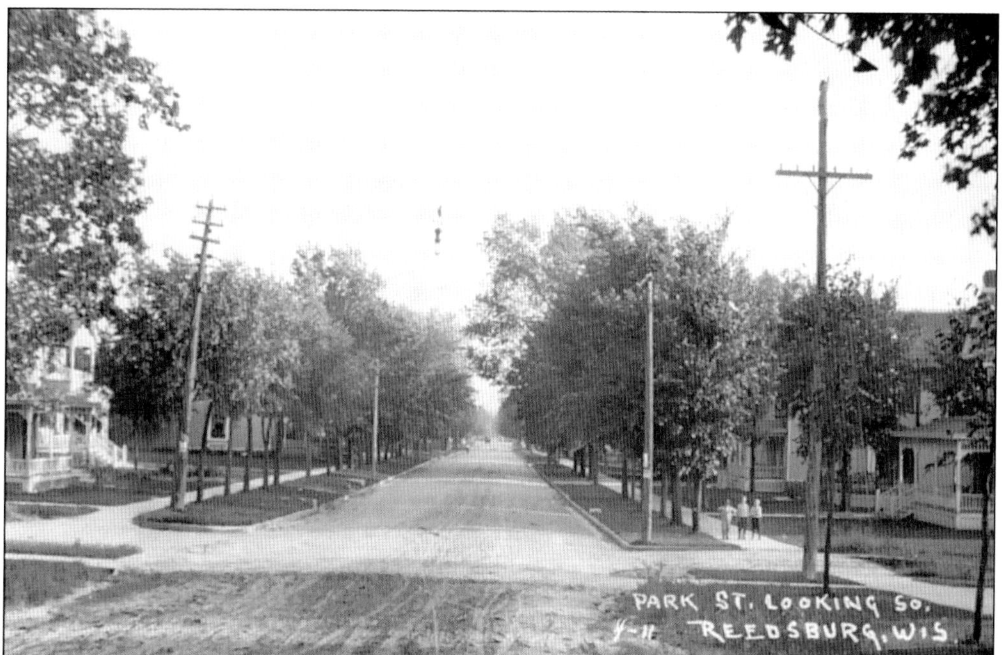

It was some time before the first street was paved with brick and even later before the dust was settled by blacktopping. Park Street was used at one time for a soapbox derby because of its gentle hill. The hospital at the top of the hill allowed sledding in the back during the winter months. For a time, the carriage barns were visible before horsepower replaced the horse stall.

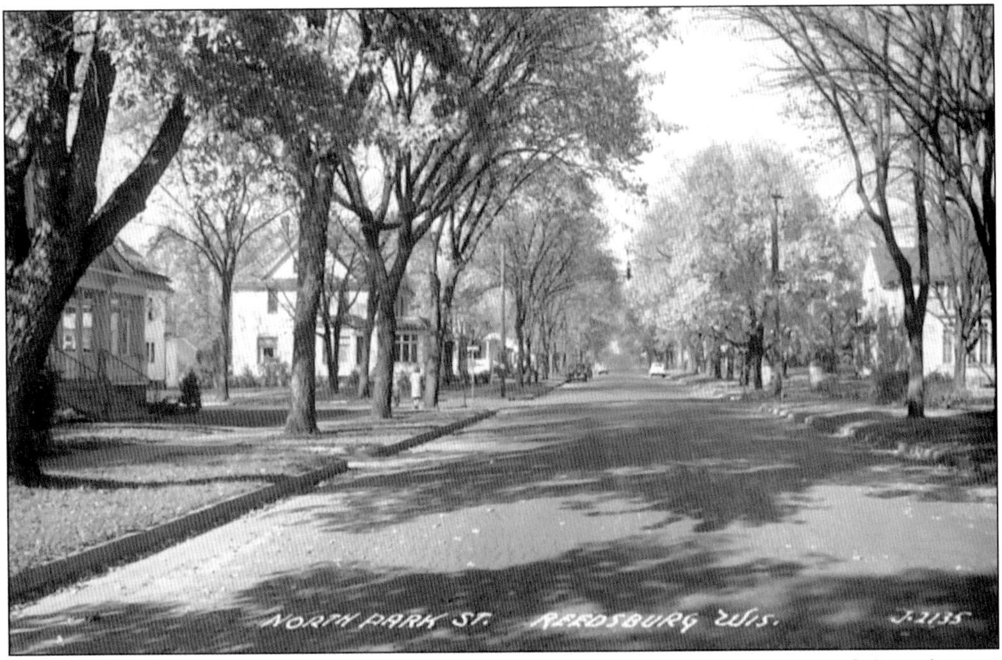

Park Street was and is a serene shaded street of many large homes. Several of these homes were built by local builders and painted by local painters. It was only a short walk to several of the churches. The City Park is the anchor of the street, only a short stroll to the grocery store, meat market, or shoemaker. A milliner or the doctor was only a short walk away. The milkman delivered bottles to many of these homes. At that time, a card was placed in the window to let the iceman know how much you would need on that delivery day. The large front porches were utilized for play on a rainy day or conversation with the neighbors.

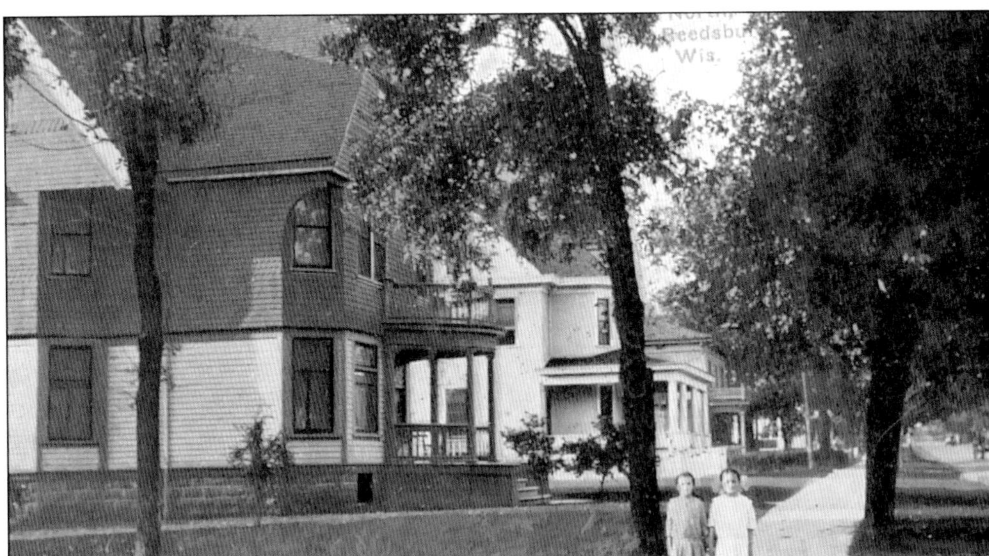

This postcards shows a shaded walk heading north from the main business district. The house on the left had and still has a "courting window"—a chair in the recessed window that allowed a young couple privacy on the front porch.

Nine

Nature's Wrath

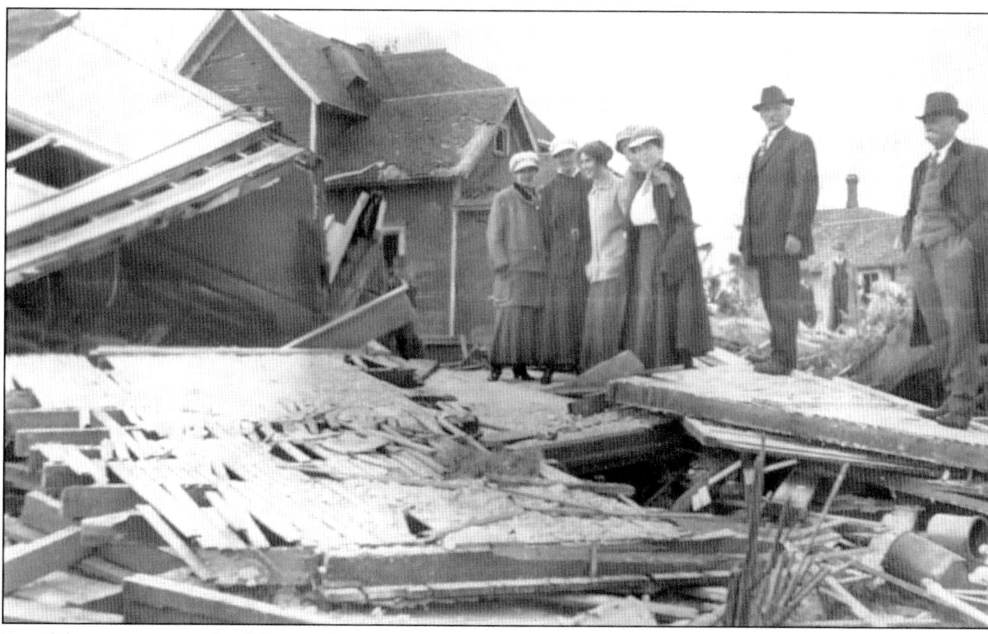

Reedsburg was touched by wicked tornadoes more than once. In 1907, a storm bore down on the town from the northwest causing much damage. The Sherwood farm lost every building but the house. A horse was found still chained in the middle of the debris without a scratch on him. In 1915, another tornado hit the city, killing one man and injuring several others. A woman and child survived, but were pinned under the timbers. C.W. Willard was the owner of a very valuable horse. He felt the horse so valuable that he refused to take the animal around to various events. "Peerless Pete" remained unharmed after the storm.

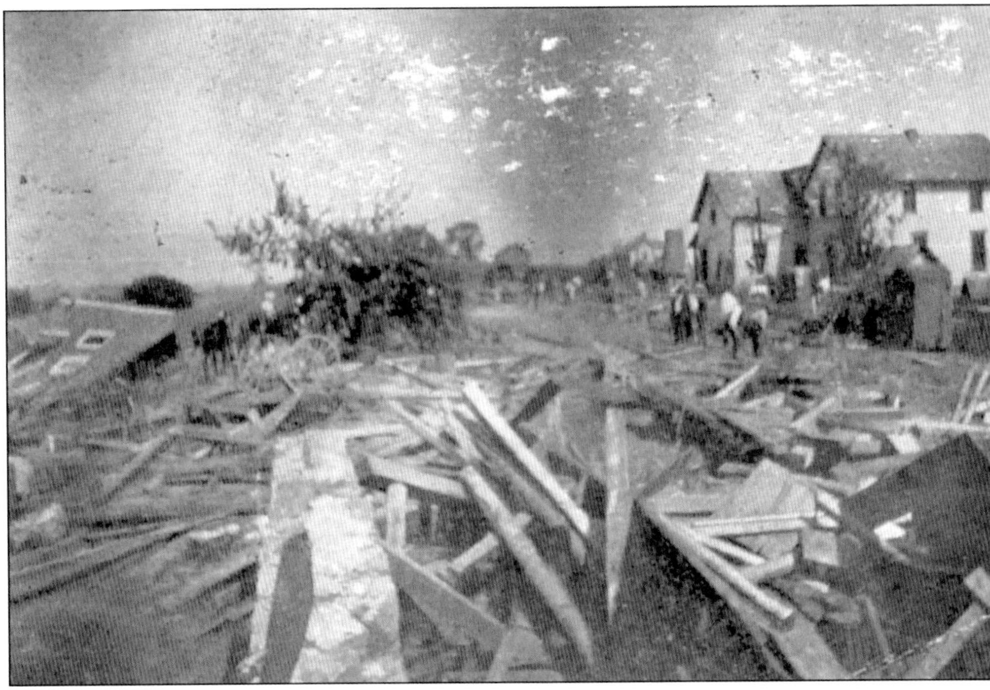

The Gates's house and barn after a tornado July 3, 1907.

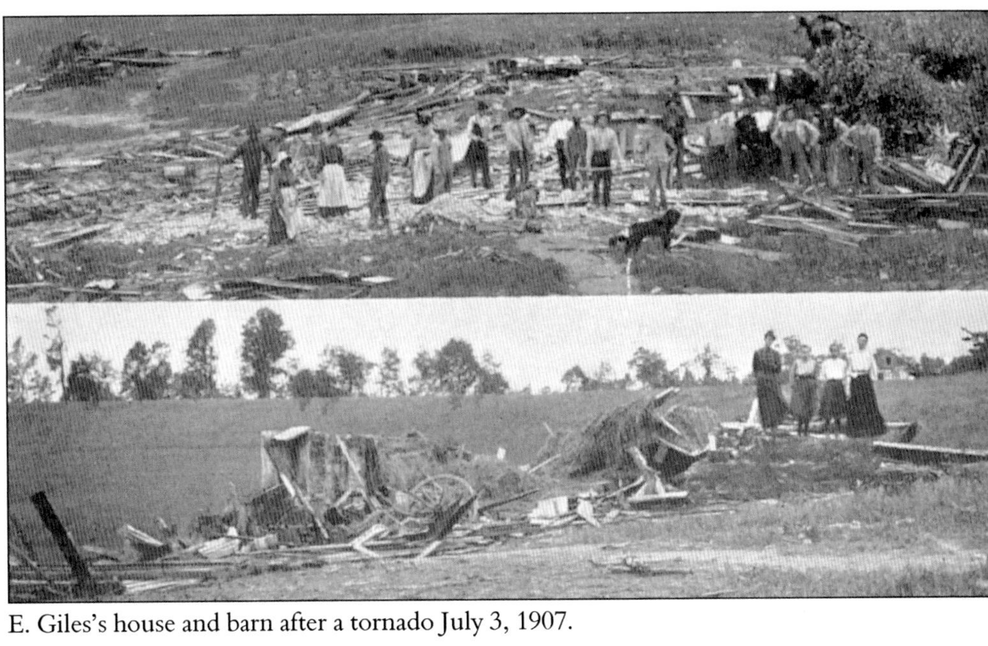

E. Giles's house and barn after a tornado July 3, 1907.

Ten

Our Next Door Neighbors

In 1964, N.E. Isaacson pursued his vision of a manmade lake just a few short miles from Reedsburg. "Ike" visited about 25 homeowners at the site of the future lake. Many moved to a new location, but several chose to reserve a small portion of their property to become lakefront homeowners. The natural springs and creeks did their jobs and by 1967 the lake was a reality. The artificial lake has approximately 650 acres of water with over 17 miles of shoreline. The once hilly farmland was converted to a recreation area, as well as a permanent residence for many people. The area once boasted a ski slope, Mt. Redstone, and was a wonderful site for fishing, sailing, waterskiing, and ice fishing. Although Mr. Isaacson moved from the area after the project was completed, his vision is enjoyed by hundreds of people year round. The venture greatly improved the economy of the area.

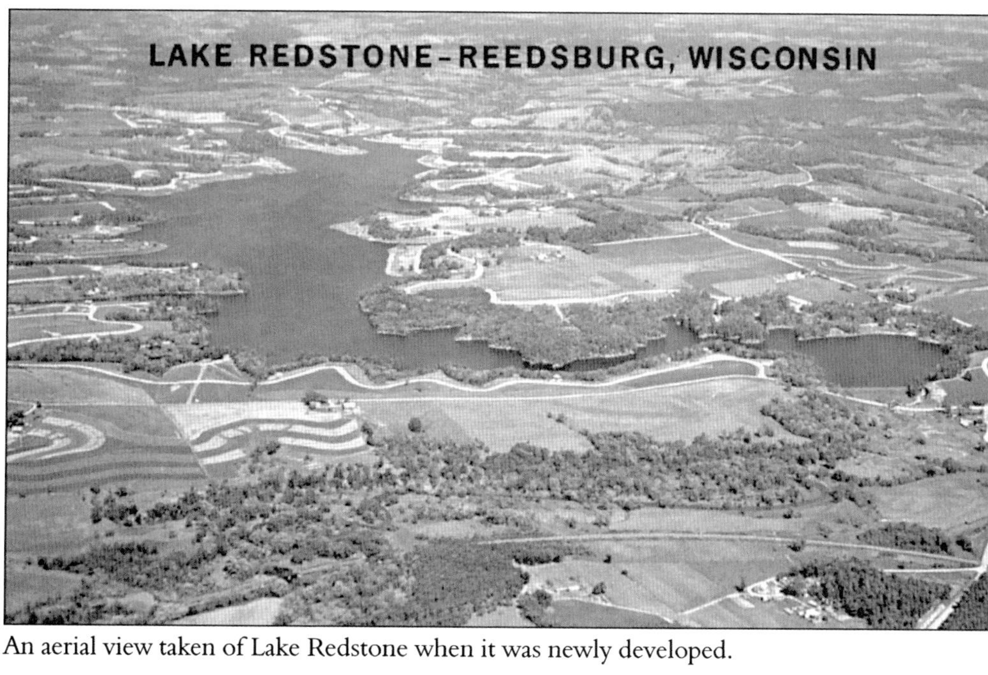

An aerial view taken of Lake Redstone when it was newly developed.

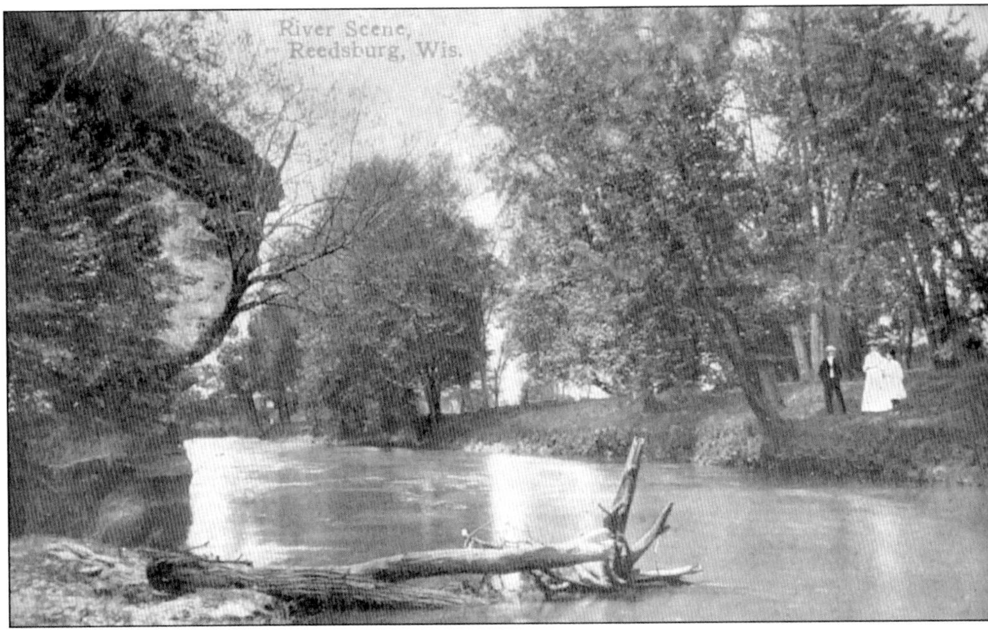

The Dells to the east of Reedsburg have always had ties to the city. Tourists from near and far have thrilled at the sight of the natural splendor. Fern Dell was platted many years ago. In a platbook dated 1905, Fern Dell was planned for several building lots and parks to be constructed on the banks of Dell Creek where it flows into Mirror Lake. Sandstone bluffs are on either side of the creek. When towns were being settled and planned, a lot depended on the railroads. If a railroad did not reach your planned city, there was not much hope for great growth. As we look at things now, it is pleasant to have such untainted places left on a rides through the nearby countryside.

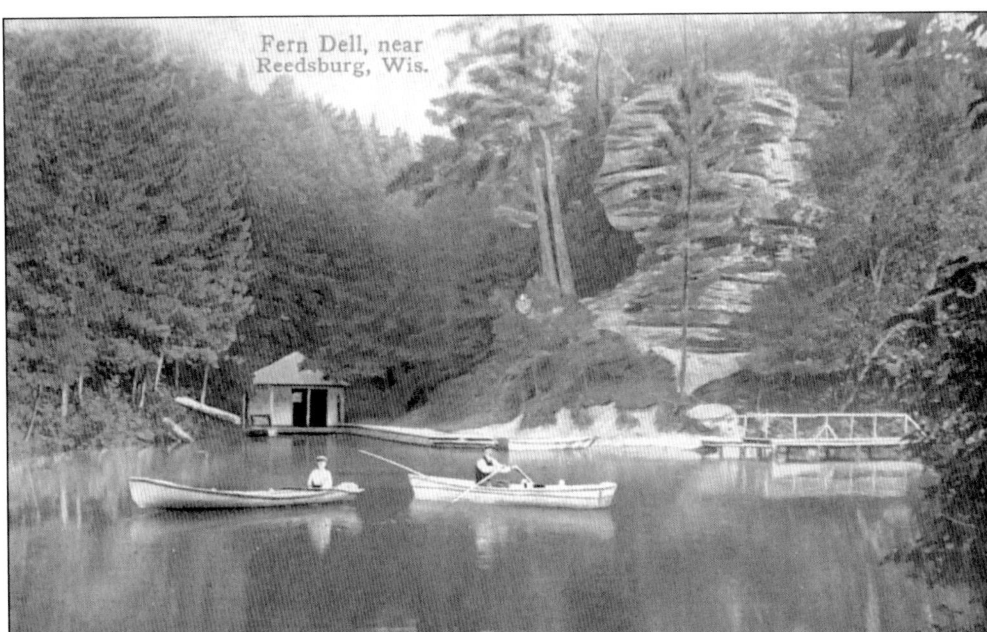

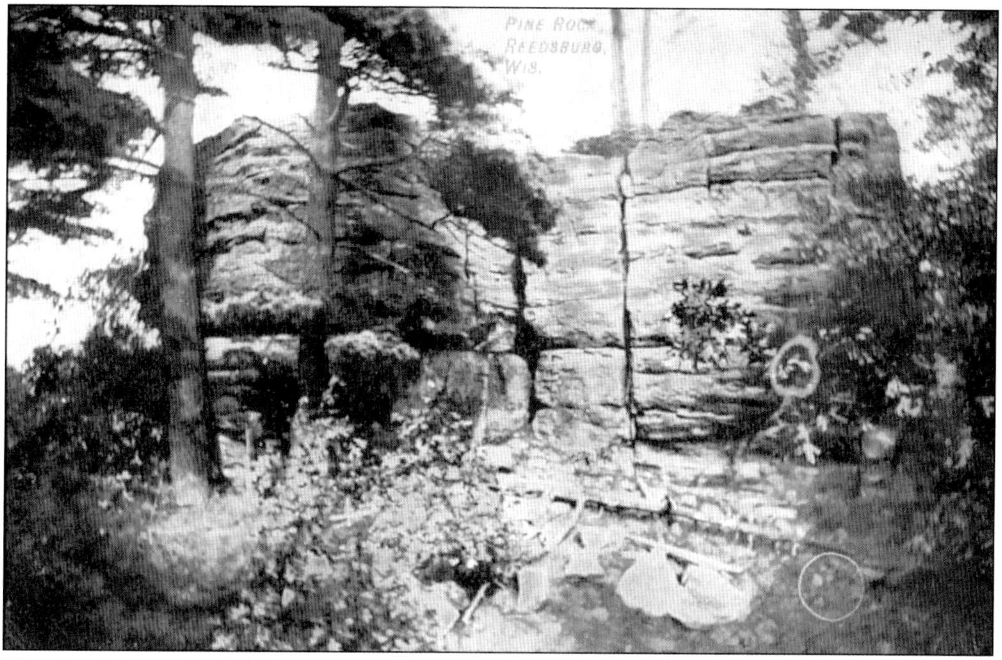

Pine Rock is north of the city on a county highway and has been a landmark for years past, as well as years to come. Only God can form such a structure.

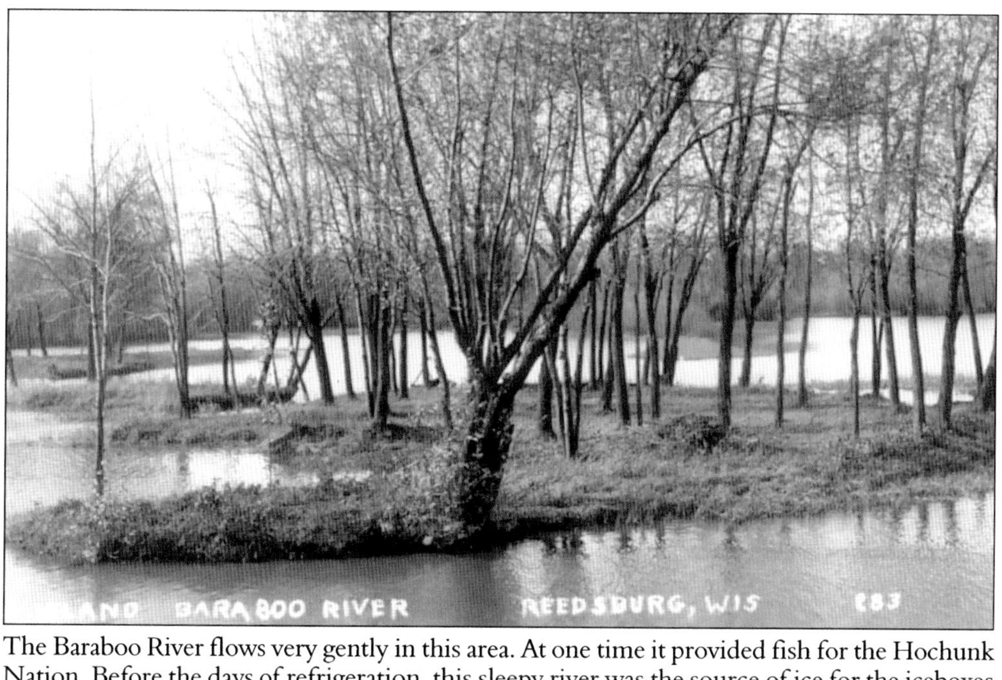

The Baraboo River flows very gently in this area. At one time it provided fish for the Hochunk Nation. Before the days of refrigeration, this sleepy river was the source of ice for the iceboxes in town. The Boat Club took several Sunday afternoon excursions up or down the river.

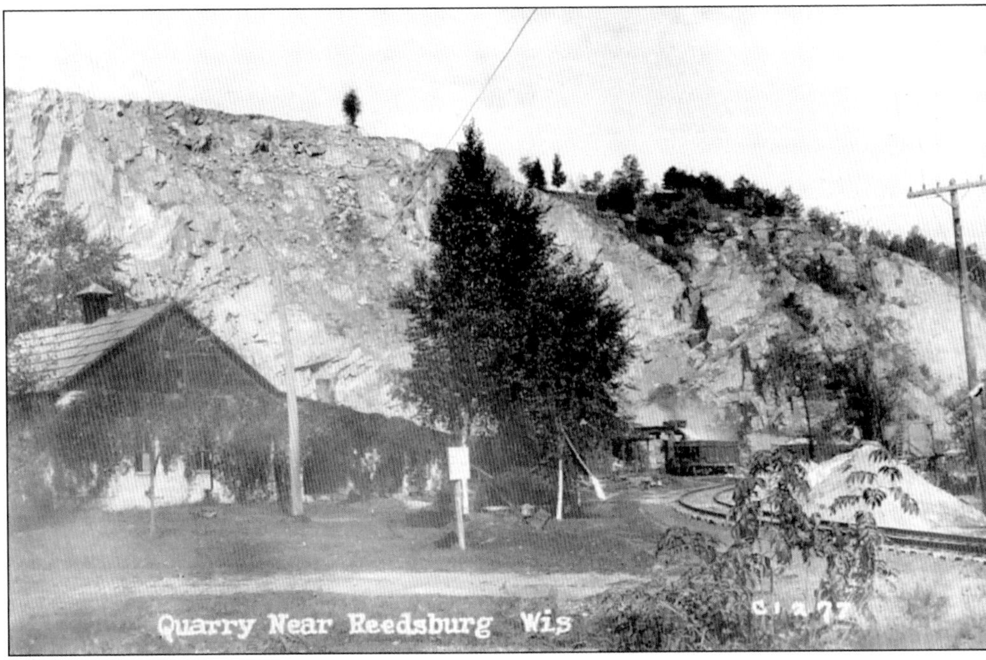

Just a few miles east of Reedsburg on Highway 136 there is a quartzite bluff. The Chicago and Northwestern railroad shipped many carloads of crushed quartzite from these bluffs. Travelers have enjoyed the scenery as they wind their way between the towering bluffs and alongside of the Baraboo River. Spring water flows abundantly from an artesian well in this area. A rock of national significance, named VanHise Rock, is located just below the bluffs. Now the rock is protected with a guard rail, but in the past several cars received a dent or two when the driver failed to navigate the corner.

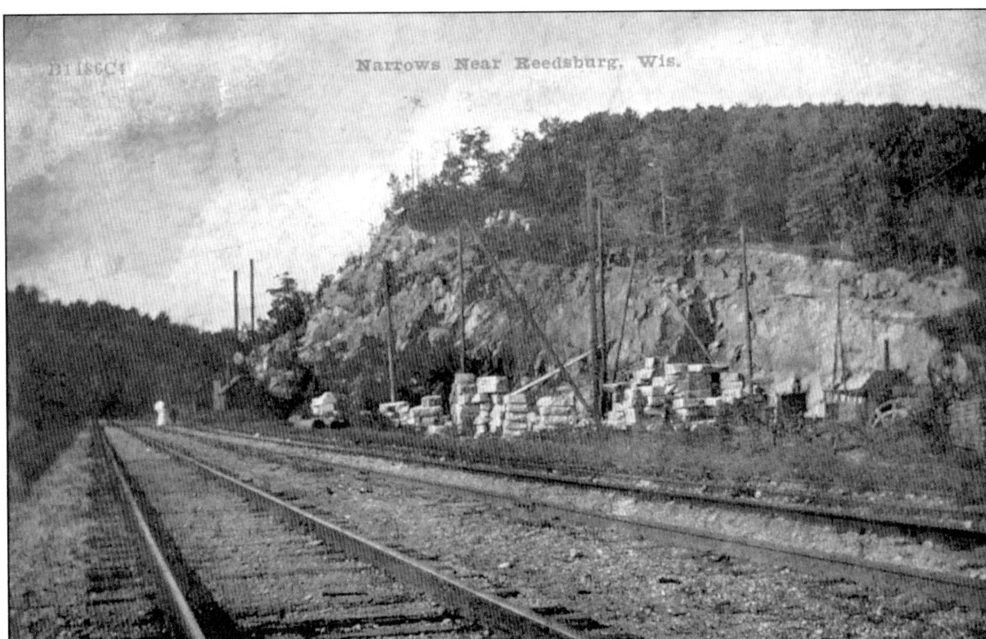

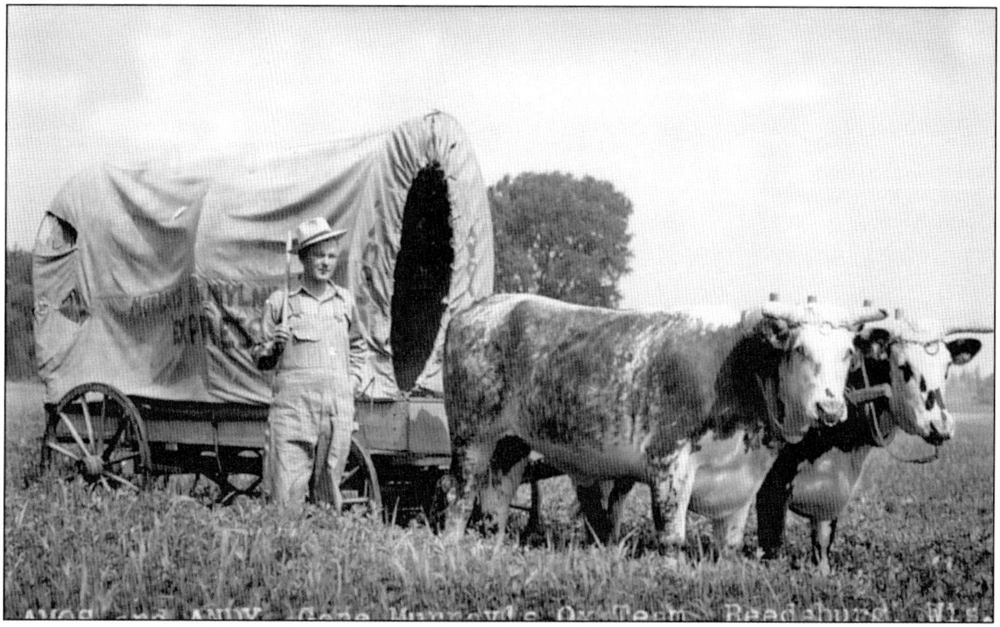

Gene Murray with his team of oxen which answered to the names Tom and Jerry.

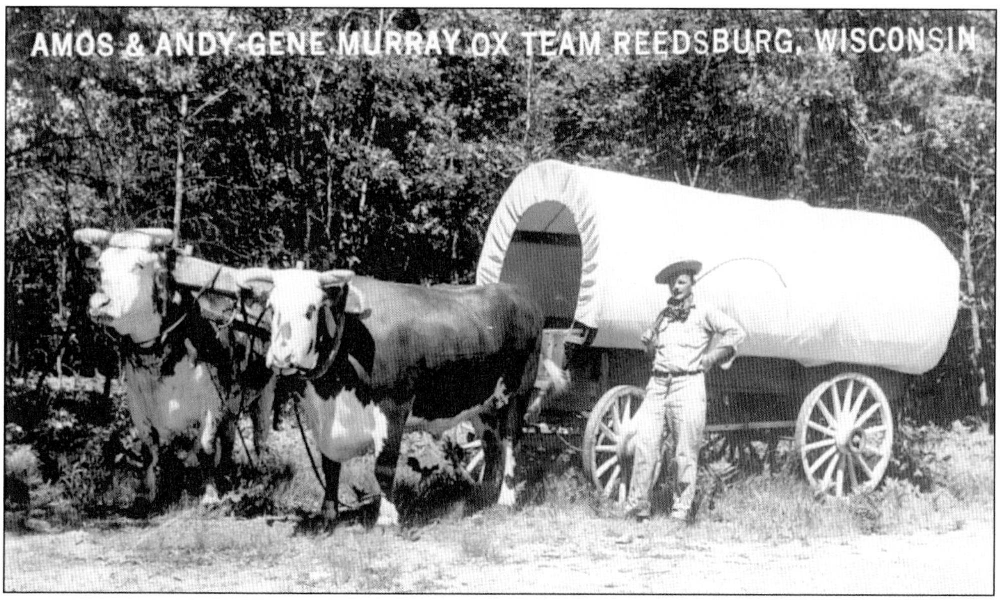

Gene Murray, a farmer and prominent resident of Dellona Township, had a unique hobby. He tended and trained several different teams of oxen to pull a covered wagon and to perform at local and regional events. They appeared in many parades, the opening of Interstate 90-94, Farm Progress Days, and the Wisconsin State Fair. Gene and his teams were a very well-known sight between 1951 and 1975. The animals that helped to settle the west and were a common sight in this area, even a hundred years after the need for moving and breaking the land was a necessity. Gene kept the spirit alive.

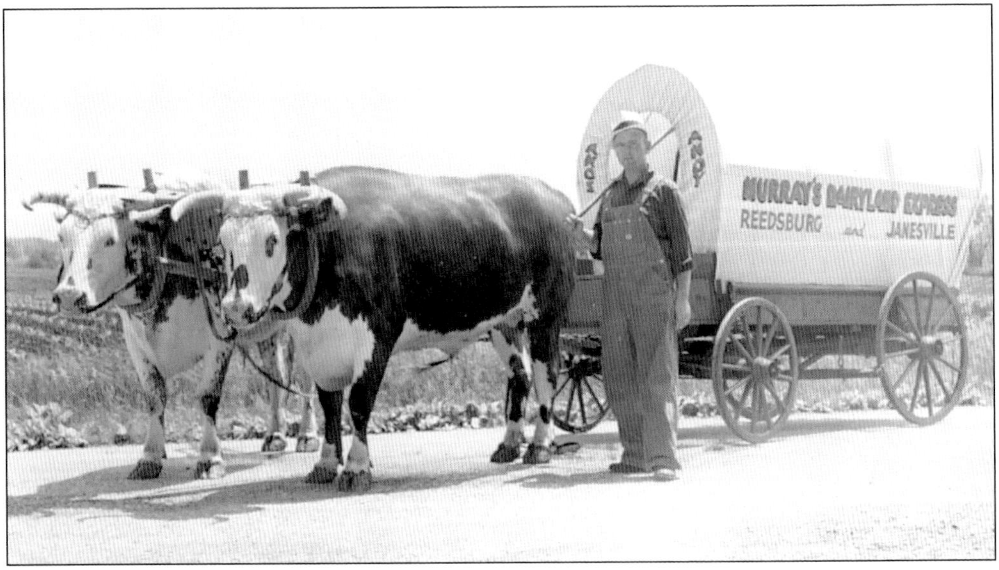

Gene Murray with Amos and Andy, one of his teams of oxen.

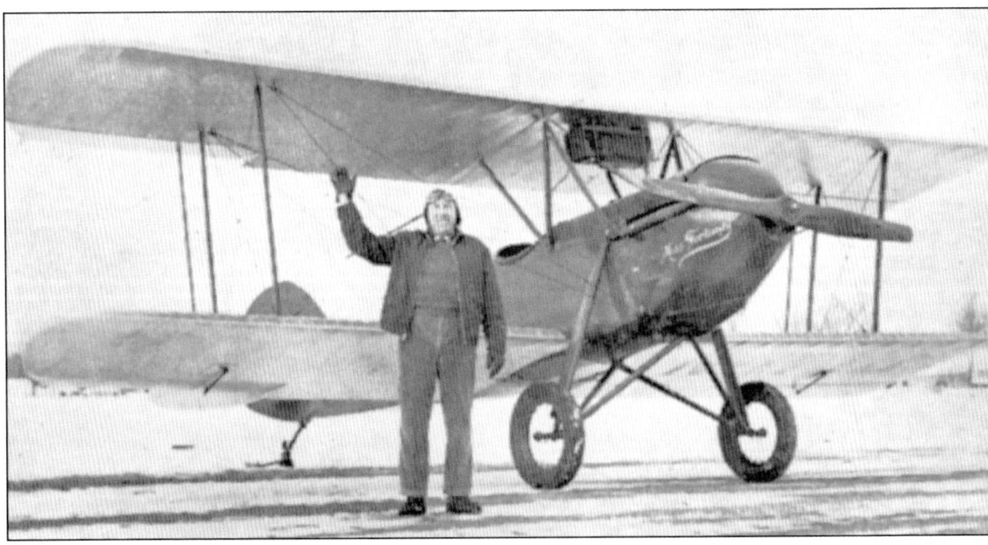

Cecil Hess. Although this is not a postcard, I felt this should be included in the cards of Reedsburg. Mr. Hess had this as a Christmas card. In 1928, Reedsburg saw its first airplane arrive as a permanent resident. Cecil Hess, with an army pilot, flew this 1928 Waco biplane into the city of Reedsburg. The city had talked of having an airport for several months and with the arrival of "Miss Fortune," flown in by Cecil, the dream became a reality. Land was at first rented and then purchased on the east side of town. Cecil built the first hangar and the federal government was asked to furnish the lights. The plane survived many barnstorming flights. Cecil was a colorful local personality and many tales are told of his days here with "Miss Fortune."